NOVEL SENSATIONS

Edinburgh Critical Studies in Modernist Culture
Series Editors: Tim Armstrong and Rebecca Beasley

Available

Modernism and Magic: Experiments with Spiritualism, Theosophy and the Occult
Leigh Wilson

Sonic Modernity: Representing Sound in Literature, Culture and the Arts
Sam Halliday

Modernism and the Frankfurt School
Tyrus Miller

Lesbian Modernism: Censorship, Sexuality and Genre Fiction
Elizabeth English

Modern Print Artefacts: Textual Materiality and Literary Value in British Print Culture, 1890–1930s
Patrick Collier

Cheap Modernism: Expanding Markets, Publishers' Series and the Avant-Garde
Lise Jaillant

Portable Modernisms: The Art of Travelling Light
Emily Ridge

Hieroglyphic Modernisms: Writing and New Media in the Twentieth Century
Jesse Schotter

Modernism, Fiction and Mathematics
Nina Engelhardt

Modernist Life Histories: Biological Theory and the Experimental Bildungsroman
Daniel Aureliano Newman

Modernism, Space and the City: Outsiders and Affect in Paris, Vienna, Berlin, and London
Andrew Thacker

Modernism Edited: Marianne Moore and the Dial *Magazine*
Victoria Bazin

Modernism and Time Machines
Charles Tung

Primordial Modernism: Animals, Ideas, transition (1927–1938)
Cathryn Setz

Modernism and Still Life: Artists, Writers, Dancers
Claudia Tobin

The Modernist Exoskeleton: Insects, War, Literary Form
Rachel Murray

Novel Sensations: Modernist Fiction and the Problem of Qualia
Jon Day

Forthcoming

Modernism and the Idea of Everyday Life
Leena Kore-Schröder

Hotel Modernity: Literary Encounters with Corporate Space
Robbie Moore

Modernism and Religion: Poetry and the Rise of Mysticism
Jamie Callison

Abstraction in Modernism and Modernity: Human and Inhuman
Jeff Wallace

The Modernist Anthropocene: Nonhuman Life and Planetary Change in James Joyce, Virginia Woolf and Djuna Barnes
Peter Adkins

www.edinburghuniversitypress.com/series/ecsmc

NOVEL SENSATIONS

Modernist Fiction and the Problem of Qualia

Jon Day

EDINBURGH
University Press

Edinburgh University Press is one of the leading university presses in the UK. We publish academic books and journals in our selected subject areas across the humanities and social sciences, combining cutting-edge scholarship with high editorial and production values to produce academic works of lasting importance. For more information visit our website: edinburghuniversitypress.com

© Jon Day, 2020, 2022

First published in hardback by Edinburgh University Press 2020

Edinburgh University Press Ltd
The Tun – Holyrood Road, 12(2f) Jackson's Entry, Edinburgh EH8 8PJ

Typeset in 10/12.5 Adobe Sabon by
IDSUK (DataConnection) Ltd

A CIP record for this book is available from the British Library

ISBN 978 1 4744 5839 9 (hardback)
ISBN 978 1 4744 5840 5 (paperback)
ISBN 978 1 4744 5841 2 (webready PDF)
ISBN 978 1 4744 5842 9 (epub)

The right of Jon Day to be identified as the author of this work has been asserted in accordance with the Copyright, Designs and Patents Act 1988, and the Copyright and Related Rights Regulations 2003 (SI No. 2498).

CONTENTS

Acknowledgements	vii
Series Editors' Preface	ix
Introduction: Modernist Fiction and the Problem of Qualia	1
1 Cognitive Realism, Qualia and the Inward Turn	11
2 What Virginia Didn't Know: Knowledge, Impressionism and the Eye	31
3 What is it Like to be Leopold Bloom?	59
4 Neuromodernism and the Explanatory Gap	80
5 Samuel Beckett and Modernism's Narratives of Reduction	104
6 Hollow Men and Chinese Rooms: Wyndham Lewis and the Will-to-Automatism	131
Conclusion: Modernism, Qualia and the Narratives of Behaviourism	167
Bibliography	175
Index	189

ACKNOWLEDGEMENTS

I am extremely grateful to Michael Whitworth, a rigorous and supportive supervisor of the DPhil thesis from which this book originated, and to Christopher Butler and Patricia Waugh, who were attentive and generous examiners. I thank the Arts and Humanities Research Council for a grant that supported my initial research, and the staff of the Bodleian Library, the Library of St John's College, Oxford, and the British Library for their assistance.

Many teachers and readers have contributed to my understanding of the ideas discussed in this book, particularly David Bradshaw, Andrew Gaedkte, Peter Hacker, David Herman, John Kelly, Carolyne Larrington, Sowon Park and Nathan Waddell. I thank especially Colin Watts, an inspirational teacher of philosophy.

Tim Armstrong and Rebecca Beasley have been wonderfully helpful editors. I thank them and everyone at Edinburgh University Press for the care with which they've ushered this book into being.

I thank all my colleagues in the English Department at King's College, London, especially Rowan Boyson, Josh Davies, Edmund Gordon, Lara Feigel, Janet Floyd, Seb Franklin, Brian Hurwitz, Clara Jones, Richard Kirkland, Sarah Lewis, Brian Murray, Anna Snaith, Max Saunders, Ed Sugden, Mark Turner, Neil Vickers, Lawrence Warner and Patrick Wright. Jo Malt provided invaluable last-minute help. I thank, too, all of the participants of my MA module 'Modernist Mindscapes' over the years, whose discussions have been invaluable in shaping the arguments of this book. Jo Hamya's research assistance has been essential. All mistakes are my own.

Many friends have contributed ideas or other support. I am especially grateful to Ben Coffer, Alex Feldman, Jonathan Gharraie, Oren Goldschmidt, Agostino Inguscio, Damian Le Bas, Alys Moody, Thomas Marks, Alex Niven, Aaron Rosenberg, Stephen J. Ross, Matthew Sperling, Will Tattersdill, Thomas Walker and Liesl Yamaguchi.

My parents, Peter and Romee, have been constantly supportive, as have my siblings: Lizzie, Anna and Ben. I thank them all.

Most of all, I thank my children, Dora and Ivo, and Natalya Dragicevic, who has put up with it all, and supported me at every turn.

SERIES EDITORS' PREFACE

This series of monographs on selected topics in modernism is designed to reflect and extend the range of new work in modernist studies. The studies in the series aim for a breadth of scope and for an expanded sense of the canon of modernism, rather than focusing on individual authors. Literary texts will be considered in terms of contexts including recent cultural histories (modernism and magic; sonic modernity; media studies) and topics of theoretical interest (the everyday; postmodernism; the Frankfurt School); but the series will also re-consider more familiar routes into modernism (modernism and gender; sexuality; politics). The works published will be attentive to the various cultural, intellectual and historical contexts of British, American and European modernisms, and to inter-disciplinary possibilities within modernism, including performance and the visual and plastic arts.

Tim Armstrong and Rebecca Beasley

For Natalya

INTRODUCTION: MODERNIST FICTION AND THE PROBLEM OF QUALIA

Walter Pater's contention that 'all art constantly aspires to the condition of music'; Gustave Flaubert's statement that 'When I write a novel I aim at rendering a colour, a shade', and that 'In *Madame Bovary*, all I wanted to do was to render a grey colour, the mouldy colour of a wood-louse's existence'; Joseph Conrad's claim that his aim as a novelist was 'above all, to make you see'; D. H. Lawrence's appeals to the 'blood consciousness'; Clement Greenberg's call for an art designed for 'eyesight alone'; James Joyce's declaration that modern man 'has an epidermis rather than a soul': in these and other modernist dictums, the senses are held to be essential both to the consumption and to the production of art.[1] If modernism has been characterised by what Sara Danius has called a 'crisis of the senses', then many modernists themselves seemed to view this crisis as distinctly liberatory.[2] Modernism has frequently been understood as an aesthetic of the human body, as a literature which sought to engage directly with eyes and ears (and even with the proximate senses: with tongues and hands and noses). At the same time, from the mid-nineteenth to the early twentieth centuries the senses became the fraught frontier of a philosophical reappraisal of the nature of consciousness itself, a reappraisal conducted primarily through the burgeoning disciplines of physics, psychology, and associated sciences and philosophies of mind.

Despite their apparent disparateness, these distinct disciplines (we might add phenomenology and psychoanalysis to the mix) can be read retrospectively as being engaged in what was at times a fairly unified theoretical project, one which sought to scrutinise the relationship between minds, brains and the external world as mediated by the senses. Within analytical philosophy, experimental psychology, neurology and physics, ever-finer distinctions were made between sensations as they were experienced, and what the objects of those sensations – be they waves, particles or neurons – could be said to consist of. These distinctions often mirrored those made within contemporary aesthetic theory and practice between linguistic descriptions of sensations and the kinds of experience those descriptions were taken to be descriptions *of*. The radical reinterpretation of the human sensorium associated with modernity has often led to claims that modernist literature was able to make the senses legible: that it was indeed possible both to encode sensory experiences in language, and to share those experiences with other minds without any loss.

These conversations, and the controversies they generated, have persisted. Now they make their influence felt particularly within the melded fields of 'cognitive cultural studies' or 'cognitive narratology' and 'neuroaesthetics': critical approaches to literature and art informed by advances in brain science that have their origins in the post-Theory era of the 1990s and 2000s, and that tend to interpret modernism's supposed 'inward turn' in often quite straightforwardly literal ways. They have been accompanied in contemporary literary fiction over the past two decades by a renewed interest in cognitive impairment and neuroatypicality as a feature of plot and style. With the rise of what Marco Roth has termed the 'neuronovel' – a strand of fiction that engages directly with the relationship between neurology and narrative (and often – strikingly – with the legacies of modernism) – the assumptions underpinning the neuroaesthetic project have been put under productive scrutiny. And, as Laura Salisbury has shown, the origins of these controversies can be seen to lie within the modernist moment itself.[3] Read in this way, modernism didn't just constitute a rupture in aesthetic understandings of the senses, but in epistemic ones too, and this rupture is one that contemporary literary critics and novelists are still grappling with.

The radical reappraisal of the nature of sensation, which has come to be associated with a fairly uncontested, if narrow, canon of modernist texts, was, as Friedrich Kittler, Tim Armstrong and Sara Danius have all argued, encouraged by the development of mnemonic technologies – telephone, gramophone, cinematograph – which in the late nineteenth and early twentieth centuries allowed sense-data to be stored in a neutral medium and reproduced almost perfectly for the first time in human history.[4] In *Discourse Networks* Kittler showed how anxieties over technology's ability to use media to neutrally capture sensation, and replicate it perfectly, were prefigured by literary attempts to do precisely the same thing.[5] Jesse Matz has shown that for a long time within modernist critical discourse the category of the 'impression' has played the role of nebulous mediator between textual and sensory representations of the world.⁶ In *The Renaissance*, Walter Pater offered his influential *détournement* of Matthew Arnold's definition of the role of the critic, relocating the burden of criticism from analysis of the external world to analysis of individual perceptions. '"To see the object as in itself it really is," has been justly said to be the aim of all true criticism whatever', Pater wrote, 'and in aesthetic criticism the first step towards seeing one's object as it really is, is to know one's impression as it really is, to discriminate it, to realise it distinctly.'⁷ After Pater, living in the moment and attending to the minute particularities of subjective perceptual experience was taken to be fundamental to aesthetic experience, a commitment to the senses that would flow through modernist discourse. But the questions raised by privileging subjective impressions over 'scientific' or 'objective' descriptions of the external world were immediately felt, both within literary criticism and within philosophy, some schools of which began to conceive of consciousness itself as little more than the 'having' of fleeting and temporally disconnected sensory experiences.

Modernism's preoccupation with what Danius has identified as a 'crisis of the senses' was, therefore, manifested across a wide range of philosophical, psychological and aesthetic arguments, the origins of many of which can be traced to Pater's assertion. As early as 1926 I. A. Richards was already blaming Pater's Conclusion to *The Renaissance* for the 'too great insistence upon the quality of the momentary *consciousness*' which 'has in recent times been a prevalent critical blunder'.⁸ Just as scrutiny of the impression as a conceptual entity eventually placed it under unendurable epistemological strain, so did philosophers and psychologists soon recognise that, no matter how closely they could be identified with particular brain events, sensory experiences remained stubbornly mute, resisting translation into any form of language. This soon led to a conceptual and scientific fragmentation of the human sensorium. Eventually modernity's new models of cognition – particularly those provided by the descriptionist, localising projects of Hermann von Helmholtz and Ernst Mach, among others – would lead to a theoretical relocation of the Cartesian *res cogitans* into individual instances of sense-perception and, within philosophy, to the identification and isolation of properties of consciousness that have subsequently been labelled 'qualia'.

Qualia are defined in the *Oxford Dictionary of Philosophy* as

> The felt or phenomenal qualities associated with experiences, such as the feeling of a pain, or the hearing of a sound, or the viewing of a colour. To know what it is like to have an experience is to know its qualia.⁹

According to philosophers such as Thomas Nagel, Frank Jackson and John Searle, qualia account for what David Chalmers has identified as the 'hard problem' of consciousness: the apparent impossibility of explaining just how it is that wet, grey brains can give rise to ineffable, irreducible, and ontologically subjective mental experiences.[10] Chalmers argues that such phenomena have 'a *qualitative feel* – an associated quality of experience', and that the 'problem of explaining these phenomenal qualities is just the problem of explaining consciousness.'[11] In Thomas Nagel's terms qualia are the 'what-is-it-like-ness' of all conscious mental states whatever.[12] Frank Jackson defines them as 'certain features of the bodily sensations especially, but also of certain perceptual experiences, which no amount of purely physical information includes.'[13]

It is important to note that qualia, then, are not neutral features of consciousness. Using the term brings with it a particular perspective on the mind body problem, one that often seems to usher in the spectre of dualism. The existence of qualia is taken by those who endorse the term to be the cause of a metaphysical rupture which Joseph Levine has termed the 'explanatory gap' between brain and mind: the seemingly uncrossable gulf of understanding that lies between our knowledge of neurological or functional states of the body and the conscious experiences those states cause or, indeed, are identical with.[14] It is partly for this reason that Ned Block has identified the debate over the existence of qualia the 'greatest chasm in philosophy of mind – maybe even all of philosophy'.[15]

This book is not a work of philosophy. My own methodology is not philosophical but historicist, and it must be acknowledged that qualia remain a hugely disputed concept within contemporary philosophy of mind.[16] While qualiaphile philosophers such as Jackson, Nagel and Searle believe that qualia constitute phenomena that any explanation of consciousness *must* explain in order to be complete, many others argue that they are an incoherent notion founded on a metaphysical sleight of hand, representing the last vestiges of a Cartesian inheritance which ought to be done away with.[17] For Daniel Dennett, a vocal denier of the existence of qualia, consciousness 'has *no* properties that are special in *any* of the ways qualia have been supposed to be special.'[18] 'Philosophers', he asserts in *Consciousness Explained*:

> have adopted various names for the things in the beholder (or properties of the beholder) that have been supposed to provide a safe home for the colors and the rest of the properties that have been banished from the 'external' world by the triumphs of physics: 'raw feels', 'sensa' 'phenomenal qualities', 'intrinsic properties of conscious experiences', the 'qualitative content of mental states' and of course 'qualia' . . . There are subtle differences in how these terms have been defined, but . . . I am denying there are any such properties.[19]

For those, like Dennett, hostile to them, qualia are a meaningless conceptual unit referring to vaguely ethereal properties which are said to attend all conscious states whatever, but which, in being invoked, actually obscure the issues under discussion. Here I am less interested in asking (let alone answering) the question of whether or not qualia exist than I am in tracing their emergence within philosophy of the early to mid-twentieth century, and conceptualising the ways the concept has intersected with literary accounts of consciousness from the same period. But my project is not *only* to historicise a philosophical debate. Whether or not they exist, it is clear that qualia continue to cause substantial conceptual headaches both for critical narratives of modernism's inward turn and for neuroaesthetic accounts of literature. They keep alive the spectre of the Cartesian theatre in an age of materialist reductionism, chasing *res cogitans* into individual instances of sense-perception, and haunting materialist accounts of consciousness as a new ghost in the old machine.

What is striking about the qualia debate from the perspective of literary and cultural history is therefore that it represents a way of conceiving of consciousness – and the problems of describing sensations – that is mirrored in debates over the materiality of the mind, and the relation of language to the body, within modernist aesthetics. Qualia were first defined in the context of philosophy of mind by the American pragmatist philosopher C. I. Lewis in 1929, but they emerged directly from the Cambridge neo-realist tradition: from G. E. Moore's notion of 'sense data' and Bertrand Russell's category of 'sensibilia'. Thus as a philosophical entity the quale is broadly contemporaneous with the artefacts of high modernism.

The question of the existence of qualia is a much contested one within contemporary philosophy, and I have no intention of contributing to that philosophical debate here. I want, if I can, to remain neutral on the possible existence of qualia. Instead my aim in this book is threefold. First, to historicise the qualia debate, providing a genealogy of the term and reading its emergence alongside works of literary fiction. Second, to ask what the consequences of a more rigorously historicised understanding of qualia have for our understanding of modernist aesthetics. Third, to suggest that such readings have implications for contemporary 'neuroaesthetic' or 'cognitive' approaches to literature. I want to ask: what happens to our interpretation of works of literature when we historicise the epistemological questions attending them? And what do these questions mean for current discussions over what it is that fictional descriptions of minds, as opposed to scientific or psychiatric ones, can be said to be *doing* to us?

Typically, accounts of modernism's engagement with sensation and philosophy of mind have concentrated on the 'explanatory gap' – between sensations and brain states, or between sensations and language – in its material and scientific contexts. Many critics have attempted to 'read' the human sensorium in relation to the emergence of mnemonic and reproductive technologies, medical breakthroughs, or the trauma of war.[20] Walter J. Ong and Marshall McLuhan both engaged provocatively with notions of orality and literacy in the age of mass culture and a mass readership, arguing that the rise of print culture had long-lasting (and generally deleterious) influences on the relationship between literature and the senses.[21] Other accounts of the senses in modernism have drawn attention to the apparent 'fragmentation' of the human subject associated with an impressionist aesthetic project.[22]

At the same time, the novel has for a long time been interpreted as a literary form which engages explicitly and in sustained fashion with Thomas Nagel's question of 'what it is like to be' another mind. For Ian Watt, famously, the rise of the novel coincided with the invention (or discovery) of a new kind of human subjectivity.[23] In *Consciousness and the Novel* David Lodge called the novel 'man's most successful effort to describe the experience of individual human beings moving through space and time.'[24] More recently, Terence Cave has argued that 'literature offers a virtually limitless archive of the ways in which human beings think, how they imagine themselves and their world.'[25] Many voices, as I will show, could be added in support of the thesis that what we value in fiction is its ability to represent mental states, of which sensations are often held to be the most significant, because the least falsifiable.

The 'problem' of qualia I propose to explore here, then, has to do with the problem the existence of qualia would pose for symbolic or linguistic descriptions (either mathematic, scientific or literary) of mental states, especially when those descriptions make special claims (or have been interpreted as making special claims) of mimetic veracity. It is one thing to claim that the qualia of 'what it is like to read *Ulysses*' is conveyed when we read *Ulysses*; quite another to claim, as some have, that reading *Ulysses* allows us to experience the mind-world of Leopold Bloom (even if that mindworld is itself a confection: the product of Joyce's own ability to trick us into thinking we're overhearing the thought-stream of a real, living mind). I am therefore less interested in what modernist writers themselves thought of this debate (although, as we shall see, some did engage directly with its philosophical forerunners), than in what subsequent critics have claimed the novel can do on behalf of these writers. If qualia do exist, then Flaubert's 'mouldy colour of a wood-louse's existence' simply cannot be conveyed within language, however refined or experimental or accomplished that language may be. And if you believe that qualia don't exist, argue philosophers who endorse the concept, then you are denying some of the very properties of consciousness that the novel, as a form, has often been celebrated for accommodating. Thus the problem of qualia is one that engages with broader aesthetic debates of the twentieth century, specifically with those over narrative fiction's supposed 'inward turn', and its capacity to portray consciousness in what we might think of as a realist, or at least more veridical, manner. It may come as no surprise that the problem of qualia emerged in relation to fictional representations of consciousness at precisely the point at which the representative claims of those fictional representations themselves came under unprecedented and sustained attack.

In Chapter 1 I frame these connected questions by examining a critical paradigm which conceives of how fiction represents consciousness in terms that I, following Emily Troscianko, have called 'cognitive realism'.[26] Cognitive realism, I will suggest, is a distilled version of the more general inward turn identified by Mark S. Micale and many others as attending the emergence of literary modernism as well as, within philosophy, the qualia thesis. Cognitive realism is now enshrined most obviously within the burgeoning field of 'neuroaesthetics', but its origins lie in the modernist moment itself. Cognitive realism, like qualia, was conditioned by the material conditions of modernity, and by technological developments that threatened the unity of the human sensorium in the late nineteenth and early twentieth centuries.

Following the work of S. P. Rosenbaum, Ann Banfield and David Herman, a central assumption of this argument is therefore that modernist literary techniques influenced philosophical methodologies in the period, often in quite direct ways. 'Significantly', observes David Herman, it is also true that 'many of the arguments about qualia in the philosophy of mind are couched in the form of stories or story-like thought experiments.'[27] As we shall see, during the early twentieth century many scientific and psychological introspectionist narratives (which were themselves taken to be the 'data' any theory of mind should be capable of explaining in order to be sufficient) took the form of short stories – on this issue the traffic between the two cultures was decidedly two-way.

Thus several of my subsequent chapters are structured around influential contemporary thought experiments that argue for the existence of qualia. Chapter 2, 'What Virginia Didn't Know', provides an analysis of Woolf's epistemological inheritance from Cambridge philosophy and the status of literature as an object of knowledge. Its title is taken from Frank Jackson's anti-functionalist thought experiment 'What Mary Didn't Know' (itself named in reference to Henry James's *What Maisie Knew* – the epistemological inheritance runs deep). Chapter 3, 'What is it Like to be Leopold Bloom?' reads James Joyce's *Ulysses* alongside Thomas Nagel's paper 'What is it Like to be a Bat?' to test what David Herman has called modernism's 'phenomenological ecologies' in relation to the problem of qualia.

Chapters 4 and 5, 'Neuromodernism and the Explanatory Gap' and 'Samuel Beckett and Modernism's Narratives of Reduction', examine the neuroscientific contexts of these debates, and the origins of modernism's reductionist impulses. Finally Chapter 6, 'Hollow Men and Chinese Rooms', considers the work of Wyndham Lewis alongside John Searle's 'Chinese Room' argument, reading what David Trotter terms modernism's pronounced 'will-to-automatism' alongside debates over the notion of the 'philosophical zombie' and the difference between semantic and syntactic intentionality.

Chapter 6 represents something of an end point of my investigation into modernism's relationship with philosophy of mind. In it I show how Lewis's fiction proposes a radical solution to the literary impasse created by the possible existence of qualia. This is a solution which was endorsed within philosophy and experimental psychology by behaviourist accounts of consciousness, but is in the end one that threatens more traditionally humanistic interpretations of fiction which are, perhaps paradoxically, often defended by contemporary cognitive narratologists and neuroaestheticians: that literature provides a repository of the human mind. As a philosophical thesis behaviourism denies qualia, yet in doing so it allows the novel to claim for itself certain representational capabilities – in particular the ability to represent all types of cognition, including sensation – that it would otherwise be denied. Cognitive or neuroaesthetic approaches to literature which engage with the qualia debate are therefore often forced to navigate between an understanding of consciousness which reduces persons to bodies, machines, automata or empty-headed literary characters, and one which makes it impossible to make any special mimetic claims for literature (at least in terms of its representation of consciousness and sensation) at all.

In considering the interactions between modernist literature and the senses through the context of philosophy of mind my aim is to shift the focus of the debate over modernism's often fraught relationship with sensation from one which dwells on the modernist sensorium's fragmentation under the weight of technological advances to one which takes into account the broader theoretical issues concerning the interrelations of the senses in a range of contexts – medical, philosophical, and aesthetic. I thus employ qualia as a concept with which to contextualise and challenge narratives of the mind – philosophical, literary and scientific – from the period. In doing so I hope to further historicise modernism's 'crisis of the senses', locating this argument in a broader theoretical space and questioning the relevance (and novelty) of contemporary approaches to reading the senses of modernism.

NOTES

1. Walter Pater, *The Renaissance: Studies in Art and Poetry*, ed. by Adam Phillips (Oxford: Oxford University Press, 1986), p. 86; Gustave Flaubert, qtd in Edmond de Goncourt, *Pages from the Goncourt Journal*, ed. and trans. by Robert Baldick (London: Oxford University Press, 1962), p. 58; Joseph Conrad, 'Author's Note', *New Review*, 17 (December 1987), 628; D. H. Lawrence, *Fantasia of the Unconscious* (London: M. Secker, 1930), p. 68; Clement Greenberg, 'Sculpture in Our Time', in *The Collected Essays and Criticism*, ed. by John O'Brian, 4 vols (Chicago and London: The University of Chicago Press, 1993), vol. 4, *Modernism with a Vengeance 1957–1969*, p. 59; James Joyce, *James Joyce in Padua*, ed. and trans. by Louis Berrone (New York: Random House, 1977), p. 21.

2. Sara Danius, *The Senses of Modernism: Technology, Perception, and Aesthetics* (Ithaca, NY and London: Cornell University Press, 2002), p. 3.
3. Laura Salisbury, 'Narration and Neurology: Ian McEwan's Mother Tongue', *Textual Practice*, 24.5 (2010), 883–912.
4. Friedrich Kittler, *Discourse Networks 1800–1900*, trans. by Michael Metteer and Chris Cullens (Stanford, CA: Stanford University Press, 1990), p. 8.
5. See Friedrich A. Kittler, *Gramophone, Film, Typewriter*, trans. by Geoffrey Winthrop-Young and Michael Wutz (Stanford, CA: Stanford University Press, 1999).
6. See Jesse Matz, *Literary Impressionism and Modernist Aesthetics* (Cambridge: Cambridge University Press, 2001).
7. Pater, *The Renaissance*, p. xix.
8. I. A. Richards, *Principles of Literary Criticism* (London: Kegan Paul, Trench, Trubner & Co., Ltd, 1925), p. 132.
9. Simon Blackburn, *The Oxford Dictionary of Philosophy*, 2nd edn (Oxford: Oxford University Press, 2008), p. 302.
10. David Chalmers, 'Facing Up to the Problem of Consciousness', *Journal of Consciousness Studies*, 2.3 (1995), 200–219 (p. 200).
11. David Chalmers, *The Conscious Mind: In Search of a Fundamental Theory* (New York and Oxford: Oxford University Press, 1996), p. 4.
12. Thomas Nagel, 'What is it Like to be a Bat?', *The Philosophical Review*, 83.4 (1974), 435–450 (p. 435).
13. Frank Jackson, 'Epiphenomenal Qualia', *The Philosophical Quarterly*, 32.127 (1982), 127–136 (p. 127).
14. See Joseph Levine, 'Materialism and Qualia: The Explanatory Gap', *Pacific Philosophical Quarterly*, 64.4 (1983), 354–361.
15. Ned Block, 'Mental Paint', in *Reflections and Replies: Essays on the Philosophy of Tyler Burge*, ed. by Martin Hahn and Bjørn Ramberg (Cambridge, MA: The MIT Press, 2003), p. 165.
16. For a good introduction to the debates for and against the existence of qualia, see John R. Searle *The Mystery of Consciousness* (London: Granta, 1997) and *The Case for Qualia*, ed. by Edmond Wright (Cambridge, MA: The MIT Press, 2008).
17. Dennett's most sustained argument along these lines is outlined in *Consciousness Explained* (London: Allen Lane, The Penguin Press, 1992).
18. Daniel C. Dennett, 'Quining Qualia', in *Consciousness in Contemporary Science*, ed. by A. J. Marcel and E. Bisiach (New York: Oxford University Press, 1988), p. 44.
19. Daniel C. Dennett, *Consciousness Explained* (London: Allen Lane, The Penguin Press, 1992), p. 372.
20. See Tim Armstrong, *Modernism, Technology, and the Body: A Cultural Study* (Cambridge: Cambridge University Press, 1998); Santanu Das, *Touch and Intimacy in First World War Literature* (Cambridge: Cambridge University Press, 2005); Ulrika Maude, *Beckett, Technology and the Body* (Cambridge: Cambridge University Press, 2009); Yoshiki Tajiri, *Samuel Beckett and the Prosthetic Body: The Organs and Senses in Modernism* (Basingstoke: Palgrave Macmillan, 2007); and Danius, *The Senses of Modernism*.

21. See Walter J. Ong, *Orality and Literacy: the Technologizing of the Word* (London: Methuen, 1982); and Marshall McLuhan, *The Gutenberg Galaxy: The Making of Typographic Man* (Toronto: University of Toronto Press, 1962).
22. Danius, *The Senses of Modernism*, p. 3.
23. Ian Watt, *The Rise of the Novel Studies in Richardson, Defoe, Fielding* (London: Chatto & Windus, 1957).
24. David Lodge, *Consciousness and the Novel* (London: Secker & Warburg 2002), p. 10.
25. Terence Cave, *Thinking with Literature: Towards a Cognitive Criticism* (Oxford: Oxford University Press, 2016), p. 14.
26. See Emily Troscianko, *Kafka's Cognitive Realism* (London: Routledge, 2016).
27. David Herman, *Basic Elements of Narrative* (Chichester: Wiley-Blackwell, 2009), p. 154.

1

COGNITIVE REALISM, QUALIA AND THE INWARD TURN

> My task which I am trying to achieve is, by the power of the written word, to make you hear, to make you feel – it is, above all, to make you see. That – and no more, and it is everything.
>
> Joseph Conrad, preface to *The Nigger of the 'Narcissus'*

Cognitive Realism and the Inward Turn

That modernist fiction was particularly successful at representing consciousness has become almost a truism. Eric Kahler's definition of modernist narrative's 'inward turn' – the idea that during the twentieth century the novel demonstrated what he identified as a 'progressive internalization of events, an increasing displacement of outer space by what Rilke has called inner space, a stretching of consciousness' – continues to be influential.[1] Mark S. Micale has extended Kahler's turn inward beyond literature, arguing that a much wider reconfiguration of subjectivity occurred during the late nineteenth and early twentieth centuries, during which both 'psychiatric medicine and the creative arts' underwent 'a thoroughgoing psychologization of their methods, subjects and intentions.'[2]

Within literary studies the inward turn has often been understood as an argument about the representational claims of literature, an argument founded on two related ideas. The first is that the mind is a relatively stable and ahistorical object or phenomenon: essential and unchanging through time. The second is that it was only with modernity that consciousness was finally pinned down in language: that, as Micale summarises, from the latter half of the nineteenth century both psychiatry and the arts 'pioneered new techniques of narration to capture the inner workings of the human mind and the moment-by-moment experience of individual consciousness.'[3] That modernism constituted a turn inward is therefore often founded on the assumption that modernist writers were committed to a representative logic of 'cognitive realism': the idea, more or less forcibly expressed, that it is indeed possible to describe not just the functions of consciousness but also its phenomenological properties through the development and judicial deployment of new literary techniques, and that those descriptions can take on a kind of perceptual immanence that is unavailable to other kinds of discourse.[4]

As David Herman has shown, historically the cognitive realist thesis has been approached primarily through considerations of the idea of the 'stream of consciousness', a phrase used both to describe a literary technique and as a metaphor for the mind itself. Whether or not May Sinclair had William James's definition in mind when she first applied the term to fiction, by the mid-twentieth-century critics were confident in associating the phrase with a new kind of cognitive immediacy.[5] In *The Psychological Novel*, for instance, Leon Edel argued that 'the most characteristic aspect of twentieth-century fiction [is] its inward turning to convey the flow of mental experience.'[6] For Melvin Friedman the 'stream of consciousness method' allowed for 'a direct, immediate presentation of consciousness'.[7] According to Robert Humphrey, such narratives represent 'a type of fiction in which strong emphasis is placed on exploration of the prespeech levels of consciousness' and, as such, constitute 'attempt[s] to create human consciousness in fiction'.[8] In Edward Bowling's definition stream of consciousness fiction allows for '*a direct quotation of the mind* – not merely of the language area but of the whole consciousness'.[9] More recently, critics have been minded to frame the relationship between the stream-of-consciousness novel and consciousness as a phenomenological reality in terms of the latter's ability to 'render' or 'embody' the former.[10]

Yet the plurality of the terms employed in these discussions might be read as an index of a profound (and longstanding) ontological confusion. Do such novels 'convey' the mind, or 'present' it? Do they 'capture' it, or 'portray' it? Do they 'render' it or, perhaps, 'create' it? Does it even make sense to conceive of the mind as an 'it' – a thing separate or separable either from the human subject, or the experiential states which that subject supposedly 'has', or even from those literary and aesthetic techniques which are used to represent it? Finally, do such works really 'enact' or 'embody' conscious states in a way that other forms of narrative – scientific, say, or philosophical – do not and can never?

In many of these accounts, what Robert Humphrey called the 'pre-speech levels of consciousness' are argued to be distinct from more considered and rational descriptions of character or behaviour. One implication of the idea of an inward turn within narrative fiction is, therefore, that personhood can be divided between character (reduced to a set of biographical idiosyncrasies – a life story which can be narrated without loss), and that character's 'stream of consciousness', conceived as a separate object composed of mental states themselves: simple, irreducible qualities that are essential, consistent, and shared universally. Our minds are built of the same sensations and perceptions, this argument presumes, and one of modernism's great innovations was to bring to light these fundamental and, in the Woolfian sense, atomistic components of consciousness, rather than to dwell on the idiosyncratic biographical particularities of a character's life story. In many of these accounts, therefore, an abstract object – the mind – is seen as synonymous with the techniques used to represent it.

Interpreting modernism's inward turn as a kind of extended or spilt realism goes back to the origins of modernism itself, of course. Writing in the *Egoist* in 1918, in a review which first applied the term 'stream of consciousness' to fiction, May Sinclair described Dorothy Richardson's technique in *Pilgrimage* as 'getting closer to reality than any of our novelists who are trying so desperately to get close' to it.[11] Virginia Woolf's influential critique of the 'materialists' in her seminal essay 'Mr Bennett and Mrs Brown' argued that in their commitment to a kind of exhaustive cataloguing of objects Bennett, Wells and Galsworthy left out something important from their description of character, and it was this something that the modernists alone could provide. All such theories, therefore, *pace* the criticisms made by Erich Auerbach over literary modernism's degenerating mimetic facility in his seminal chapter on Woolf in *Mimesis*, generally describe a relationship between the object – be it 'mind', 'consciousness' or the 'stream-of-consciousness' – and the means of its representation in language which might be broadly conceived of as realist.[12]

This has proved to be a persistent relational claim within modernist studies. In *Towards a 'Natural' Narratology*, Monika Fludernik identifies what she calls the 'consciousness novel' as 'the culmination point in the development of narrative realism rather than its first regrettable lapse into idiosyncratic preoccupations with the non-typical and no-longer-verisimilar of human subjectivity.'[13] David Herman too has argued that literary modernism might be read not as a rejection of the realist paradigm, but as a development of it. 'It is . . . possible', he writes in *The Emergence of Mind*, 'to hold that modernist narratives move from external reality to an inner mental domain without viewing modernism as being fundamentally discontinuous with realism.'[14] Endorsing Pericles Lewis's assertion that modernism's radical experimentalism was an attempt 'to show not necessarily how things really are, but how things are experienced, what it feels like to be alive', Herman goes on to argue that 'stories emulate through their temporal and perspectival configuration the what-it's-like dimension of conscious awareness itself . . . [e]nacting and not just representing ways of experiencing.'[15] In his allusion to Thomas Nagel's definition of qualia as constituting the 'what-is-it-like-ness' of mental states, Herman here suggests that the right kind of story can 'enact' rather than merely 'represent' consciousness. This is a vital starting point in my consideration of the relationship between qualia and fiction, but it leaves much tantalisingly unanswered. Are fictional stories the only kinds of writing that are able to 'enact' consciousness in this way? And what, in the end, is the difference between 'ways of experiencing' experiences and the 'having' of those experiences themselves?

It may be that in objecting to the idea that the mind is a stable entity while maintaining that literary representations of it are always and inevitably historically contingent, we are confronting a deeper disagreement between the two cultures. 'There is a sense in which science attempts to establish, or at least strains towards, truths that are permanent, atemporal, universal', writes Terence Cave in a recent intervention on the subject.[16] 'In cognitive neuroscience and psychology', he continues,

> the aim is to uncover the architecture and functioning of the brain and thus show how the mind works, how humans think, how animals, babies, and children think, and so on. Literary specialists worry about the essentialism or 'innatism' those aims seem to imply; most of the materials we work with belong to a cultural order, and culture is relative to particular groups and societies.[17]

For scholars of literary modernism, however, what is so striking about this ongoing debate is that it seems to have its origins in a particular historical moment. And modernist aesthetic innovations are often still held up – by critics on both sides – as exemplars of precisely what is at issue when we think of the novel as a form of literature particularly suited to representing or rendering or describing the mind. Those who hold essentialist views on the nature of consciousness tend to conceive of modernist innovation as an aberration – as, in the novelist Ian McEwan's words, a literary movement that committed 'a dereliction of duty' with regards to plot (and, the implication is, to personhood) – whereas those who view the mind as a diachronic, more culturally contingent set of capacities tend to interpret modernism's radical experimentalism as an example of the flexibility and plasticity not just of literary forms, but of brains, and therefore of minds, themselves.[18]

Sense-Data and the New Physics: Historicising Qualia

What can we be said to be aware of when we encounter the world through the senses? What is made present to our minds when we experience a sensation? Does the phenomenological nature of sensation constitute a distinct form of knowledge? These questions, which lie at the crux of the qualia debate, became particularly vexed within philosophy and physics during the early twentieth century. The debate over qualia had a direct antecedent in philosophical debates over the nature of 'sense-data', particularly within the Cambridge analytical tradition, and these debates were for the most part driven by new evidence provided by science. As Gillian Beer and Michael Whitworth have shown, advances in physics during the late nineteenth and early twentieth centuries contributed to an understanding that matter was in some sense fictional – a mental construct – and conceptually divided the world ever more firmly between what John Locke had identified, in *An Essay Concerning Human Understanding*, as its 'primary' and 'secondary' qualities. As matter became ever more unknowable, so the sensorium came under intense scrutiny as our only source of reliable information about the external world.

The radical sensory doubt associated with the new physics was mirrored in philosophical, scientific and psychological writings which often sought to relocate epistemology's explanatory burden from the external to the internal. Popular science stressed that the waves which dominated the new physics were imaginary: were, in the French physicist Louis de Broglie's phrase, 'ondes fictives' which, as James Jeans suggested, existed only 'in our minds'.[19] Matter came to be thought of as 'constructed' in the period primarily because it appeared to differ so fundamentally from our folk or perceptual intuitions about it. It became increasingly apparent that it was the human mind that supplied the raw data of the world – whether they be waves in motion, olfactory compounds, or the kinetic energy of molecules in contact with skin – with their phenomenological qualities.[20] In essence the external world itself was, it was thought, inert. As Alfred North Whitehead put it

> the poets are entirely mistaken. They should address their lyrics to themselves, and should turn them into odes of self-congratulation on the excellency of the human mind. Nature is a dull affair, soundless, scentless, colourless; merely the hurryings of material, endlessly, meaningless.[21]

Attempts to map sensory experiences onto these waves, particles and compounds required new psychological and philosophical methodologies. The physicist and philosopher Ernst Mach's influential call for a science founded upon the analysis of sensations promoted an approach that, he hoped, would allow for the basic units of conscious experience to be isolated, and thus named. For Mach – and for many of those who followed him – such a process depended on attending to the subtle actualities of sensation as it was experienced, and on converting those actualities into prose, prose which often took the form of a kind of short story about the subject's reported perceptual experiences. An early section of Mach's *The Analysis of the Sensations* reads as a sort of impressionist sensory reverie:

> Thus, I lie upon my sofa. If I close my right eye, the picture represented in the accompanying cut is presented to my left eye. In a frame formed

> by the ridge of my eyebrow, by my nose, and by my moustache, appears a part of my body, so far as visible, with its environment. My body differs from other human bodies – beyond the fact that every intense motor idea is immediately expressed by a movement of it, and that, if it is touched, more striking changes are determined than if other bodies are touched – by the circumstance that, it is only seen piecemeal, and, especially, is seen without a head.[22]

As Michael Whitworth has argued, this Machian methodology – and many of the scientific and philosophical projects which grew out of it – was founded on 'descriptionism': the idea that scientific language represented an efficient economisation of thought, and that its value therefore lay in its ability to provide ever more succinct and accurate formulas with which the world could be described and interpreted.[23] Mach's was just one of many attempts to invent a new language of the body in the period, a language that, he hoped, would allow minds and sensations to be reduced to a series of stable, and shareable, propositional statements. But the passage above does much to destabilise that very desire. Bodies, as Mach says, feel distinct and special to those who have them. Yet although they are formed of the same component parts, other peoples' bodies can only ever encountered 'piecemeal'.

Tim Crane has argued that many of the concerns of the qualia-thesis were prefigured by debates over the status of 'sense-data' inspired by Mach's reductive project, particularly in the work of G. E. Moore and Bertrand Russell. Often these debates centred on the relationship between language, sensation and the external world of physical objects. 'Language offers us no means of referring to such objects as "blue" and "green" and "sweet"' wrote G. E. Moore in 1922, 'except by calling them sensations; it is an obvious violation of language to call them "things" or "objects".'[24] Moore's neo-realist epistemological project, developed by Russell, represented a Machian attempt to isolate and name sensations more rigorously, and he tried to achieve it by conceptually deconstructing the world of objects into their component parts. When we encounter the world through the senses, argued Moore, we do not, strictly speaking, see pens and desks and other objects at all. Instead, we perceive only the sense-data of which these object are composed: caused by, but independent of, those objects themselves.

From its inception, therefore, the sense-data thesis, like Mach's descriptionist project before it, was reductive and impressionistic, emphasising that it was the mind itself that constructed objects and gave them continuity through time. Sense-data were not themselves physical, but neither were they considered to be fully psychical. They embodied something of the paradoxes of the model of wave/particle duality that had precipitated their definition:

both present in the mind but also born of interaction with the material world. As the philosopher H. H. Price later summarised, as a concept the sense-datum was not supposed to bring with it any particularly metaphysical baggage. It was intended to be 'a *neutral* term' which did not 'imply the acceptance of any particular theory.'[25] Thus both the Machian descriptionists and the sense-data theorists were engaged in similar projects: to identify and name the objects of experience, and to place them in relation to the material objects of the world (chairs and tables, but also the elementary particles uncovered by the new science). Yet it was not until 1929 that a term appeared which could suitably replace the relatively ambiguous 'sense-data' to describe the peculiar ontology of the new phenomena under discussion.

In *Mind and the World Order*, the American philosopher C. I. Lewis described the 'two elements' which, he said, are inherent to our 'cognitive experiences': the immediate data of sense which are presented or given to the mind, and the form, construction, or interpretation of those data which represents the activity of thought.[26] Lewis felt that the difficulty of naming precisely what constitutes the 'second element' of cognitive experience – it was in his words a 'construction', or an 'interpretation' – was unsatisfactory, and so he clarified the point by invoking a new term that he hoped would remove the ambiguities associated with sense-data. The content of any sensory 'presentation' within consciousness, is, he said,

> either a specific quale (such as the immediacy of redness or loudness) or something analyzable into a complex of such. The presentation as an event is, of course, unique, but the qualia which make it up are not. They are recognizable from one to another experience. Such specific qualia and repeatable complexes of them are nowadays sometimes designated as 'essences'.[27]

Whereas sense-data could be discussed or analysed on their own terms – while their status remained perilously ambiguous – for Lewis qualia stood more as a philosophical cipher or algebraic place-holder for those qualities of consciousness that by definition resisted any such classification. As Lewis continued, 'such qualia, though repeatable in experience and intrinsically recognizable, have no names.'[28] With his coinage, Lewis hoped merely to clarify precisely what was at issue when attempts were made to analyse sensations in a Machian manner. But in doing so he gave birth to a metaphysical dilemma that has become central to debates within philosophy of mind over the nature of sensation, and the relationship between minds and bodies. This dilemma, as we shall see, has also impacted on the way in which modernist fiction's supposed turn inward has been formulated.

Qualia, Bergson and Modernist Aesthetics

It is tempting to read the emergence of philosophical debates over the status of qualia as mirroring those associated with modernism's wider aesthetic and psychological revolutions. Just as the mnemonic and cognitive functions of the mind became threatened by technological advances (gramophone, typewriter, camera) in the period, and the essence of the human was sought in ever more specific and atomised qualities of consciousness, so did much modernist art and literature begin to focus its attention on the minutiae of sensory experience. In policing the dividing line between real and artificial minds – and between the machine and the human – qualia embodied some of the political and ethical tensions implicit to the modernist project also. Here was a concept that promised to draw clear lines between affect and its absence; between the individual artist and the mob; between recognising the epiphanies of significant form, style and colour and being forever ignorant of them.

As we shall see in Chapter 2, when invoked in relation to aesthetics the quale – like the 'impression', the 'sensation' and the 'sense-datum' before it – has often been employed as a binary marker, and associated with a state of childish, prelapsarian consciousness unburdened by rational thought. This association, too, had its origins within modernism. Virginia Woolf's ambivalent engagement with Cambridge epistemology and James Joyce's radical experiments in narrative perspective can both be understood as resulting from a perceived dichotomy between knowledge of objective 'facts' and knowledge of one's own sensations that was first proposed by William James (and later taken up by Bertrand Russell) in his distinction between 'knowledge by acquaintance' and 'knowledge by description'. This contested boundary between perception and knowledge had literary as well as philosophical origins. In Henry James's *What Maisie Knew*, for instance, a naïve child with limited experience of the world is asked to make sense of her experiences in much the same way that we as readers are asked to encounter fictional worlds when we read novels. The trope of the 'naïve eye', which, as Michael Whitworth has shown, was enshrined within so much modernist fiction was in its first incarnation essentially a scientific eye: one focused on the relationship between experience, hypothesis and experimentation.[29] Just as art became conceived of as a way of 'probing reality' – engaged in an experimental process not because it represented an 'experiment' in form that might succeed or fail, but because it actively experimented *on* the viewer (the canvas becoming a photographic plate, the novel a laboratory) so the sciences quickly internalised the languages and styles of literary modernism. This interrelation between scientific discourse, philosophy and literary aesthetics was particularly evident in the work of Henri Bergson.

Bergson's theories were enormously influential within both literary and philosophical circles in Britain in the early 1900s.[30] He was, according to Jesse Matz, 'the century's first pop psychologist', representing, for some modernists, a revolution in ways of conceiving of subjectivity and consciousness.[31] As Michael Levenson and Mary Ann Gillies have argued, Bergson's influence on Anglo-American literary modernism, was in many cases quite direct.[32] For others he was the leader, in Wyndham Lewis's words, of a 'childish time-cult' that privileged sensation over analysis.[33] Mapping Bergson's theories onto the qualia debate is difficult, not least because it is hard to isolate a stable position in his writing as to whether sensory experience could ever be successfully 'written' at all.[34] Nevertheless, a Bergsonian desire to enshrine the senses at the heart of a mutually constituted philosophical and aesthetic project clearly mirrors many of the debates over the status of sense-data in the period, and anticipates some of the central controversies within the qualia debate later in the century. Despite his claim, in *Time and Free Will*, that 'the art which gives only sensations is an inferior art', elsewhere Bergson subscribed to an aesthetics of immediacy which quite clearly privileged the experiential over the descriptive.[35]

One of the most obvious instances of the similarities between Bergson's theories and the doctrine of qualia can be seen in his philosophy as it related to concepts of time, in particular in his differentiation between *durée* and *temps* which he saw as central both to the complex reality of sensory experience and to the central problems of philosophy. *Durée* – like qualia – was held by Bergson to be experiential, ontologically subjective, irreducible, and impossible to convey in third-person terms. In *Creative Evolution* he defined *durée* as 'the continuous progress of the past which gnaws into the future and which swells as it advances', concluding that 'we do not *think* real time. But we *live* it, because life transcends intellect.'[36] Like qualia, then, duration could only be known through experiential introspection: not from the outside, but only as lived experience. As such it was inherently resistant to any symbolic representation. As Bergson wrote in *An Introduction to Metaphysics*, translated into English by T. E. Hulme, duration 'can be presented to us directly in an intuition . . . it can be suggested to us indirectly by images, but . . . it can never – if we confine the word concept to its proper meaning – be enclosed in a conceptual representation'.[37]

Temps, on the other hand, and the kind of knowledge it represented, *could* be 'enclosed in conceptual representation' successfully. Clock time was, Bergson argued, impersonal, public, and, crucially, could be shared with others through intermediary devices, or through language. Yet, as such, *temps* was also inevitably impoverished and partial: it was only, in Bergson's formulation, 'a diagram, a simplified reconstruction, often a mere symbol, in any case a motionless view of the moving reality.'[38] It falsified the experience of movement which was essential to duration, ignoring its phenomenological nature and thus misleading us as to the true nature of underlying reality. Abstract concepts, ideas, measurements and language all removed consciousness from contact with what was real. One of the most pressing errors of contemporary philosophy, so Bergson believed, lay 'in believing that we can reconstruct the real with these diagrams'.[39]

Bergson's theories therefore endorsed a dichotomy between ways of knowing the world that were very similar to those espoused by contemporary philosophers interested in sense-data, which would be developed by later philosophers engaged with the problem of qualia. And, as with the qualia debate, they were constantly under pressure from those who saw them not as ushering in a new era of Vitalist art and psychology, but as obfuscating precisely what the relationship between sensation and the arts should look like. This tension is particularly evident through the work of T. E. Hulme, who was a leading translator and populariser of Bergson's theories in the English-speaking world (but who, as Michael Levenson and Jesse Matz have shown, radically altered his opinion of Bergsonism in the 1910s).[40] Though she claimed never to have read him, Virginia Woolf too was certainly familiar with Bergson's philosophy, due in part to the fact that her sister-in-law, Karin Stephen, was a leading Bergsonian.[41] Her influential call, in 'Modern Fiction', for novelists to capture the 'incessant shower of innumerable atoms as they fall' upon the mind suggests sympathy, as many critics have noted, with Bergson's ideas.[42] In a 1922 book which did much to popularise Bergson's ideas to the British public, Karin Stephen presented his philosophical method as an inversion of what was by then a well-established rational hierarchy when it came to studying the mind. Stephen used the example of contemporary art to elucidate the practice of discrimination and categorisation she saw as antithetical to Bergson's philosophy:

> If, for instance, you look at a very modern painting, at first what you are directly aware of may be little more than a confused sight: bye and bye, as you go on looking you will be able to distinguish colours and shapes, one by one objects may be recognised until finally you may be able to see the whole picture at a glance as composed of four or five different colours arranged in definite shapes and positions. You may even be able to make out that it represents a human figure, or a landscape.[43]

This process of 'reading' a picture – gradually building up its meaning from the immediate sense-data of which it is composed – so Stephen argued, limits understanding by diminishing one type of experience by focusing only on those elements of the painting that pertain to 'action': on the kinds of judgements made by a rational mind on behalf of the body. 'Actual knowledge' emerges from this examination of the senses, but it was in the 'virtual' knowledge left over, so Stephen (following Bergson) argued, that pure sensation dwelt.

Hulme too had stressed the Bergsonian dichotomy between those cognitive functions he associated with 'action' – which were rational, abstracted and inherently misleading – and those associated with pure sensation. According to the aesthetic theory outlined in his essay 'Bergson's Theory of Art', the tyranny of this classification, and the failure of language to accommodate 'the individuality and freshness of things', created space for a separate class of perceiver, one which Hulme identified with the figure of the artist.[44] But this separation also meant that the arts were only ever rarely – if ever – able to grasp sensory reality directly. 'What I see and hear', he wrote, 'is simply a selection made by my senses to serve as a light for my conduct. My senses and my consciousness give me no more than a practical simplification of reality.'[45] Because of this simplification, Hulme continued, 'we never ever perceive the real shape and individuality of objects. We only see stock types. We tend to see not *the* table but only *a* table.'[46] Applying Bergson's ideas to poetry, Hulme went on to discuss Keats's poem 'Isabella; or, The Pot of Basil', specifically focusing on the line 'And she forgot the blue above the trees' and asking:

> Why . . . did he put 'blue above the trees' and not 'sky'? 'Sky' is just as attractive an expression. Simply for this reason, that he instinctively felt that the word 'sky' would not convey over the actual vividness and the actuality of the feeling he wanted to express. The choice of the right detail, the blue above the trees, forces that vividness on you and is the cause of the kind of thrill it gives you.[47]

Here literary originality is conceived of as figurative – meaning, a new kind of knowledge, resides in the creation of novel metaphorical connections founded on the primacy of sensation. The deconstruction and alienation of the visual field that were central to the Imagist and Impressionist projects is therefore of a piece with the general reductive impulses of modernity that will be examined in Chapter 5. But it is also suggestive of the central fault lines of the qualia thesis itself. Stripping away extraneous markers of knowledge to concentrate on essential 'meaning' (however elusive this meaning proves to be) was, argued Hulme, the source not only of accurate knowledge of the external world, but also of good poetry. The atomisation of sensation into its constituent visual synecdoche was for Hulme a characteristic of literary language that could never be achieved in the tokenistic exchanges of scientific writing. 'It is only where you get these fresh metaphors and epithets employed', he argued, 'that you get this vivid conviction which constitutes the purely aesthetic emotion that can be got from imagery.'[48] For Hulme, once language had lost its power to convey sensation it became subsumed within the residuum of algebraic designation, entombed in the museum of dead metaphors. According to this reading, any attempt by philosophical or scientific writing to get to grips with sensations as they are experienced was doomed to failure.

The strategy of defamiliarisation associated with sense-data theory, Bergsoniansim, and later with qualia can be seen therefore to have been incorporated across modernist discourse as a kind of general aesthetic principle that was never fully realised. But the various tensions between sensation and language, or between qualia and materialist accounts of consciousness, which lay at the heart of the Bergsonian project made it an unstable scaffold on which to build a general aesthetic theory. While Hulme did much to popularise Bergson's theories in Britain and America, for other leading modernists Bergson was an obfuscating charlatan committed to what Wyndham Lewis called the 'inner method' of Gertrude Stein, Woolf and Joyce. 'Time for the bergsonian or relativist' Lewis argued in *Time and Western Man*, 'is fundamentally sensation; that is what Bergson's *durée* always conceals beneath its pretentious metaphysic.'[49] By 1912, Matz writes, even Hulme himself 'had turned from Bergsonism to embrace an opposing position' consisting of those 'anti-psychologistic positions' endorsed by Husserl, Moore and others.[50] 'Rejecting Bergson', Matz concludes, 'Hulme led modernism's effort to exclude psychology from definitions of culture.'[51]

The particular tensions inherent in the debate over the relation of sense-data to physics was clearly mirrored in aesthetic debates over the status and utility of sensation formulated by Bergson and shared in the English speaking world by writers and artists broadly associated with modernism. And one way in which this particular aspect of Bergson's psychologism can be seen to have persisted within Anglo-American philosophy was through the qualia debate. By the 1910s physics, aesthetics and philosophy were motivated to differentiate between those elements of consciousness that were secret, ontologically subjective and unshareable (but essential and unchanging), and those aspects of it which were public, available to language, and shareable. Just as the origins of qualia as a philosophical concept lie in the modernist moment, then, so too do aesthetic debates surrounding the possibility of literature ever being able to properly 'capture' or 'convey' or 'render' them.

Qualia and the Critics

As we have seen, both modernist aesthetics and the philosophical debate over qualia manifest an (often fruitful) anxiety over the role, purpose and possibilities of various forms of reduction. The reductive impulses of modernity – whether inculcated in Ezra Pound's Imagist project, which sought 'direct treatment of the "thing," whether subjective or objective'; or in the analytical philosophical tradition's interest in 'sense data'; or in Husserl's phenomenological campaign which sought, via the process of 'epoché' or 'bracketing', to get 'back to the "things themselves"' – were internalised across the arts in the period to become something of a general aesthetic principle.[52] But these impulses also led to profound psychological, scientific and literary reappraisals of what, precisely, those 'things' or 'objects' of the mind could or should be said to consist of once they had been isolated. These reappraisals raised some obvious questions. How can literature, an art composed of words, hope to acquaint us with non-verbal mental experiences, experiences which can by definition mean nothing in and of themselves? How can imaginative literature peopled by invented characters ever claim to represent 'real' minds? Modernism's hyper-subjectivity often sought to strip character of story, yet in doing so it brought about a notable paradox. The very components that were said by some to constitute the fundamental building blocks of consciousness – whether they were called sensations, phenomenological experiences, or qualia – often turned out, both within the novel-form and within the philosophical and psychological traditions attendant to it, to be the most elusive and least shareable.

Over the past twenty years critical narratives of modernism's inward turn have begun to engage with qualia, yet those critics who have discussed the concept have often downplayed the difficulties qualia pose for reductive theories of mind, and for the cognitive realist thesis. Within philosophical discourse qualia are generally held to be incompatible with reductively materialist accounts of consciousness: if they exist, then the mind can never be reduced to a model or theory or diagrammatic account of its workings.[53] Accepting the existence of qualia would seem, therefore, to necessitate a rejection of the belief that consciousness is a stable entity that can be reduced to written descriptions, whether scientific, philosophical, or literary.

Many contemporary critics, especially those aligned with a 'neuroaesthetic' or 'cognitive' approach to literature, have been minded to deny simple physicalist or reductive conceptions of mind in theory, while at the same time endorsing the novel as a literary mode which is able to successfully encode qualia within language (denying the possibility of conveying sensation directly through the straightforward reporting of sensory experiences, for instance, while maintaining that certain stylistic literary strategies are able to circumvent these limitations). They would therefore seem to rely on some form of reductive materialism to justify their arguments. Though the relationship between materialist theories of consciousness and literary modernism have generally focused on modernism's debt to contemporary philosophy (as, for instance, in the work of S. P. Rosenbaum and Ann Banfield, or in analyses of literary applications of Bergson's legacies, as examined above), more recently, with the cognitive turn in cultural studies, critics have begun to engage in the question of qualia by seeking to justify modernism's formal experimentation solely in terms of its ability to render consciousness in a cognitive realist mode.

In a book which is exemplary of this kind of approach – *Consciousness and the Novel* – David Lodge makes an argument which is representative of these neo-humanist attempts to defend the status of fiction as a repository of qualia. 'Literature' he asserts, 'is a record of human consciousness, the richest and most comprehensive we have. Lyric poetry is arguable man's most successful effort to describe qualia. The novel is arguably man's most successful effort to describe the experience of individual human beings moving through space and time.[54] For Lodge the novel is conceived as a kind of cognitive virtual reality machine, representing mankind's 'most successful effort to describe the experience' of consciousness. Here Lodge, like many cognitive realist theorists of the novel, understands the use of the first-person pronoun to be equivalent to the direct presentation of qualia. Imaginative literature, he argues, offers something that objective, scientific writing cannot, and it is precisely that *something* that is equivalent with qualia. 'The first-person pronoun is not used in scientific papers', he continues, if 'there were any hint of qualia in a scientific paper . . . it would be edited out.'[55]

In Lodge's account, which is typical of these kinds of cognitively informed approaches to fiction, qualia are treated as properties of language rather than as ontologically distinct qualities of mind. On this point Lodge echoes the neuroscientists V. S. Ramachandran and Sandra Blakeslee, who have argued that solving the problem of qualia would involve nothing more than reconciling 'the first-person and third-person accounts of the universe.'[56] But to interpret 'first-person and third-person accounts' in this context as referring to narrative positioning rather than to ontological properties is to misrepresent the more radical problem presented by the qualia thesis. In *The Mystery of Consciousness* John Searle made an influential distinction between two different kinds of subjectivity: 'epistemic' and 'ontological.' 'In one sense', he argued:

> the objective/subjective distinction is about claims to knowledge. I call this the epistemic sense. A claim is said to be objective if its truth or falsity can be settled as a matter of fact independently of anybody's attitudes, feelings, or evaluations; it is subjective if it cannot . . . In another sense, the objective/subjective distinction is about modes of existence. I call this the ontological sense. An entity has an objective ontology if its existence does not depend on being experienced by a human or animal subject; otherwise it is subjective. For example, mountains, molecules, and tectonic plates are ontologically objective. Their experience does not depend on being experienced by anybody. But pains, tickles, and itches only exist when experienced by a human of animal subject. They are ontologically subjective.[57]

For Searle the kind of subjectivity invoked by first-person narratives is only ever epistemic – it is about claims to public knowledge, even if those claims pertain to a fictional world. A series of sensory statements, such as those that make up the opening section of Virginia Woolf's *The Waves* – 'I see a ring', 'I see a slab of yellow', 'I hear a sound' – have no greater claims on subjective ontology than if they were written in the third person.[58] Inadmissible to a scientific paper though such sensory declarations may be, they do not suddenly become *less* ontologically subjective by being re-written in the third person. To read 'I see a ring' rather than 'he sees a ring' is still to be at one remove from the ring seen. The subjective ontology of qualia should not be seen as equivalent to the apparent intimacy and immediacy generated by first-person narrative, argues Searle. Indeed, it is a category mistake to conflate the two. For if qualia exist then the 'hint of qualia' Lodge identifies above as being 'edited out' of scientific discourse can never be 'present' in *any* form of discourse. If qualia exist then they could not be edited out of a scientific paper, for they could never have been there in the first place.

Adherents of cognitive realism often invoke the more 'literary' qualities of imaginative writing – especially the use of figurative language, and literary techniques associated with modernist aesthetics – as allowing it to overcome the problems posed by qualia. For Lodge metaphor and simile allow writers to avoid the reductive constraints of scientific writing about consciousness, so that they are somehow able to 'render' qualia. 'In literature', he writes, 'by describing each quale in terms of something else that is both similar and different . . . the object and the experience of it are vividly stimulated. One sensation is invoked to give specificity to another. The nonverbal is verbalised.'[59] In *Imagining Minds*, Kay Young too argues that the figurative nature of literary discourse allows writers to address the senses directly, sidestepping the representative limitations qualia maintain. The philosopher, she argues, 'writes ideas as arguments about the nature of being' whereas the novelist 'embodies ideas as representations of being'.[60] Philosophers 'write . . . arguments' whereas artists 'represent . . . in metaphor'.[61]

Similarly, by resisting particular contextual information and obscuring the individual who may be doing the speaking, so Lodge argues, lyric poetry achieves an affective phenomenological fidelity: a faithful replication of a specific sensory experience. Quoting from a discussion of Marvell's 'The Garden' from his novel *Thinks . . .* , which dealt with similar concerns, he continues:

> Let me point out a paradox about Marvell's verse, which applies to lyric poetry in general. Although he speaks in the first person, Marvell does not speak for himself alone. In reading this stanza we enhance our own experience of the qualia of fruit and fruitfulness. We see the fruit, we taste it and smell it and savour it with what has been called 'the thrill of recognition' and yet it is not there, it is the virtual reality of fruit, conjured up by the qualia of the poem.[62]

Yet endorsing the existence of qualia while maintaining that literary language can somehow cross the explanatory gulf their existence would create is inherently contradictory. Thomas Nagel's influential formulation of qualia as constituting the 'what-is–it-like-ness' of consciousness is explicitly meant to *not* be a comparative statement. As Ned Block has pointed out, to focus on the comparative or figurative capabilities of literary language, and to anoint them with some special status or ability which allows them to overcome the problem of qualia and write sensation directly, is to misrepresent precisely what is at issue in the debate. Metaphor is no way out of the qualial impasse. Although in 'The Garden' we are told something about the 'fruit of the vine', and of some of its properties, to say that 'we see the fruit, taste it and smell it' through reading is, in an important sense, simply not true. 'Ecrite la merde', noted Roland Barthes, 'ne sent pas'.[63]

What's particularly striking here is that in their analyses of the role of metaphor in conveying qualia, critics like Lodge and Young often subscribe to an understanding of the possibilities of figurative language which itself took hold during the modernist moment. The idea that stylistically experimental forms of expression might be better able to convey the reality of our inner lives was manifested particularly in the Symbolist inheritance of Imagist poetics, where the poet was figured as the source of new language able to meet the demands of fractious modernity. In his essay on 'Bergson's Theory of Art', for instance, T. E. Hulme (in a passage very suggestive of Ralph Waldo Emerson's poetics) argued that though metaphors 'soon run their course and die', it was

> necessary to remember that when they were first used by the poets who created them they were used for the purpose of conveying over a vividly felt actual sensation. Nothing could be more dead now than the conventional expressions of love poetry, the arrow which pierces the heart and the rest of it, but originally they were used as conveying over the reality of the sensation experienced.[64]

The tendency for critics engaged, even tangentially, with the question of qualia to identify 'literature' in general, and figurative language in particular, as somehow more suited or more successful at conveying certain types of knowledge than scientific language is itself a product of this historical moment. In this, as in so many other ways, we live in the shadow of modernism.

Many critics have interpreted the specific problems of representing the mind in fiction as emerging directly from attempts to understand consciousness in the positivist, scientific terms associated with modernity. In this account modernist aesthetics self-consciously grapples with its Cartesian legacy and our increasingly sophisticated knowledge of the biological workings of the brain by retreating into stylistic obfuscation and difficulty. Often, debates over the status of qualia within literature are channelled into discussion of the presence (or absence) of 'the body' more generally within fiction. Partly, as Terry Eagleton has argued, this desire to re-insert an abstracted 'body' into literary discourse is the product of a nostalgia for the origins of aesthetics.[65] And yet in one important sense, if qualia exist then bodily ways of knowing simply cannot be accommodated within literature, however much we'd like that to be the case. Indeed the void between bodily and analytical knowledge which debates over the existence of qualia continue to grapple with was, as Patricia Waugh has argued, itself produced by the conditions of modernity:

> The incertitude of the void is the abyss which opens between the Cartesian subject and the Newtonian universe, and the specifically modern aesthetic is formulated as a heroic struggle toward the plenitudinous form of a concrete universal where, somehow, the wound of self-consciousness might be healed, where embodied experience might be reunited with the reflective idea of itself, mind with body, and consciousness with cosmos. Literature exists in this heroic vision to give presence to what is made unavailable by science.[66]

While offering a compelling justification for literature being our most affective and accurate record of individual human consciousness, therefore, the claims made by cognitive realists such as Lodge and Young, when they engage with the question of qualia, offer little methodical exegesis. It is not enough to simply claim that literary language is more 'embodied' or 'vital' or 'sensory' than other forms of language use. By invoking the term, many critics give credence to the concept of qualia while at the same time maintaining that the dualist void the existence of such properties would create can be crossed by certain types of writing, and thus commit what we might term the 'fallacy of qualia.' To see why it is that these ontological slippages took hold in such a wide range of contexts during the modernist moment it is necessary to return to intellectual origins, to provide a historical account of the emergence of qualia, and to read the philosophical debates which gave rise to the concept alongside those fictional representations of sensory experience that mirrored (and, in some senses, contributed to) their development. This is what I shall begin to do in the following chapters.

Notes

1. Eric Kahler, *The Inward Turn of Narrative*, trans. by Richard and Clara Winston (Princeton, NJ: Princeton University Press, 1973), p. 5.
2. Mark S. Micale, 'Introduction: The Modernist Mind – A Map', in *The Mind of Modernism: Medicine, Psychology and the Cultural Arts in Europe and America 1880–1940*, ed. by Mark S. Micale (Stanford, CA: Stanford University Press, 2004), p. 2
3. Micale 'Introduction: The Modernist Mind', p. 2.
4. Emily Troscianko, *Kafka's Cognitive Realism* (London: Routledge, 2016); Terence Cave, *Thinking With Literature* (Oxford: Oxford University Press, 2016).
5. See Anne Fernihough, 'Consciousness as a Stream', in *The Cambridge Companion to the Modernist Novel*, ed. by Morag Shiach (Cambridge: Cambridge University Press, 2007).

6. Leon Edel, *The Psychological Novel: 1900–1950* (London: Rupert Hart-Davis, 1955), p. ix.
7. Melvin Friedman, *Stream of Consciousness: A Study in Literary Method* (New Haven, CT: Yale University Press, 1955), p. 27.
8. Robert Humphrey, *Stream of Consciousness and the Modern Novel* (Berkeley and Los Angeles, CA: University of California Press, 1962), pp. 4, 6.
9. Lawrence Edward Bowling, 'What is the Stream of Consciousness Technique?', *PMLA*, 65.4 (1950), 333–345 (p. 345) (emphasis in original).
10. See Fernihough, 'Consciousness as a Stream', p. 72; and David Lodge, *Consciousness and the Novel* (London: Secker & Warburg 2002), p. 10.
11. May Sinclair, 'The Novels of Dorothy Richardson', *The Egoist*, 5.4 (1918), 57–59 (p. 58).
12. Erich Auerbach, *Mimesis: The Representation of Reality in Western Literature*, trans. by Willard R. Trask (Princeton, NJ: Princeton University Press, 1953), p. 525–553.
13. Monika Fludernik, *Towards a 'Natural' Narratology* (London and New York: Routledge, 1996), p. 170.
14. David Herman, 'Re-minding Modernism', in *The Emergence of Mind: Representations of Consciousness in Narrative Discourse in English*, ed. by David Herman (Lincoln, NE and London: University of Nebraska Press, 2011), p. 252–253.
15. Herman, 'Re-minding Modernism', p. 253.
16. Cave, *Thinking with Literature*, p. 17.
17. Cave, *Thinking with Literature*, pp. 17–18.
18. Ian McEwan, interview with Michael Silverblatt, Bookworm, KCRW, 11 July 2002. On the cultural and philosophical implications of neuroplasticity see, especially, Catherine Malabou, *What Should We Do with Our Brain?* (Ashland, OH: Fordham University Press, 2008).
19. Gillian Beer, 'Wave Theory and the Rise of Literary Modernism', in *Open Fields: Science in Cultural Encounter*, ed. by Gillian Beer (Oxford: Clarendon Press, 1996), p. 295; James Jeans, *The Mysterious Universe* (Cambridge: Cambridge University Press, 1930), p. 79.
20. Michael H. Whitworth, *Virginia Woolf* (Oxford: Oxford University Press, 2005), p. 116.
21. Alfred North Whitehead, Science and the Modern World: Lowell Lectures, 1925 (New York: Mentor Books, 1925), p. 55.
22. Ernst Mach, *The Analysis of Sensations and the Relation of the Physical to the Psychical*, trans. by C. M. Williams (Chicago, IL and London: The Open Court Publishing Company, 1914), p. 18–19.
23. See Michael H. Whitworth, *Einstein's Wake: Relativity, Metaphor, and Modernist Literature* (Oxford: Oxford University Press, 2001), pp. 83–110.
24. G. E. Moore, Philosophical Studies (London: Kegan Paul, Trench, Trubner & Co. Ltd, 1922), p. 19.
25. H. H. Price, *Perception* (London: Methuen & Co. Ltd, 1932), p. 19.
26. C. I. Lewis, *Mind and the World Order* (New York: Dover Publications, Inc., 1929), p. 38.
27. Lewis, *Mind and the World Order*, p. 60.

28. Lewis, *Mind and the World Order*, p. 61.
29. See Whitworth, *Einstein's Wake*, p. 97.
30. See especially, Shiv Kumar, *Bergson and the Stream of Consciousness Novel* (London and Glasgow: Blackie & Son, 1962); Paul Ardoin, S. E. Gontarski and Laci Mattison, eds, *Understanding Bergson, Understanding Modernism* (New York: Bloomsbury, 2013); and Mary Ann Gillies, *Henri Bergson and British Modernism* (Montreal and London: McGill-Queen's University Press, 1996).
31. Jesse Matz, 'T. E. Hulme, Henri Bergson, and the Cultural Politics of Psychologism', in *The Mind of Modernism*, ed. by Micale, p. 341.
32. See Gillies, *Henri Bergson and British Modernism*; and Michael H. Levenson, *A Genealogy of Modernism A Study of English Literary Doctrine 1908–1922* (Cambridge: Cambridge University Press, 1984). For an excellent discussion of Bergson's influence on his contemporaries, see Frederick Burwick and Paul Douglas, eds, *The Crisis in Modernism: Bergson and the Vitalist Controversy* (Cambridge: Cambridge University Press, 1992). Giles Deleuze argued for a return to Bergsonism in his *Bergsonism*, trans. by Hugh Tomlinson and Barbara Habberjam (New York: Zone Books, 1988), and Mark Antliff has examined the cultural politics of Bergsonism in *Inventing Bergson: Cultural Politics and the Parisian Avant-Garde* (Princeton, NJ: Princeton University Press, 1993).
33. Wyndham Lewis, *Time and Western Man*, ed. by Paul Edwards (Santa Rosa, CA: Black Sparrow Press, 1993), p. 27.
34. This is partly due to the difficulty, as Stephen E. Robbins has noted, of accommodating the temporal dimension into models of consciousness that accommodate qualia. See Stephen E. Robbins, 'Time, Form and the Limits of Qualia', *The Journal of Mind and Behavior*, 28.1 (2007), 19–43.
35. Henri Bergson, *Time and Free Will: An Essay on the Immediate Data of Consciousness*, trans. by F. L. Pogson (London: George Allen & Company, Ltd, 1910), p. 17.
36. Henri Bergson, *Creative Evolution*, trans. by Arthur Mitchell (London: Macmillan and Co., Ltd, 1911), pp. 5, 49.
37. Henri Bergson, *An Introduction to Metaphysics*, trans. by T. E. Hulme (London: Macmillan and Co., Ltd, 1913), p. 19.
38. Bergson, *An Introduction to Metaphysics*, p. 41.
39. Bergson, *An Introduction to Metaphysics*, p. 41.
40. See Levenson, *A Genealogy of Modernism*, and Matz, 'T. E. Hulme, Henri Bergson, and the Cultural Politics of Psychologism', p. 339.
41. In a letter to Harmon H. Goldstone (dated 16 August 1932), Woolf wrote 'I may say that I have never read Bergson and have only a very amateurish knowledge of Freud and the psychoanalysts; I have made no study of them'. Virginia Woolf, *The Sickle Side of the Moon: The Letters of Virginia Woolf Volume V: 1932–1935*, ed. by Nigel Nicolson (London: Chatto & Windus, 1979), p. 91.
42. Virginia Woolf, 'Modern Fiction', in *The Essays of Virginia Woolf*, vol. IV, ed. by Stuart N. Clarke (London: The Hogarth Press, 2009), p. 161.
43. Karin Stephen, *The Misuse of Mind* (London: Kegan Paul, Trench, Trubner & Co., Ltd, 1922), p. 25.

44. T. E. Hulme, 'Bergson's Theory of Art', in *The Collected Writings of T. E. Hulme*, ed. by Karen Csengeri (Oxford: Clarendon Press, 1994), p. 201.
45. Hulme, 'Bergson's Theory of Art', pp. 198–9.
46. Hulme, 'Bergson's Theory of Art', p. 199.
47. Hulme, 'Bergson's Theory of Art', p. 201.
48. Hulme, 'Bergson's Theory of Art', p. 195.
49. Wyndham Lewis, *Time and Western Man*, p. 27.
50. Matz, 'T. E. Hulme, Henri Bergson, and the Cultural Politics of Psychologism', p. 340.
51. Matz, 'T. E. Hulme, Henri Bergson, and the Cultural Politics of Psychologism', p. 340.
52. Ezra Pound, *Literary Essays* (New York: New Directions, 1935; repr. 1968), p. 35; Edmund Husserl, *Logical Investigations*, ed. by Dermot Moran, trans. by J. N. Findlay, 2 vols (London and New York: Routledge, 2001), vol. i, p. 168.
53. See, for instance, Clyde L. Hardin, 'Qualia and Materialism: Closing the Explanatory Gap', *Philosophy and Phenomenological Research*, 48.2 (1987), 281–298.
54. Lodge, *Consciousness and the Novel*, p. 10.
55. Lodge, *Consciousness and the Novel*, p. 11.
56. V. S. Ramachandran and S. Blakeslee, *Phantoms in the Brain: Probing the Mysteries of the Human Mind* (New York: Morrow & Co., 1998), p. 229.
57. John R. Searle, 'The Mystery of Consciousness Continues', *The New York Review of Books,* 9 June 2011, p. 50. See also John R. Searle, *The Mystery of Consciousness* (London: Granta, 1997), pp. 112–122.
58. Virginia Woolf, *The Waves* (London: The Hogarth Press, 1931), p. 7.
59. Lodge, *Consciousness and the Novel*, p. 13.
60. Kay Young, *Imagining Minds: The Neuro-Aesthetics of Austen, Eliot and Hardy* (Columbus, OH: The Ohio State University Press, 2010), p. 95.
61. Young, *Imagining Minds*, p. 95.
62. Lodge, *Consciousness and the Novel*, p. 12.
63. Roland Barthes, *Sade, Fourier, Loyola* (Paris: Editions du Seuil, 1980), p. 140.
64. Hulme, 'Bergson's Theory of Art', p. 195. Christopher J. Knight points out that where Hulme differs from Emerson is in his belief that one could 'transcend this difficulty. Hume believes that while the ordinary course of both perception and language is one that caters to the habitual, it is possible, with a powerful degree of determination, not only to "see things as they really are" but also "to force the mechanism of expression out of the way in which it tends to go and into the way he wants."' See Christopher J. Knight, *The Patient Particulars: American Modernism and the Technique of Originality* (Lewisburg, PA: Bucknell University Press; London: Associated University Press, 1995), p. 72.
65. Terry Eagleton, *The Ideology of the Aesthetic* (Oxford: Blackwell, 1990), p. 13.
66. Patricia Waugh, 'Revising the Two Cultures Debate: Science, Literature and Value', in *The Arts and Sciences of Criticism*, ed. by David Fuller and Patricia Waugh (Oxford: Oxford University Press, 1999), p. 36.

2

WHAT VIRGINIA DIDN'T KNOW: KNOWLEDGE, IMPRESSIONISM AND THE EYE

> Oh, yes, my body, me alive, *knows*, and knows intensely. And as for the sum of all knowledge, it can't be anything more than an accumulation of all the things I know in the body, and you, dear reader, know in the body.
> D. H. Lawrence, 'Why the Novel Matters'

Knowledge and the Novel

Literature in general, and the novel in particular, has often been considered capable of conveying kinds of knowledge that are resistant to other forms of representation. But the nature of this knowledge is various, and it has altered over time. Technological advances in the early twentieth century changed fundamentally our understanding of what knowledge itself consisted of. 'What one can know of a human being today', wrote Friedrich Kittler in *Discourse Networks*, 'has nothing to do with the 4,000 pages that Sartre, posing the same question, devoted to the psychology of Flaubert. One can record people's voices, their fingerprints, their parapraxes.'[1] The newly invented mnemonic technologies of gramophone and photograph which Kittler identified as the principal catalysts for this epistemological renegotiation allowed for a simulacrum of personhood to be captured through recording the data streams which make up the human sensorium. In the 'Hades' episode of James Joyce's *Ulysses* Leopold Bloom contemplates the ways in which such technology made people recordable and reproducible as never before. 'Besides how could you remember everybody?', Bloom asks himself,

'Eyes, walk, voice. Well, the voice yes: gramophone. Have a gramophone in ever grave or keep it in the house . . . Remind you of the voice like a photograph reminds you of the face.'[2] By offering a model of perfect sensory reproduction, such technology threatened to render the human subject dead or, at any rate, dying. Under the scrutiny of the reductive sciences, bolstered by mnemonic technologies able to capture sensation seemingly without loss, an understanding of personhood, and of what constituted literary character, began to be sought in new places.

When read alongside the qualia thesis, the idea that literature might provide a way of making up the knowledge deficit associated with modernity – that it might convey to its readers the kind of knowledge that D. H. Lawrence calls, in 'Why the Novel Matters', 'emphatic and vital' – is clearly problematic. Although, as Lawrence writes in that essay, the 'body, me alive, *knows*, and knows intensely', if qualia exist then this knowledge seems doomed forever to exist outside of language, whether that language is scientific, literary, or analytical.[3] And yet modernist narrative fiction has often been interpreted very much in terms of its ability to make us think that the overtly 'literary' body is, in Patricia Waugh's words 'in some sense' more alive than other textual manifestations of it. 'Literary language', Waugh has argued, 'is in some sense more embodied, closer to and arising out of the rhythms and pulsations of the body, and more able to produce bodily effects in its readers, than the so-called transparent language of science.'[4] As we have seen, invoking the notion of qualia complicates this established picture of the written or literary body, however, forcing us to be more rigorous in our associations of certain forms of writing with certain forms of 'bodily' knowledge.

This anxiety – over the status of knowledge and its relationship both to the body and to writing – manifests itself explicitly within modernist narrative fiction. Alan Palmer has suggested that modernist literature is often 'oriented toward the investigation of such issues as perception and cognition, perspective, the subjective experience of time, and the circulation and reliability of knowledge', and that it is 'preoccupied with such questions as, What is there to know about the world? Who knows it, and how reliably? How is knowledge transmitted, to whom, and how reliably?'[5] Many literary critics have emphasised the modernist novel's catholic nature: the form's heteroglossic capacity to contain competing yet often complementary forms of knowledge, and also to comment on or interpret these ways of knowing from within. 'The flexibility of [the novel's] narrative modes and uses of voice', Waugh writes, 'allows for complex metalevel reflection on the relations between language, feeling and cognition in the representation of *qualia*.'[6] Yet the question of whether it makes sense to speak of the representability of qualia in terms of competing forms of sensory knowledge is a vexed one, and in this chapter I will explore this question by focusing on what has come to be termed the 'knowledge argument' for the existence of qualia, an argument that intersects in provocative ways with many of the preoccupations of literary modernism.

As with the qualia debate, the philosophical conditions of the knowledge argument were prefigured in debates over the status of sense-data in the Cambridge philosophical tradition, and are writ large in the work of Virginia Woolf. Much of Woolf's fiction frames the problem of representing consciousness as a problem of representing different, and often competing, forms of knowledge. This has important implications for the status of the novel, for the epistemological limits of fiction, and for the possibilities of reductive critical theories of literature more generally. For Woolf, attempts to reconcile the surfeit of consciousness with the apparent poverty of language seem doomed to a particularly interesting kind of failure, and it is this failure – considered as a failure of conveying a certain kind of knowledge – that I would like to explore here. To do so, in the first part of this chapter it will be necessary to define more clearly a type of knowledge that literature – despite the protestations of D. H. Lawrence and others – seems inherently incapable of containing.

Woolf, Modernity and the Economies of Knowledge

Despite Bloomsbury's declared educative project, Virginia Woolf never felt entirely at ease with the state of her own knowledge. She claimed to have been denied a formal education, and pursued her learning largely autonomously, culling it from books in her father's library.[7] Consequently, Woolf always professed to be insecure about her knowledge of certain academic subjects: languages, economics, philosophy and especially epistemology, a form of knowledge that engaged explicitly and often tortuously with what we can know, and how we can come to know it. Difficult knowledge assaulted her, and she often described learning as a visceral, bodily process. In a letter to Clive Bell she wrote about the experience of reading G. E. Moore as a kind of cognitive assault:

> I split my head over Moore every night, feeling ideas travelling to the remotest parts of my brain, and setting up a feeble disturbance hardly to be called thought. It is almost a physical feeling, as though some little coil of brain unvisited by any blood so far, and pale as wax, had got a little life into it at last; but had not strength to keep it.[8]

The language with which Woolf discusses the difficulty of Moore's writing here suggests that of a proto-neuroscience, but she also stresses the affective mechanisms by which difficulty makes itself known to the body. The 'little coil of brain' stands as a physical marker, registering mental work almost as a biomechanical phenomenon.[9] For Woolf knowledge, it seems, could be *felt* even as it could not be known.

Elsewhere Woolf suggested that her ignorance of doctrinal philosophical systems of knowledge was liberating, declaring 'I don't want a "philosophy" in the least',[10] and arguing, in an essay on George Meredith:

> when philosophy is not consumed in a novel, when we can underline this phrase with a pencil, and cut out that exhortation with a pair of scissors and paste the whole into a system, it is safe to say that there is something wrong with the philosophy or with the novel or with both.[11]

As S. P. Rosenbaum has noted, these 'remarks were not written by someone hostile or even indifferent to philosophy and its importance for fiction', but they do suggest that for Woolf the novel's forms of knowledge were different to those made available by philosophy.[12] Similarly, the flights of mystical fancy engaged in by more esoteric philosophies were anathema to her, and are nicely punctured in *Jacob's Room* by the figure of Miss Marchmont, whose synaesthetic research in the British Museum reading room is made to seem absurdly vague:

> What was she seeking through millions of pages, in her old plush dress, and her wig of claret-coloured hair, with her gems and her chilblains? Sometimes one thing, sometimes another, to confirm her philosophy that colour is sound – or, perhaps, it has something to do with music. She could never quite say, though it was not for lack of trying.[13]

Despite her suspicion of systematised forms of knowledge, however, it seems clear that Woolf, more than many writers, repeatedly 'consumed' certain philosophical arguments within her fiction. As Rosenbaum and Ann Banfield have both shown, many of Woolf's works, particularly her shorter fictions and late novels, demonstrate familiarity with the central epistemological problems posed by philosophers in the British empirical tradition, especially G. E. Moore and Bertrand Russell.[14] And, as Banfield has argued, it was the question of knowledge itself – in all its social, artistic and political manifestations – that most exercised these philosophers.[15]

The title of this chapter alludes to Frank Jackson's anti-physicalist thought experiment 'What Mary Didn't Know', and with it I do not wish to cast further aspersions on the state of Woolf's learning, but to suggest that distinctions between various types of knowledge manifest themselves throughout Woolf's work in ways that anticipate quite directly contemporary debates over the mind–body problem and the status of qualia. Frank Jackson's thought experiment concerns a savant-like neuroscientist, 'Mary' (itself an auspicious name: in *A Room of One's Own* Woolf introduced us to her own Mary saying 'call me Mary Beton, Mary Seton, Mary Carmichael or by any name you please – it is not a matter of any importance'), who has been permanently confined since birth in a monochrome room of her own.[16] While there she is, writes Jackson,

> educated through black-and-white books and through lectures relayed on black-and-white television. In this way she learns everything there is to know about the physical nature of the world. She knows all the physical facts about us and our environment, in a wide sense of 'physical' which includes everything in completed physics, chemistry, and neurophysiology, and all there is to know about the causal and relational facts consequent upon all this, including of course functional roles. If physicalism is true, she knows all there is to know. For to suppose otherwise is to suppose that there is more to know than every physical fact, and that is just what physicalism denies . . . It seems, however, that Mary does not know all there is to know. For when she is let out of the black-and-white room or given a color television, she will learn what it is like to see something red, say. This is rightly described as learning – she will not say 'ho, hum.' Hence, physicalism is false.[17]

Jackson's thought experiment poses a challenge to functionalist, physicalist, and other reductively materialist accounts of consciousness which hold that the mind is completely explainable solely in terms of material processes and physical interactions. For it seems that no matter how comprehensive the state of Mary's learning is (and it is significant that the experiment depends upon the notion of what Jackson identifies as a 'completed' science of perception: Mary does not just know all that *we* know about such subjects, she knows everything it will ever be *possible* to know), she will inevitably be unacquainted with qualia: with the particular qualities of perceptual knowledge as it is experienced by a mind connected with the world. The knowledge Mary gains when experiencing colour for the first time exists independently of any system of representation we could invent to communicate it. For Jackson qualia are claims to knowledge of certain properties of the external world as it is experienced. The problem of qualia outlined here is that which the concept poses to *descriptions* of sensory experience, therefore, and it is this particular kind of knowledge that asserts its peculiarities throughout much of Woolf's work. According to Jackson's thought experiment (and sometimes – though crucially not always – to Woolf herself) no language, no matter how exhaustive, seems capable of conveying this kind of knowledge to any reader, no matter how sensitive or imaginative she may be.

Ann Banfield argues that the eye was the sensory organ through which Bloomsbury's epistemological debates were most frequently framed. 'The visual', she writes, was 'in Bloomsbury is synecdochic for the sensible, for "those senses which are stimulated so briskly by the moderns; the senses of sight, of sound, of touch."'[18]

Bloomsbury's oculocentrism was in part a response to the peculiar paradoxes thrown up by contemporary science, which, as we saw in Chapter 1, exposed the tensions between the observed properties of the external world at a macro level and science's explanation of its workings at the micro as never before. It is undoubtedly the case that the 'sensory crisis' identified by many critics as occurring in the early twentieth century had its genesis in scientific developments which made it ever more difficult to reduce what we know to what we feel. Scientific developments led philosophers to conceive of the sensorium not as a cohesive, synaesthetic whole but as a fragmented and specialised set of almost reflexive sensory responses. How to represent those isolated instances of perception within the unified linearity of the sentence became one of Woolf's most pressing aesthetic concerns.

Seeing has, of course, since Aristotle been intimately associated with 'knowing'; with interpreting the real world in dispassionate and rational terms. It is a bias enshrined in phrases such as 'do you see?' as a synonym for understanding, and in our implicit faith in the eye as a neutral arbiter of external reality. The dominance of the eye and its close association with enlightenment principles has led some to identify it as an organ which has had a disproportionate influence on western sensory discourse. For hundreds of years, so it is argued by critics such as Martin Jay, Jonathan Crary and Karen Jacobs, the eye was enshrined as the organ of sense and rationality, and 'Cartesian perspectivalism' dominated the western sensorium. According to Jacobs, it was precisely this conception of seeing as knowing which came under attack in the late nineteenth and early twentieth centuries, when the 'God's eye view' of Cartesian perspectivalism – a vision of the world in which, according to Paul Ricoeur, 'the whole of objectivity is spread out like a spectacle on which the *cogito* spreads its sovereign gaze' – was directly challenged.[19]

Distinguishing between sensory experience and its analysis in terms of competing types of knowledge is certainly not new. In his *Essay Concerning Human Understanding* John Locke recalled a 'studious blind Man who had mightily beat his Head about visible Objects', attempting to 'understand those names of light and colours which often came in his way' and:

> bragg'd one day, That he now understood what *Scarlet* signified. Upon which, his friend demanding, what Scarlet was? the blind Man answered, It was like the Sound of a Trumpet. Just such an Understanding of the name of any other simple *Idea* will he have, who hopes to get it only from a Definition, or other Words made use of to explain it.[20]

Like Jackson's Mary, Locke's studious blind man was forced to transcend his sensory limitations by approaching knowledge of the qualia of vision obliquely, via figurative comparison and the imagination. The knowledge argument thus often hinges on a dichotomy between sensory and abstracted knowledge. Such thought experiments therefore display some anxiety over a life of the mind, or a life lived through books, as inherently impoverished. Attempts to transcend the gulf of feeling using the traditional tools of literature – comparison, metaphor, and imagination – seem on these accounts to be doomed to failure.

Many nineteenth-century philosophers followed Locke in maintaining a dualism between experiential knowledge and indirect or descriptive knowledge. In 1865 John Grote identified the distinction as an implicit feature of many languages, noting that in most cases natural language 'distinguishes between these two applications of the notion of knowledge, the one being γνωναι, noscere, kennen, connaître, the other being ειδεναι, scire, wissen, savoir.'[21] Later, Hermann von Helmholtz was struck by the difficulties of reconciling 'das Kennen' (knowledge constitutive of 'mere familiarity' with phenomena), and 'das Wissen' ('the knowledge of [phenomena] which can be communicated by speech').[22] Following Helmholtz and Grote, in 1890 William James made his influential distinction between knowledge by acquaintance and knowledge by description. 'I am acquainted', he wrote,

> with many people and things, which I know very little about, except their presence in the places where I have met them. I know the color blue when I see it, and the flavor of a pear when I taste it; I know an inch when I move my finger through it; a second of time, when I feel it pass; an effort of attention when I make it; a difference between two things when I notice it; but about the inner nature of these facts or what makes them what they are, I can say nothing at all. I cannot impart acquaintance with them to any one who has not already made it himself. I cannot describe them, make a blind man guess what blue is like, define to a child a syllogism, or tell a philosopher in just what respect distance is just what it is, and differs from other forms of relation. At most, I can say to my friends, Go to certain places and act in certain ways, and these objects will probably come.[23]

It is striking that this dichotomy – between a kind of knowledge that is intimate and conveyed by the senses directly, and a kind which exists only in relation to representational systems of public language – came to the fore within philosophy alongside material and technological developments in the natural sciences which suggested it might be possible to decipher the workings of the sensorium itself, and to represent its workings in empirically objective terms. As technological changes began to threaten the notion of a unified and coherent sensorium – separating out the data streams which supplied the mind with its representations of the world – the contrast between the experiences of the senses and their representation in language became ever more fraught.

It was within Cambridge philosophy that the dualist implications of contemporary epistemology were most severely tested. Bertrand Russell once stated that the new epistemologies espoused by himself and G. E. Moore were prompted by 'the gulf between the world of physics and the world of sense', a gulf that could be refigured as one between experiences of the world and scientific accounts of it.[24] As we saw in Chapter 1, the relation of sense-data to physics, the title of an influential talk given by G. E. Moore, was a central concern for those attempting to establish a new science of consciousness. For Russell, sensory knowledge was intimate, infallible, and independent both of the cultural knowledge which underpinned other forms of perception, and of the matter described by physics which was its ultimate source.[25] In *Problems of Philosophy* he developed James's distinction between knowledge by acquaintance and knowledge by description.[26] 'We shall say we have *acquaintance*', wrote Russell,

> with anything of which we are directly aware, without the intermediary of any process of inference or any knowledge of truths. Thus in the presence of my table I am acquainted with the sense-data that make up the appearance of my table – its colour, shape, hardness, smoothness, etc.; all these are things of which I am immediately conscious when I am seeing and touching my table. The particular shade of colour that I am seeing may have many things said about it – I may say that it is brown, that it is rather dark, and so on. But such statements, though they make me know truths *about* the colour, do not make me know the colour itself any better than I did before: so far as concerns knowledge of the colour itself, as opposed to knowledge of truths about it, I know the colour perfectly and completely when I see it, and no further knowledge of it itself is even theoretically possible.[27]

Knowledge by description, in contrast, depended on language: on mental categories and concepts which could be used to organise sense-data into objects, and on appealing to what Russell termed 'universals' in order to define the meanings of those objects:

> My knowledge of the table as a physical object, on the contrary, is not direct knowledge. Such as it is it is obtained through acquaintance with the sense-data that make up the appearance of the table . . . There is no state of mind in which we are directly aware of the table; all our knowledge of the table is really knowledge of *truths*, and the actual thing which is the table is not, strictly speaking, known to us at all. We know a description, and we know that there is just one object to which this description applies, though the object itself is not known to us.[28]

According to Russell, therefore, knowledge by acquaintance is immediate, irrefutable and unmediated. Knowledge by description, on the other hand, is indirect, analytical and, ultimately, what might be termed *literary*: dependent on descriptive skill and linguistic fluency, and deriving its authority from an established system of language.

As we saw in Chapter 1, the sense-data thesis was founded on the notion that 'common-sense' perceptions of the world could be fundamentally misleading. In his 1910–1911 lectures, G. E. Moore defined sense-data by using the example of looking at a white envelope, claiming that what we see (and what escapes scientific description) when we attend closely to our sensations is not the envelope itself, but a series of ill-defined patches of colour and shapes: 'These things: this patch of a whitish colour, and its size and shape I did actually see. And I propose to call these things, the colour and size and shape, *sense-data*, things given or presented to the senses.'[29]

Equivocations regarding the status of sense-data – over whether they are independent of mind or not – continued (as Tim Crane notes, by 1952 Moore admitted 'that he should have called the *patch* the sense-datum, and not the properties of the patch').[30] But Moore's neo-realism, like Jackson's qualia-thesis, was always committed to the belief that sensations constitute objects of knowledge.[31] 'A sensation', he later wrote, 'is, in reality, a case of "knowing" or "being aware of" or "experiencing" something. When we know that the sensation of blue exists, the fact that we know is that there exists an awareness of blue.'[32]

In a definition of sensation which probably, as S. P. Rosenbaum has shown, influenced Woolf's short piece 'Blue & Green' (a short sketch in which a perceiving consciousness considers the images thrown off by light striking a chandelier) Moore went on to define colours in terms of their inherently subjective nature, identifying 'consciousness' itself as a property of colour sensations as they are experienced:

> The term 'blue' is easy enough to distinguish, but the other element which I have called 'consciousness' – that which the sensation of blue has in common with the sensation of green – is extremely difficult to fix. That many people fail to distinguish it at all is sufficiently shown by the fact that there are materialists. And, in general, that which makes the sensation of blue a mental fact seems to escape us: it seems, if I may use a metaphor, to be transparent – we look through it and see nothing but the blue; we may be convinced that there *is something* but *what* it is no philosopher, I think, has yet clearly recognised.[33]

Here the notion of an executive, centralised consciousness peering out at the world through the sensory organs but located somewhere inside us is abandoned in favour of a more radical cognitive model. Consciousness, for Moore here, is a quality or property of all sensations whatever. Here the mind is figured as something to be seen *through*: not to be made present or objectified on its own terms. Throughout Woolf's fiction too consciousness is represented as a perspective, or a set of capacities, which mediate between the world of physical reality and the mental states that are themselves representations of that reality. The mind is the 'luminous halo, semi-transparent envelope' described in Woolf's essay 'Modern Fiction'; or it is like 'lying in a grape and seeing through a film of semi-transparent yellow', as she wrote in *A Sketch of the Past*.[34] Woolf's definitions of the mind often suggest the Impressionist practice of looking through half-closed eyes in order to get a truer sense of the forms and colours which were being perceived, encouraged by Sir Joshua Reynolds who, in his *Discourses* (edited by Roger Fry in 1905), advised the painter to perceive scenes through dilated pupils.[35] The act, like Woolf's description of her own consciousness, forces us to attend not to the clear and specific world of physical objects, but to a more general sensory field composed of forms, shapes and colours made alien and therefore seen anew. Woolf's advice to the painter Mark Gertler, recorded in her diary, point to her belief in the importance of the creation of distance between artist and material, subject and creator: 'I advised him, for arts sake, to keep sane; to grasp & not exaggerate, & put sheets of glass between him & his matter.'[36]

In many manifestations of the knowledge argument therefore – be they literary or philosophical – the mind, considered as an executive centre of consciousness (as *res cogitans* or ego or ghost in the machine of the body) is eroded in favour of theories of sensation as immanent phenomena. 'I think therefore I am' is replaced as a philosophical certainty with 'there are sensations'. Like Russell's distinction between knowledge by acquaintance and by description, and Moore's identification of the 'sense-datum' as neutral bearer of material information, Jackson's thought experiment dramatises the irreducibility of qualia and consequently of perceptual experiences in general. In this it is an emergentist theory, supposing that the vast complexities of perceptual experience cannot be put back into the box from whence they spring. According Jackson's thought experiment qualia are epiphenomenal. They are dependent on, but never reducible to, brain states, photon streams. But nor are they straightforwardly identical with the named objects which populated the external world.

Conceiving of the argument over consciousness in terms of categories of knowledge in this way has a precedent in the descriptionist science of the early twentieth century examined in Chapter 1. Ernst Mach's *The Analysis of Sensations* and Karl Pearson's *The Grammar of Science* both posited what Otto Neurath would later term a 'physicalist' model of consciousness – a reductive view of the mind that maintained it must be possible to explain consciousness solely in terms of physical processes. This was a development of materialist doctrine which itself depended on new conceptions of the role of science for its justification. In 1925 the Cambridge philosopher C. D. Broad outlined the limitations of such approaches using his own version of the knowledge argument, invoking the figure of the 'mathematical archangel' in his book *The Mind and its Place in Nature*. Such a being, argued Broad, though endowed with unlimited analytical skills and 'gifted with the further power of perceiving the microscopic structure of atoms', could not predict the full nature of, say, the smell of ammonia, for he would always lack knowledge of one essential quality of that substance until he experienced it.[37] As Broad put it:

> He [the archangel] would know exactly what the microscopic structure of ammonia must be; but he would be totally unable to predict that a substance with this structure must smell as ammonia does when it gets into the human nose. The utmost that he could predict on this subject would be that certain changes would take place in the mucous membrane, the olfactory nerves and so on. But he could not possibly know that these changes would be accompanied by the appearance of a smell in general or of the peculiar smell of ammonia in particular, unless someone told him so or he had smelled it for himself.[38]

Here Broad's 'mathematical archangel' is figured as something like the neuroscientist Mary, able to predict 'certain changes in the mucous membrane, the olfactory nerves and so on', but unable to connect these observations with sensory affect. Like Locke's studious blind man and Jackson's Mary, here is a subject isolated from the economies of knowledge, representing the life of the pure mind, isolated from the shocks of the world in the monadic room of the laboratory.

WOOLF AND GENDERED KNOWLEDGE

'What Mary Didn't Know' and its philosophical predecessors engage with perceptual and epistemological economies, as well as with issues of gender and knowledge, echoing the ways in which Woolf 'consumed' such questions within her fiction. The knowledge argument is really a literary thought-experiment, and not just in terms of its form: that of a short story about a woman trapped in a room. Mary's monadic, monochrome world is composed almost entirely of symbols – it is a world composed of books and print rather than of sensation. Yet Mary's gender is significant also: symptomatic of the changes within the academy that Woolf herself looked forward to in *A Room of One's Own* and elsewhere.[39] As Friedrich Kittler notes, speaking of another female modernist-neuroscientist, Gertrude Stein, despite the masculine nature of the knowledge associated with it, the laboratory was during the period becoming a place of potential liberation for women:

> In the methodic isolation of her laboratory, cut off from all the classical determinations of woman and integrated into the new desexualized

university, an ideal student speaks and writes as if the rejected truth of Western thought had returned. Psychophysics thus took the place of occult media (read: women). Alone and dazed, a Pythia sits on the tripod again, and men or priests whisper to her the secret ideas of the people.[40]

An engagement with the economies of knowledge runs through much of Woolf's work, and she often distinguishes between these forms in terms of a dichotomy between 'feeling' and 'knowing'. In her short story 'A Society', for instance, Woolf identified men as the creators of infinite unreadable books, producers of the streams of information which threatened to overload the modern consciousness. In the story a group of women form a reading group around one of their number, Poll, whose father has bequeathed her inheritance only on the condition that she reads all the books in the London Library. 'While we have borne the children', says Poll, 'they, we supposed, have borne the books and the pictures. We have populated the world. They have civilised it. But now that we can read, what prevents us from judging the results?'[41] Poll's Borgesian task leads to a discussion about the nature of 'truth' (aesthetic, cultural and scientific), and of what constitutes knowledge itself. While she masters much of the knowledge of her time – contained in those bastions of masculine discourse, contemporary novels, scientific articles, and leader articles in the *Times* – Poll becomes increasingly aware of the inherent emptiness of such ways of knowing. Learning, or at any rate the learning prized by patriarchal society, is presented as a fall from innocence to experience. 'If we hadn't learned to read' Poll says, bitterly, 'we might still have been bearing children in ignorance and that I believe was the happiest life after all.'[42]

Elsewhere Woolf pursued this gendered dichotomy of knowledge by contrasting the classificatory and taxonomic principles of genealogy with the writing of evocative sketches, a dichotomy she described in an essay on biography as divided between the 'granite' of fact and the 'rainbow' of fictional evocation.[43] In her short story 'The Journal of Mistress Joan Martyn', for instance, she described a female historian who was more interested in showing 'vividly as in a picture, some scene from the life of the time' than in listing the dry, statistical if, perhaps more 'objective' information of names and dates gleaned from her studies.[44] She is criticised by her fellow historians who say that such digressions 'have nothing to do with the system [of] mediaeval land tenure' and that she has 'no materials at [her] side to stiffen these words into any semblance of the truth.'[45] Knowledge of ancestry, that ongoing concern of Woolf's, is here conceived of as something that can be read in two ways: as a heraldic progression of dates, rents and quantities, true but not 'vivid', or as the rich record of unique and idiosyncratic individual lives.

This tension over lived experience – over how it should be represented in literature and whether it can be reconciled with semantic or descriptive knowledge – recurs throughout Woolf's fiction, and is often contained in narratives that themselves mirror the formal structure of philosophical thought experiments. In her short sketch 'The Mark on the Wall', for instance, the phenomenological investigations of an individual consciousness are triggered by a visual experience so slight as to almost defy description:

> In order to fix a date it is necessary to remember what one saw. So now I think of the fire; the steady film of light upon the page of my book; the three chrysanthemums in the round glass bowl on the mantelpiece. Yes, it must have been the winter time, and we had just finished our tea, for I remember that I was smoking a cigarette when I looked up and saw the mark on the wall for the first time.[46]

Here a visual impression is presented as the starting point for analytical speculation. An anonymous narrator, stripped of all the usual trappings of literary characterisation, sits in a monadic room and explores the implications of her own epistemological assumptions. The narrating consciousness uses the visual impression – the sense-datum of the mark on the wall – as an anchor to structure thought, a way of obtaining temporal placement (the cold hard date must be fixed with reference to an ephemeral visual experience), and locating the mind in a past which it is no longer able to possess directly. This meditation on the visual is then presented as something essentially limiting: intrinsically difficult to share with others and eternally hampered by the material and cultural constraints that attend it. The mind is predisposed to interpret the world of sensations, Woolf's narrator observers. 'How readily our thoughts swarm upon a new object', she thinks, 'lifting it a little way, as ants carry a blade of straw so feverishly and then leave it.'[47] And in interpreting such marks, they end up inevitably being assimilated into the world of objects and categories associated with a kind of knowing that Woolf often characterised as masculine.

In navigating through a host of semiotic 'readings' of the mark, the narrator of 'The Mark on the Wall' engages in a kind of epistemological enquiry which creates a distinction between sensations and other forms of knowledge, therefore. 'No, no', she eventually declares,

> nothing is proved, nothing is known. And if I were to get up at this very moment and ascertain that the mark on the wall is really – what shall I say? – the head of a gigantic nail, driven in two hundred years ago, which has now, owing to the patient attrition of many generations of housemaids, revealed its head above the coat of paint, and is taking its first view of modern life in the sight of a white-walled fire-lit room, what should I gain? Knowledge? Matter for further speculation? I can think sitting still as well as standing up. And what is knowledge?[48]

The type of objective knowledge the narrator would gain were she to get up and investigate the mark is in the story associated with 'masculine' values, knowledge which seeks to pin down and categorise, knowledge associated with 'Whittaker's table of precedency', recalling 'leading articles, cabinet ministers – a whole class of things indeed which as a child one thought the thing itself, the standard thing, the real thing.' It is 'generalisation', a type of knowledge sought by 'learned men'.[49]

In her story 'Monday and Tuesday' this quest for masculine knowledge and 'truth' is internally reconciled with sensation by creating a sharp delineation between the two types of information and how they are conveyed. The faithful replication of a train of thought is relayed in words stripped of their categorical specificity, and the distillation of language is associated with the narrator's constant quest for truth:

> desiring truth, awaiting it, laboriously distilling a few words, for ever desiring – (a cry starts to the left, another to the right. Wheels strike divergently. Omnibuses conglomerate in conflict) – for ever desiring – (the clock asseverates with twelve distinct strokes that it is midday; light sheds gold scales; children swarm) – for ever desiring truth.[50]

The technique of bracketing off primary sensory experiences from the main thrust of the narrative, suggesting a literary simultaneousness that Woolf would wield so effectively in *To the Lighthouse* and *Mrs. Dalloway*, can be discerned in embryo. Here it creates a hierarchy of cognition. Specificities of sensory description are confined to parenthesis. External action punctuates – typographically – the distillation process which is described. But the lament is one which never really reaches a conclusion. The external world constantly and forcefully intrudes on thought, never allowing us to settle on any particular definition of the 'truth'.

What all these moments share is a tone and narrative form which is very similar to that of the thought experiment as conducted within the analytical philosophical tradition. These are stories which embody some of the very epistemological questions they raise: can writing be considered a means of gaining knowledge about the world? What does it mean to describe the experiences of a perceiving subject in language? It seems significant, observes David Herman, that 'many of the arguments about qualia in the philosophy of mind are couched in the form of stories or story-like thought experiments', and this seems particularly true of Woolf's shorter fictions, which often seem more concerned to stage a series of interventions, or to pose epistemological questions, than to establish character and linear narrative.[51] Woolf herself was well aware that the form of the thought experiment was one of analytical philosophy's most forceful argumentative tools. Many of her novels fictionalise the central paradoxes of subjectivity in terms of the conflicted status of the observing agent and explicitly connect this figure with contemporary philosophical incarnations of it. The 'Time Passes' section of *To the Lighthouse*, for instance, which attempts to present a narrative of unobserved passivity, in many ways forms a structural correlative to Andrew's definition of his father's work in *To the Lighthouse*: '"think of a kitchen table then," he told her, "when you're not there"'.⁵² In 'Time Passes', passivity is the defining feature of the unobserved world: 'Not only was furniture confounded; there was scarcely anything left of body or mind by which one could say "this is he" or "this is she."'⁵³

But what happens when the individual consciousness is removed from participating in the visual economy while retaining, outwardly, the potential for vision: for seeing, and thus for knowing? Mr Ramsay is described in *To the Lighthouse* in precisely these terms:

> Indeed he seemed to her sometimes made differently from other people, born blind, deaf and dumb, to the ordinary things, but to the extraordinary things, with an eye like an eagle's. His understanding often astonished her. But did he notice the flower? No. Did he notice the view? No. Did he even notice his own daughter's beauty or whether there was pudding on his plate or roast beef?⁵⁴

Later in the novel, Mrs Ramsay considers her husband's inability to appreciate the subtleties of vision:

> And looking up, she saw above the thin trees the first pulse of the full-throbbing star, and wanted to make her husband look at it; for the sight gave her such keen pleasure. But she stopped herself. He never looked at things. If he did, all he would say would be, Poor little world, with one of his sighs.⁵⁵

In Woolf's work sensory pathology is frequently associated with masculinity. Here there is a doubled distancing of sensations from knowledge. Astronomy was a central concern for many of Woolf's contemporaries, and Bertrand Russell had argued that astronomy was a unique science that 'differs from terrestrial physics because of its exclusive dependence upon sight.'⁵⁶ As such, astronomy (hinted at above in the 'pulse of the full-throbbing star') in some respects represented an older, discredited model of knowledge, one that depended upon the making of stories, and upon trusting our increasingly untrustworthy sensorium as to the true nature of the world.

Indeed Woolf often invoked tactility as a more definite and objective sense than vision, a sense that was opposed to the abstractions of the eye. Certain recurring motifs in her work continue the tradition, identifiable in Descartes' 'Argument from Illusion' (but arguably Biblical in origin), of privileging touch over sight as a source of definite knowledge of the world. Thus in *The Waves* Bernard taps his knuckles 'smartly upon the edges of apparently solid objects' and asks 'Are you hard?' and later states 'I strike the table with a spoon. If I could measure things with compasses I would, but since my only measure is a phrase, I make phrases.'[57] Like doubting Thomases, many of Woolf's protagonists require the confirmation of solidity to be conducted by hand or foot rather than by eye. In *The Waves,* for instance, the boot becomes the measure of the real, the banisher of figments and phantoms: 'These are fantastic pictures – these are figments, these visions of friends in absence, grotesque, dropsical, vanishing at the first launch of the toe of a real boot.'[58]

Yet solidity and materialism are not straightforward concepts in Woolf's work. In her essay 'Phases of Fiction' Woolf wrote of the 'truth tellers' – Defoe, Swift and Trollope – who mimic reality by focusing on solidity itself. What 'they describe happens actually before our eyes', she said. 'We get from their novels the same sort of refreshment and delight that we get from seeing something actually happen in the street below.'[59] In Defoe, especially, she continues, we 'seem wedged among solid objects in a solid universe'.[60] And yet this conjuring up of a solid, literal world cannot hold our attention for long. Denied variation of 'realities', and presented at all times with the material facts of characters interacting, concentration is lost. 'We begin to crave for something to vary it that will yet be in harmony with it.'[61] Matter, which as we have seen became with modernism a paradoxically un-solid substance, is tested by the boot of reason. There are frequent references to the kicking of stones and to the solidity of boots in Woolf's work (as when Mr Ramsay describes the boots of his own design to Lily Briscoe in *To the Lighthouse,* or, later, when he considers the ephemerality of human endeavour, thinking 'The very stone one kicks with one's boot will outlast Shakespeare'),[62] a lineage of kicking which is surely an echo of Boswell's report of Dr Johnson's refutation of Bishop Berkeley's idealism, in which he recounts:

> After we came out of the church, we stood talking for some time together of Bishop Berkeley's ingenious sophistry to prove the nonexistence of matter, and that every thing in the universe is merely ideal. I observed, that though we are satisfied his doctrine is not true, it is impossible to refute it. I never shall forget the alacrity with which Johnson answered, striking his foot with mighty force against a large stone, till he rebounded from it – 'I refute it *thus.*'[63]

In Woolf's writing the visual is frequently challenged by the paradoxes of solidity, and by the knowledge we can gain of the world through our other sensory organs. The problem of what objectivity can ever remain once Berkeleyian idealism, guaranteed by an observing God, has been rejected (one thinks of the hymn recalled by Jacob in *Jacob's Room*, with its Christian idealist mantra which amounts to a plea or a request for epistemological certainty: 'Great God, what do I see and hear?', invoking God as a means of justifying perceptual experiences themselves) is, however, not solved by the implicit placement of an observing god-narrator.[64] Idealism and neo-realism do battle on the pages of Woolf's novels, manifesting their influence in the exploratory essays on the limits of knowledge 'consumed' within much of her work, and constituting a sustained engagement with the status of sensation within fiction more generally.

As I argued in Chapter 1, the category of sense-data tended to relocate Cartesian arguments about the relationship between mind and matter onto individual instances of sense perception, and as such maintained or indeed reinstated certain kinds of dualism within contemporary philosophy. But cast in this way, Woolf's is a form of dualism that has less to do with how we define the mind than how we understand the causal connections between objects and their representation. Bertrand Russell himself recognised a 'dualism' implicit to the new doctrine, one which 'has nothing to do with any "mind"' that I may be supposed to possess', and indeed 'exists in exactly the same sense if I am replaced by a photographic plate.'[65] Whether or not it had a bearing on philosophy of mind, such a dualism therefore posed difficulties for the status of literature, as it problematised the types of knowledge that could be conveyed through language. Woolf's dismissal of certain types of analytical, masculine, quantitative knowledge in favour of a subjective knowledge of sense and emotion is in some sense incompatible with such a conception of mind and world.

As such, and as Banfield contends, the central question asked by Woolf throughout her fiction is one that can never finally be answered. It was a question that she articulated in straightforward terms in *The Waves*: 'But how describe the world seen without a self?'[66] The problem of describing a world seen without a self was for her not one of ontology but of language. When dealing with the primary sensation it often feels as if there are simply 'no words. Blue, red – even they distract, even they hide with thickness instead of letting light through.'[67] Woolf's frequent calls for a literature which would allow one to 'record . . . impressions in words of one syllable', for what she calls in *The Waves* a 'little language such as lovers use', locates the central problem of philosophy not outside consciousness – as a study in the possibility of cognitive objectivity – but inside the individual mind, as a problem of conveying sensations to others: a problem of sharing certain types of often competing knowledge.[68]

The impossibility of conveying qualia to other minds through language is something that Woolf addressed most directly in her essays. In 'On Being Ill', for instance, she noted that 'literature does its best to maintain that its concern is with the mind; that the body is a sheet of plain glass through which the soul looks straight and clear', and, further, that illness presents a special sensory case which makes its translation into language impossible.[69]

'The merest schoolgirl', she argued, 'when she falls in love, has Shakespeare or Keats to speak her mind for her; but let a sufferer try to describe the pain in his head to a doctor and language at once runs dry.'[70] Woolf's proposed solution to the problems of writing pain is a linguistic one: she expresses a Hulmean desire for a 'new language . . . more primitive, more sensual, more obscene'.[71] But she also called for a new understanding of bodily processes, 'a new hierarchy of the passions' under the auspices of which

> love must be deposed in favour of a temperature of 104; jealousy give place to the pangs of sciatica; sleeplessness play the part of villain, and the hero become a white liquid with a sweet taste – that mighty Prince with the moths' eyes and the feathered feet, one of whose names is Chloral.[72]

Here Woolf proposes a view of sensation that in some respects pre-empts what the philosophers Paul and Patricia Churchland have called 'Eliminative Materialism': the belief that our common sense or 'folk' psychological intuitions about the mind are mistaken and that, if we want to understand consciousness properly, they must be replaced with scientific terms for mental states. According to the Churchlands the notion of 'pain', for instance, is a redundant and imprecise term, merely offering a vague description of a brain state that can be describe far more precisely as 'C-Fibres firing'. For the eliminative materialists all mental states have similar brain-state equivalents, and we must become fluent in the language of neuroscience if we want to accurately describe and fully account for consciousness. Once equipped with a more accurate language of consciousness, so the Churchlands argue, the problem of qualia will cease to trouble us at all. Yet what's interesting about Woolf's account of pain in 'On Being Ill' is that once she has proposed the reduction she goes on to re-inscribe a literary model for these scientific processes into her story of illness. Love may well have to be 'deposed in favour of a temperature of 104', but sleeplessness itself becomes personified: it is a villain, to be vanquished in heroic fashion by 'that mighty Prince with the moths' eyes and the feathered feet, one of whose names is Chloral.'

In grappling with the inherently subjective nature of qualia, then, Woolf employs language in a way that suggests a Post-Impressionist focus not upon the visual as perceived through the eye, but on the world as reconstructed in the mind through the interplay between ideas and sensations. Hotness, coldness, redness, roughness, pain – Woolf's fiction is constantly returning to the primacy of felt experience which is presented as the source of all our mental being. And yet at the same time her language – like all language – immediately moves in to fossilise felt experience: to entomb it in words which ultimately threaten to deaden experience. Much of Woolf's fiction and non-fiction grapples with this central paradox: that it is only within language that we can think at all, but that in thinking, we might cease to feel at all.

Knowledge and the Naïve Eye

In his account of modernism's complex relationship with popular science, *Einstein's Wake*, Michael Whitworth identifies the trope of the 'innocent eye' as a recurring feature of philosophical literature of the time.[73] The naïve subject of the kind imagined by Bergson and Mach was an imaginary construct: a being devoid of certain kinds of knowledge, inhabiting a world of primary sensory phenomena. For many scientists and philosophers the naïve eye was a conceptual tool which allowed for the adoption of an ideologically neutral position from which to perceive the world. It involved embracing a 'common sense' perspective regarding phenomenological issues. Such positioning, they believed, would lead to the discovery of greater truth. It was a trope which the phenomenologists turned into a philosophical system, and was a founding assumption of Impressionist practice in the visual arts.[74] It is also one that intersects in provocative ways with Woolf's negotiations between visual experience and literary knowledge.

In scientific and philosophical texts this propositional naïveté was often addressed explicitly in terms of childhood, conceived as a time of perceptual innocence. The general vogue for the primitive (as well as the fears of 'degeneration' this vogue engendered during the modernist moment) can be read as an attempt to strip the world back to some original, pre-Edenic state of sensory reification. G. E. Moore's epistemological project was conceived explicitly along these lines. The self-declared aim of his philosophical project was, he once said, 'to raise some childishly simple questions as to what we are doing when we make judgements of a certain kind.'[75] The confluence between phenomenology and Impressionism, though often conflicted, was apparent to many philosophers of the period. Maurice Merleau-Ponty, consolidating Husserl's phenomenological project, was a keen advocate of Cézanne's naïve approach to perception. For Merleau-Ponty, Cézanne's art deconstructed the world of man-made objects in order to reveal 'the base of human nature upon which man has installed himself. This is why Cézanne's people are strange, if viewed by a creature of another species. Nature itself is stripped of the attributes which make it ready for animistic communions.'[76] For this reason, argued Merleau-Ponty, Cézanne and the Impressionists had contributed to an annihilation of socially constructed 'ways of seeing' which was to be celebrated. Yet such attempts, which generally involved the reduction of the visible into basic visual forms, broke from the descriptionist rubric in a variety of ways. Rather than representing 'efficient' – and therefore clearer – ways of summarising visual information, they were often conceived as alienating strategies which attempted to make us view the world afresh by making it strange. As Jesse Matz suggests, within literature in particular, 'Impressionism does aspire to something like the phenomenological synthesis, but without phenomenology's inclination to define it clearly.'[77]

Though notoriously difficult to define, Impressionism in the visual arts can thus be characterised by its interest in the representation of subjective visual sensation. The faithful representation of such experiences, unshackled from the compromising effects of cultural legacy, over-literalisation, or narrative manipulation, lay at the heart of Impressionist aesthetics. Many of these artists defined their practice as producing something realer than naturalism, ignoring externalities to provide veridical portraits of the subjective sensory experiences of an individual, idealised observer.

Virginia Woolf's literary project, outlined in her influential essay 'Modern Fiction', was based on a similar desire. There she famously urged the novelist to: 'record the atoms as they fall upon the mind in the order in which they fall, [to] trace the pattern, however disconnected and incoherent in appearance, which each sight or incident scores upon our consciousness.'[78]

In stressing that writers should remain faithful to the actualities of sensory experience, 'however disconnected and incoherent in appearance' the finished work might appear, in 'Modern Fiction' Woolf proposed a literature of sensation with aims analogous to those of Impressionist painting. Yet although similarities of style and subject between Woolf's writing and the aesthetic assumptions of Impressionism are certainly apparent, it is inevitable that, as she commented in her essay on Walter Sickert, painting and writing 'must part in the end.'[79] One of the reasons they must part is that, if qualia exist, they are inherently incompatible with the kind of knowledge it is possible to contain within language.

Though it manifested its influence across the arts, the problem of knowledge was therefore primarily a literary problem. Frank Jackson borrowed the title of his thought experiment from Henry James's *What Maisie Knew*, a work which was itself concerned with the degree to which knowledge could be shared, and which marked a revolutionary shift in the epistemic claims made on behalf of – and indeed *by* – the novel-form. In his preface to the New York edition James described Maisie as a 'light vessel of consciousness', a half-formed cipher unable to contain a fully fledged mind.[80] Maisie was a focaliser of naïveté, an innocent stand-in for the reader's eye perceiving the scene, unable to translate her experience into rich literary language because 'small children', as James pointed out, 'have many more perceptions than they have terms to translate them.'[81] Maisie, like Jackson's Mary, was supposed in one important way to know significantly *less* than those around her, and in decoding what she knew in sensory terms, but not in social ones, the reader was supposed to be drawn closer to the way in which she experienced the world.

The fragile subjectivity of perspective and focalisation proposed by *What Maisie Knew* – in which the emotional experiences of a small child are narrated in a language which reflects her limited understanding of the world – fictionalised many of the philosophical assumptions held by Henry's brother William

James, and posited the subjective impression as the focus of much contemporary fiction. The effect of this formal psychological intimacy, however, was itself paradoxically alienating, drawing attention as it did to the fact that the novel told fundamentally artificial, invented stories. Though Woolf herself was impressed with the technique, she stressed the alienating qualities of attempts to suggest the conscious mind, especially that of a child, indirectly within the novel. Maisie, Woolf wrote,

> can only affect us very indirectly, each feeling of hers being deflected and reaching us after glancing off the mind of some other person. Therefore she rouses in us no simple and direct emotion. We always have time to watch it coming and to calculate its pathway, now to the right, now to the left ... we hang suspended over this aloof little world and watch with intellectual curiosity for the event.[82]

The definition of James's novel as an 'aloof little world' is typical of Woolf's ongoing if uneasy interest in closed epistemic systems – with rooms as prototypal minds or monads, with *res cogitans* as isolated agent, passively taking in external stimuli, or with the hermetically sealed systems represented by children playing with the miniature worlds, such as the rock pools Nancy plays with in *To the Lighthouse*.[83] As a form the novel, of course, is itself a little world: a selective and particular utterance exploring certain pre-ordained limits of the mind. But it is the innocence of childhood figured as a lack of *knowledge* that is so striking a feature of James's novel, and of Woolf's and Jackson's later applications of it.

Thus naïveté and the innocent eye, both in the arts and in philosophy, represented a range of often-contradictory positions regarding the status of the perceiving agent and the representability of its perceptions in the period. In literature point of view is always and inevitably connected with the knowledge the perceiving character has of the scene perceived, but the value of that knowledge or its absence was fiercely contested in Woolf's work. For her the relationship between childhood and naïve objectivity was self-evident. 'It seems to me that a child must have a curious focus', she wrote, 'it sees an air-ball or a shell with extreme distinctness.'[84] Lacking the ability to name and therefore classify, and subsequently dull, a world composed primarily of perceptual experiences, for Woolf childhood could only be characterised after the event as the experience of:

> many bright colours; many distinct sounds; some human beings, caricatures; comic; several violent moments of being, always including a circle of the scene which they cut out: and all surrounded by a vast space – that is a rough visual description of childhood.[85]

In her fiction, childhood is often figured as a primitive state associated with synaesthetic experience and the uncontrollable assaults of sense-data. But Woolf's attempts to capture the experience of childish perceptual naïveté in prose were always tinged with elegy. Unlike James Joyce, whose attempts to render the fractured and fragmented (if associative) nature of childish discourse on the first page of *A Portrait of the Artist as a Young Man* embodied some of the limited literary abilities of a youthful consciousness, Woolf's children often speak in a sophisticated 'little language', despite often being unable to say precisely what they mean.

Much has been written about the way in which Woolf's focus on colours and shapes in her descriptive passages is suggestive of the *plein air* paintings of the Impressionists.[86] E. M. Forster's gentle dismissal of stories such as 'Kew Gardens' and 'The Mark on the Wall' as 'lovely little things' which 'seem to lead nowhere', composed as they are of 'tiny dots and coloured blobs', is symptomatic of a critical approach to her shorter fictions which treats them as interesting, yet limited, experiments in consolidating and consummating the techniques of visual impressionism in language.[87] Woolf herself described these stories in a letter to Ethel Smyth as 'mere tangles of words; balls of string that the kitten . . . has played with . . . inarticulate, ridiculous, unprintable mere outcries.'[88] Nevertheless there are certainly illuminating comparisons to be made between Woolf's work and the visual arts. Monet's famous advice to Lilla Cabot Perry could be read as a manifesto for many of Woolf's descriptive passages:

> When you go out to paint, try to forget what objects you have before you – a tree, a house, a field, or whatever. Merely think, here is a little square of blue, here an oblong of pink, here a streak of yellow, and paint it just as it looks to you, the exact colour and shape, until it gives your own naïve impression of the scene before you.[89]

A similar conception of a new method of description is a central tenet of Woolf's stylistic principles. As she states in her essay on Walter Sickert: 'The novelist . . . must often think that to describe a scene is the worst way to show it. It must be done with one word, or with one word in skilful contrast with another.'[90]

In the end the use of 'one word, or one word in skilful contrast with another' in place of realist 'description', places a semantic burden on individual words which means that they must be carefully chosen in order to achieve their effects through suggestion, rather than assertion. As she wrote elsewhere, words have 'short wings for their heavy body of meaning', and are often 'inadequate to carry them far . . . thus alighting awkwardly upon the very common objects that surrounded them.'[91]

By employing language stripped of much of its specificity, then, Woolf's impressionist descriptions seem to undermine form. Like the paintings which they are analogous to, these passages force us to imagine for ourselves the relations between the objects depicted and component parts of the visual field must be built up again internally. The description of the flowerbed in 'Kew Gardens' operates in precisely this way:

> there rose perhaps a hundred stalks spreading into heart-shaped or tongue-shaped leaves half-way up and unfurling at the tip red or blue or yellow petals marked with spots of colour raised from the surface; and from the red, blue, or yellow gloom of the throat emerged a straight bar, rough with gold dust and slightly clubbed at the end.[92]

Here we are offered a defiantly partial account of the flower bed, which strikes us as flat, lacking perspective, and are forced to reconstruct the 'scene' in a more attentive fashion than is usually required. In 'Kew Gardens' the movement between the various stages of visual description are strikingly cinematic also. The close-up intensity of domestic vision we are offered here quickly gives way to the vagaries of impressionistic description. The family move away from the implied observer (camera or eye), 'diminishing in size among the trees and looked half transparent as the sunlight and shade swam over their backs in large trembling irregular patches.' Our attention returns to the progress of the snail – a recurring symbol of specific perceptual concentration for Woolf – and again the sweep and movement of changing perspectives is suggested. The progress of the snail, occurring in a temporal frame which is alien to that which governs the progress of the characters around it, serves to focus our attention, contrasting with the more biographical narrative facts we are presented with elsewhere in the story.

In the visual arts, the interplay between the experience of the senses and their representation often forces us to attend anew to our own visual consciousness, and aesthetic satisfaction is derived from the realization that the world 'out there' is itself represented through the senses in ways which resist formal classification. The lack of visual demarcation so characteristic of Impressionism – resulting in paintings which look as though the scene were being viewed through half-closed eyes – works in precisely this way. In Woolf's fiction, however, the defamiliarisation of the subject, achieved in painting through remaining faithful to the 'exact colour and shape' of the subject, is both replicated and challenged in language which focuses on basic perceptions, rather than on categories or objects, to describe the world.

Bernard in *The Waves*, with his notebook of world-making phrases, provides the final model of a kind of utopian and direct sensory inscription which Woolf seemed to wish for throughout her writing. The fluid 'hive mind' evoked in *The Waves* is itself concerned primarily with the data of sense – with colours, smells and other sensory realities – and the novel opens with an exhaustive catalogue of sensory description, a litany of feelings and perceptions recounted in straightforward, referential prose:

> 'I see a ring,' said Bernard, 'hanging above me. It quivers and hangs in a loop of light.'
> 'I see a slab of pale yellow,' said Susan, 'spreading away until it meets a purple stripe.'
> 'I hear a sound,' said Rhoda, 'cheep, chirp; cheep, chirp; going up and down.'[93]

Here all the senses of the classical sensorium are targeted individually, in language which, though poetic and crafted, isn't particularly elaborate. As Susan contends, later on in the novel, her language is tokenistic, in the Hulmean sense: 'It is black, I see; it is green, I see; I am tied down with single words.'[94] Compared to Susan's elemental phrase-making – her fitting of words to world in the most straightforward way possible, bearing witness to the sensory phenomena she experiences – Bernard's experiments in articulation offer the promise of authorial control, a shaping of experience into art through the deployment of crafted phrases. As Susan continues: 'you wander off; you slip away; you rise higher, with words and words in phrases.'[95] Though there is a sort of fetishisation of visionary childhood here, it is one defiantly controlled: ordered and written about rather than overheard. Later in the novel Bernard outlines what amounts to a manifesto for Woolf's own method in *The Waves*: 'I notice externals only. I sit here like a convalescent, like a very simple man who knows only words of one syllable. "The sun is hot." I say. "The wind is cold."'[96]

Yet it is clear that these simple declarations of experience get us no closer to experiencing the sensations seen and felt by the characters within the novel than any more sophisticated descriptive writing would or could. As in Jackson's thought experiment, acquaintance with one particular kind of knowledge does not automatically allow for the communication of other kinds. Woolf's strategy of defamiliarising objects – taking them apart so as to describe them in terms of colour or shape – is the literary equivalent of the phenomenologist's epoché. But it never quite provides the arrival at 'things in themselves' that the phenomenologists urged that it should. Such atomised, fragmented descriptions are of course typical of modernism. But in Woolf's work they are closely aligned with philosophical projects, like Jackson's, that see such fragments of sensory knowledge both as the building blocks of analytical inquiry, and as forever inherently private, and therefore unshareable.

The paradox that lies at the heart of Impressionism's celebration of the authenticity of childhood experience, and the anxieties which attend the naïve eye in the philosophical tradition, is, therefore, reflected in Woolf's fiction. It is that a faithful correlation between analytical and sensory knowledge can never be communicated in words. The artist who attempts to present this relationship must inevitably rely on representational strategies. For Woolf any writer attempting to convey the subjective reality of childhood experience, or of any other kind of sensory experience, had two options. They could either artificially re-create the limited, fragmentary nature of the child's linguistic ability (as Joyce did in the opening sentences of *A Portrait of the Artist as a Young Man*), or they could put questions of the 'appropriateness' of language aside, and present a sort of sensory 'case study' in concrete, specific terms, while at the same time lamenting language's inability ever to bear sensation at all.

NOTES

1. Friedrich A. Kittler, *Discourse Networks 1800–1900*, trans. by Michael Metteer, with Chris Cullens (Stanford, CA: Stanford University Press, 1990), p. 237.
2. James Joyce, *Ulysses*, ed. by Hans Walter Gabler (London: The Bodley Head, 1986), 6.933. All references to James Joyce's *Ulysses* are to the Gabler synoptic edition, and are given in the form [episode number.line number].
3. D. H. Lawrence, 'Why the Novel Matters', *Study of Thomas Hardy and Other Essays*, ed. by Bruce Steele (Cambridge: Cambridge University Press, 1985), p. 194.
4. Patricia Waugh, 'Writing the Body: Modernism and Postmodernism', in *The Body and the Arts*, ed. by Corinne Saunders, Ulrika Maude and Jane Macnaughton (Basingstoke: Palgrave Macmillan, 2009), pp. 140–141.
5. Alan Palmer '1945 – Ontologies of Consciousness', in *The Emergence of Mind*, ed. by David Herman (Lincoln, NE and London: University of Nebraska Press, 2011), p. 276.
6. Waugh, 'Writing the Body: Modernism and Postmodernism', p. 139.
7. Anna Snaith and Christine Kenyon-Jones have found that Woolf may have overstated the degree to which she was self-taught. They provide evidence that 'Woolf had much more first hand experience of women's higher education than either she or her biographers have acknowledged'. See 'Tilting at Universities: Virginia Woolf at King's College London', *Woolf Studies Annual*, 16 (2010), 1–44 (p. 1).
8. Virginia Woolf, *The Flight of the Mind: The Letters of Virginia Woolf Volume I: 1888–1912*, ed. by Nigel Nicolson (London: The Hogarth Press, 1975), p. 357.
9. Woolf's frequent off-hand references to the 'nerves' (which are often presented as 'fiddle strings' to be 'vibrated' by sensory input), suggest a similar model of affect and cognition. See, for instance, *To the Lighthouse*, in which Mrs Ramsay declares: 'My nerves are taut as fiddle strings. Another touch and they will snap.' Virginia Woolf, *To the Lighthouse* (London: The Hogarth Press, 1927), p. 143.
10. Virginia Woolf, *The Diary of Virginia Woolf Volume IV: 1931–35*, ed. by Anne Olivier Bell (Harmondsworth: Penguin, 1983), p. 126.
11. Virginia Woolf, 'The Novels of George Meredith', in *The Essays of Virginia Woolf Volume V: 1929–1932,* ed. by Stuart N. Clarke (London: The Hogarth Press, 2009), p. 550.

12. S. P. Rosenbaum, 'The Philosophical Realism of Virginia Woolf', in *English Literature and British Philosophy*, ed. by S. P. Rosenbaum (Chicago, IL and London: The University of Chicago Press, 1971), p. 317.
13. Virginia Woolf, *Jacob's Room* (London: The Hogarth Press, 1922), pp. 171–172.
14. See Ann Banfield, *The Phantom Table: Woolf, Fry, Russell and the Epistemology of Modernism* (Cambridge: Cambridge University Press, 2000); and S. P. Rosenbaum, 'The Philosophical Realism of Virginia Woolf'.
15. Banfield, *The Phantom Table*, p. 17.
16. Virginia Woolf, *A Room of One's Own* (London: The Hogarth Press, 1929), p. 8.
17. Frank Jackson, 'What Mary Didn't Know', *The Journal of Philosophy*, 83.5 (1986), 291–295 (p. 291).
18. Banfield, *The Phantom Table*, p. 12.
19. Paul Ricœur, 'The Question of the Subject: The Challenge of Semiology', in *The Conflict in Interpretations: Essays in Hermeneutics*, ed. by Don Idhe (Evanston, IL: Northwestern University Press, 1974), p. 236.
20. John Locke, *An Essay Concerning Human Understanding*, ed. by Peter H. Nidditch (Oxford: Clarendon Press, 1975), p. 425.
21. John Grote, *Exploratio Philosophica: Rough Notes on Modern Intellectual Science* (London: Bell and Daldy, 1865), p. 60.
22. H. L. F. von Helmholtz, 'The Recent Progress of the Theory of Vision', *Popular Scientific Lectures*, trans. by P. H. Pye-Smith (New York: Dover Publications, 1962), pp. 93–185.
23. William James, *Principles of Psychology*, 2 vols (London: Macmillan and Co. Ltd, 1907), vol. I, p. 221.
24. Bertrand Russell, *Our Knowledge of the External World* (London: George Allen & Unwin Ltd, 1922), p. 106.
25. See Banfield, *The Phantom Table*, p. 6.
26. Bertrand Russell, *The Problems of Philosophy* (London: Thornton Butterworth Ltd, 1912), p. 72.
27. Russell, *The Problems of Philosophy*, p. 73.
28. Russell, *The Problems of Philosophy*, p. 73.
29. G. E. Moore, *Some Main Problems of Philosophy* (London: George Allen & Unwin Ltd, 1953), p. 30.
30. Tim Crane, 'The Origins of Qualia', in *The History of the Mind–Body Problem*, ed. by Tim Crane and Sarah Patterson (London: Routledge, 2000), p. 173.
31. Crane, 'The Origins of Qualia', p. 173.
32. Moore, *Philosophical Studies*, p. 24.
33. Moore, *Philosophical Studies*, p. 20.
34. Virginia Woolf, 'Modern Fiction', *The Essays of Virginia Woolf Volume IV: 1925–1928*, ed. by Andrew McNeillie (London: The Hogarth Press, 1994; repr. 2009), p. 160; Virginia Woolf, *A Sketch of the Past*, ed. by Jeanne Schulkind (London: The Hogarth Press, 1985), p. 65.
35. Joshua Reynolds, *Discourses*, ed. by Roger Fry (London: Seeley & Co. Limited, 1905), p. 189.

36. Virginia Woolf, *The Diary of Virginia Woolf Volume I: 1915–19*, ed. by Anne Oliver Bell (Harmondsworth: Penguin, 1979), p. 176.
37. C. D. Broad, *The Mind and Its Place in Nature* (London: Kegan Paul, Trench, Trubner & Co. Ltd, 1923), p. 71.
38. Broad, *The Mind and Its Place in Nature*, p. 71.
39. Woolf, *A Room of One's Own*, pp. 170–172.
40. Kittler, *Discourse Networks 1800/1900*, trans. by Michael Metteer and Chris Cullens, foreword by David E. Wellbery (Stanford, CA: Stanford University Press, 1990), p. 228.
41. Virginia Woolf, *A Haunted House: The Complete Shorter Fiction*, ed. by Susan Dick (London: Vintage, 2003), p. 119.
42. Woolf, *Haunted House*, p. 128.
43. Woolf, 'The New Biography', *The Essays,* vol. IV, p. 473.
44. Woolf, *Haunted House*, p. 34.
45. Woolf, *Haunted House*, p. 35.
46. Woolf, *Haunted House*, p. 77.
47. Woolf, *Haunted House*, p. 77.
48. Woolf, *Haunted House*, p. 81.
49. Woolf, *Haunted House*, p. 81.
50. Woolf, *Haunted House*, p. 131.
51. David Herman, *Basic Elements of Narrative* (Chichester: Wiley-Blackwell, 2009), p. 154.
52. Woolf, *To the Lighthouse*, p. 40.
53. Woolf, *To the Lighthouse*, p. 196.
54. Woolf, *To the Lighthouse*, p. 111.
55. Woolf, *To the Lighthouse*, p. 112.
56. Bertrand Russell, *The ABC of Relativity* (London and New York: Routledge, 1997), p. 14.
57. Woolf, *The Waves*, pp. 303–304.
58. Woolf, *The Waves*, pp. 126–127.
59. Virginia Woolf, 'Phases of Fiction', *The Essays,* vol. V, p. 42.
60. Woolf, 'Phases of Fiction', p. 43.
61. Woolf, 'Phases of Fiction', p. 44.
62. Woolf, *To the Lighthouse*, p. 59.
63. James Boswell, *The Life of Samuel Johnson: Including a Journal of a Tour to the Hebrides*, ed. by John Wilson Croker, 2 vols (London: Carter, Hendee and Company, 1832), vol. I, p. 209.
64. Woolf, *Jacob's Room*, p. 81.
65. Bertrand Russell, *The Analysis of Mind* (London: George Allen & Unwin, 1921), p. 130.
66. Woolf, *The Waves*, p. 314.
67. Woolf, *The Waves*, p. 314.
68. Woolf, *The Waves*, p. 323.
69. Woolf, 'On Being Ill', *The Essays*, vol. IV, p. 318.
70. Woolf, 'On Being Ill', *The* Essays, vol. IV, pp. 318–319.

71. Woolf, 'On Being Ill', *The Essays*, vol. IV, p. 319.
72. Woolf, 'On Being Ill', *The Essays*, vol. IV, p. 319.
73. Michael H. Whitworth, *Einstein's Wake: Relativity, Metaphor, and Modernist Literature* (Oxford: Oxford University Press, 2001), p. 97.
74. See, for instance, Herbert Muller, 'Impressionism in Fiction: Prism vs. Mirror', *The American Scholar*, 7.3 (1938), 355–367 (p. 356).
75. Moore, *Philosophical Studies*, p. 220.
76. Maurice Merleau-Ponty, 'Cézanne's Doubt', in *Sense and Non-Sense*, trans. by Hubert L. Dreyfus and Patricia Allen Dreyfus (Evanston, IL: Northwestern University Press, 1964), p. 16.
77. Jesse Matz, *Literary Impressionism and Modernist Aesthetics* (Cambridge: Cambridge University Press, 2001), p. 18.
78. Woolf, 'Modern Fiction', *The Essays*, vol. IV, p. 161.
79. Woolf, 'Walter Sickert: A Conversation', *The Essays*, vol. VI, p. 43.
80. Henry James, *What Maisie Knew*, ed. by Douglas Jefferson (Oxford: Oxford University Press, 1966), p. 4.
81. James, *What Maisie Knew*, p. 6.
82. Woolf, 'Phases of Fiction', in *The Essays,* vol. V, p. 64.
83. Woolf, *To the Lighthouse*, pp. 118–119.
84. Woolf, *A Sketch of the Past*, p. 78.
85. Woolf, *A Sketch of the Past*, p. 79.
86. See, for instance, Diane F. Gillespie, *The Sisters' Arts: The Writing and Painting of Virginia Woolf and Vanessa Bell* (Syracuse, NY: Syracuse University Press, 1988).
87. E. M. Forster, *Virginia Woolf* (Cambridge: Cambridge University Press, 1942), p. 11.
88. Virginia Woolf, *A Reflection of the Other Person: The Letters of Virginia Woolf Volume IV: 1929–1931*, ed. by Nigel Nicolson (London: The Hogarth Press, 1978), p. 231.
89. Qtd in Lilla Cabot Perry, 'Claude Monet's Ideas about Art', in *Impressionism and Post-Impressionism 1874–1904: Sources and Documents*, ed. by Linda Nochlin (Englewood Cliffs, NJ: Prentice-Hall, 1966), p. 35.
90. Woolf, 'Walter Sickert: A Conversation', *The Essays*, vol. VI, p. 43.
91. Woolf, *Haunted House*, p. 37.
92. Virginia Woolf, *Haunted House*, p. 32.
93. Woolf, *The Waves,* p. 7.
94. Woolf, *The Waves*, p. 15.
95. Woolf, *The Waves*, p. 15.
96. Woolf, *The Waves*, p. 201.

3

WHAT IS IT LIKE TO BE LEOPOLD BLOOM?

> What, reduced to their simplest reciprocal form, were Bloom's thoughts about Stephen's thoughts about Bloom and about Stephen's thoughts about Bloom's thoughts about Stephen?
>
> James Joyce, *Ulysses*

WHAT-IS-IT-LIKE-NESS AND THE UMWELT

In 1934, the Swedish philosopher and biologist Jakob von Uexküll published *A Foray into the Worlds of Animals and Humans*, an exploration of animal physiology and phenomenology which became a founding text for the fledgling discipline of 'biosemiotics'.[1] In it Uexküll fused a form of Machian sensory analysis with a phenomenological and ecologically minded approach to consciousness, and in doing so promoted the notion of the *Umwelt*: the perceptual mantle, which, so he argued, constituted every organism's uniquely subjective experience of the world. As Evan Thompson summarises, for Uexküll, the 'Umwelt is an animal's environment in the sense of its lived, phenomenal world, the world as it presents itself to that animal thanks to its sensorimotor repertoire.'[2] Uexküll's theory stressed the subjective specificity of perception, arguing that it was misleading to conceive of consciousness as a stable entity statically processing the sense-data of the external world. Instead, the mind should be thought of as interactive and extended, influencing the very ways in which that world is presented to the subject. The world is given significance according to the particular biological needs of the organism perceiving it, such that *In-der-Welt-sein* – the Heideggerian notion of 'being in the world' – inevitably constitutes an act of interpretation. Uexküll's method recast phenomenological analysis as poetics, arguing for a semiotic view of consciousness according to which even the most basic of organisms 'interpret' the world rather than merely 'experiencing' it.

Uexküll said that all organisms should be thought of as being accompanied by a 'soap bubble' of consciousness (a term similar to Virginia Woolf's notion of the 'translucent envelope' of consciousness described in 'Modern Fiction'), which sets the limits of experience and only occasionally overlaps with the 'bubbles' inhabited by other kinds of organism.[3] These bubbles constitute all that exists for these creatures; indeed the bubbles create the very notion of space itself, for, as Uexküll went on to comment, there 'is no space independent of subjects'.[4] Organisms are isolated from one another not merely by an inability to communicate their sensory realities, but due to the inherent impossibility of inhabiting another's bubble. What we perceive when we attempt to conceive of another's Umwelt is in fact a projection of our own environment, and the first task of the biosemiotician was, according to Uexküll, to deconstruct this nascent familiarity:

> The animal's environment . . . is only a piece cut out of its surroundings, which we see stretching out on all sides around the animal – and these surroundings are nothing else but our own human environment. The first task of research on such environments consists in seeking out the animal's perception signs and, with them, to construct the animal's environment.[5]

In contrast to Heidegger, who considered animals to be 'poor in world', and whose phenomenological project demoted animal consciousness as *less* rich than that of the human, and to the Cartesian characterisation of animals as mere automata (a thesis which was being channelled, as we shall see in Chapter 6, into J. B. Watson's behaviourist psychology during the period), Uexküll argued that the 'first principle of Umwelt theory' was that

> all animal subjects, from the simplest to the most complex, are inserted into their environments to the same degree of perfection. The simple animal has a simple environment; the multiform animal has an environment just as richly articulated as it is.[6]

Uexküll's project was therefore founded on a kind of imaginative empathy. The job of the biosemiotician, he argued, was to navigate the Umwelt of various animal consciousnesses through acts of imaginative positioning; to re-interpret the world as it was experienced by various types of organism, and thus to 'read' the 'perception marks' and 'search images' by which those organisms themselves navigated the world.

Using the example of a tick, which recent research had shown was devoid of the senses of taste, hearing and sight, Uexküll wrote what amounted to a short story about what it might be like to be possessed of such a limited sensorium:

> The tick hangs inert on the tip of a branch in a forest clearing. Its position allows it to fall onto a mammal running past. From its entire environment, no stimulus penetrates the tick. But here comes a mammal, which the tick needs for the production of offspring.
>
> And now something miraculous happens. Of all the effects emanating from the mammal's body, only three become stimuli, and then only in a certain sequence. From the enormous world surrounding the tick, three stimuli glow like signal lights in the darkness and serve as directional signs that lead the tick surely to its target . . . The whole rich world surrounding the tick is constricted and transformed into an impoverished structure that, most importantly of all, consists of only three features and three effect marks – the tick's environment [Umwelt]. However, the poverty of this environment [Umwelt] is needful for the certainty of action, and certainty is more important than riches.[7]

The tick, according to Uexküll, dwells in a world composed solely of the sense-data of scent and temperature which, although apparently limited, is just as rich in meaning for the tick as our own more complex world of signs is for us. As biosemiotician, Uexküll was therefore engaged in an act of literary interpretation: he espoused a paradoxical functionalism that denied the mechanistic nature of the Cartesian vision, but which was also uninterested in the existence or otherwise of qualia. For Uexküll, as for Woolf, the Umwelt theorist must become a *reader* of environments rather than merely an experiencer of them:

> Just as a gourmet picks only the raisins out of the cake, the tick only distinguishes butyric acid from among the things in its surroundings. We are not interested in what taste sensations the raisins produce in the gourmet but only in the fact that they become perception marks of his environment because they are of special biological significance for him; we also do not ask how the butyric acid tastes or smells to the tick, but rather, we only register the fact that butyric acid, as biologically significant, becomes a perception mark for the tick.[8]

In his introduction to *A Foray* Uexküll called his work a 'travelogue', calling upon his readers to 'come along as we wander through these worlds.'[9] This was to be, first and foremost, a guidebook to the Umwelt. To illustrate his theory,

Uexküll included a series of pictures with which he attempted to portray the world as it was perceived by various organisms. In his discussion of 'perception marks' (those features of the external world which are singled out as important by particular organisms depending on their sensorimotor needs) for instance, he argued that 'bees prefer to land on shapes that [have] a more opened form, such as stars and crosses; they avoid closed forms, such as squares and circles', accompanying this assertion with a visualisation of a 'bee's-eye' view of a field: straightforward if somewhat schematic view of a meadow of flowers. In a second image, which sought to portray the bee's Umwelt, objects were simplified in form so as to become almost abstract symbols. The horizon was reduced; the buds of the flowers become signified geometrically rather than represented more naturalistically. Where humans 'see the bees in their surroundings, a meadow in bloom, in which blossoming flowers alternate with closed buds', Uexküll argued, only 'the blooms, not the buds, have meaning for the bees.'[10]

Later in *A Foray* Uexküll included several illustrative interpretations of a street scene as it might be perceived by various different organisms. The first picture in this series was a photograph of a typical street in an alpine town, with a car in the foreground and a church spire peeping above the rooftops at the back of the image. The next image showed the same scene as it might be perceived by a fly. The bulk of the buildings was lessened, their walls and roofs warped; the human figures and the car in the foreground reduced to simple blocks of colour. Edges were softened. The image was impressionistic. A final interpretation of the scene presented the street as seen through the eye of a mollusc.[11] Here the move to abstraction was almost complete. Objects lost all quiddity, and a field of slightly modulated greys, devoid of perspective or of colour, was all that remained of the scene.

What's so striking about the images Uexküll used to outline his thesis, and what I want to draw attention to in this chapter, is the degree to which attempts to inhabit alien consciousnesses in this way are *always* and *inevitably* indebted to existing cultural and aesthetic practices, styles and assumptions. In attempting to visualise what it might be like to see the world from the perspective of a bee, a fly or a mollusc, Uexküll employed what were by 1934 quite conventional – even perhaps canonical – representative schema. When answering the question of what it might be like to perceive the Umwelt of another life form, therefore, Uexküll was forced to employ pre-established representational codes and visual tropes. In one sense this is unsurprising, and Uexküll might have responded to this criticism by pointing out that he was a scientist and philosopher, not an artist: it was not his job to create new ways of seeing the world, but to suggest new ways of thinking about it. However, my point here is that Uexküll didn't merely *illustrate* his theory using established visual forms, but that he derived the very notion of asking what it might be like to be a fly or a mollusc – arguably derived the methodological schema enshrined in the notion of an 'Umwelt' itself – from ideas that were abroad within culture more generally in the period. As we saw in Chapter 2, the vogue for the primitive, the desire to decontextualise perception so as to rid it of narrative and get back to 'things in themselves' through the figure of the naïve perceiving subject, was a fundamental driving force behind much modernist art. Uexküll's Umwelt theory, I would suggest, is a direct product of these impulses.

In this chapter I will suggest that the same thing is true of the representational strategies of literature also, especially as manifested within the work of James Joyce. The novel is a literary form particularly engaged with the question of what it might be like to inhabit another mind, and *Ulysses* in particular asks this question repeatedly. In Chapter 2 I read the work of Virginia Woolf through the prism of Frank Jackson's essay 'What Mary Didn't Know', arguing that competition between ways of knowing in the period conditioned both what a character could be said to know of the literary world they inhabited, and what a reader could be said to know about that world through reading about it. In this chapter I want to consider Joyce's novel alongside another influential pro-qualia thought experiment that engages with questions of knowledge in ways strikingly similar to Uexküll's: Thomas Nagel's influential essay 'What is it Like to be a Bat?'

WHAT IS IT LIKE TO BE A BAT?

Nagel's essay addresses the limitations of physicalist and functionalist attempts to reduce mind to brain. It does so by attending closely to the problems of encoding sensations – particularly the sense experiences associated with alien consciousnesses – in language. Written in 1974 in response to what he identified then as a 'wave of recent reductionist euphoria', it characterises consciousness in terms strikingly similar to Uexküll's, famously defining qualia as 'what it is like' for a particular consciousness to experience the world through the senses.[12] The 'fact that an organism has conscious experience *at all*', Nagel argues, means

> that there is something it is like to *be* that organism. There may even (though I doubt it), be implications about the behaviour of the organism. But fundamentally an organism has conscious mental states if and only if there is something that it is like to *be* that organism – something that it is like *for* that organism.[13]

This qualitative content of experience, so Nagel continues, 'is not captured by any of the familiar, recently devised reductive analyses of the mental, for all of them are logically compatible with its absence.'[14] Knowledge of qualia, in Nagel's terms, is knowledge of what it is like to have a particular perceptual experience: knowledge of what it is like to inhabit the mind of another being, or another person.

Nagel's thought experiment, like Uexküll's Umwelt theory, begins by attempting to imagine the perceptual field of an organism – in this case a bat – possessed of sensory modalities that are fundamentally alien in their processes to our own. Though we are generally happy to accept that bats possess minds and have a distinct phenomenology, Nagel argues that we can't begin to imagine, other than analytically, what it would be like to have such minds ourselves.[15] Bats are attractive agents for this kind of speculation because, though they are mammals and physiologically similar to humans, what Uexküll would term their 'perceptual marks' have a fundamentally alien and rather exotic otherness about them. For this reason the question of what it is like to be another being, especially when asked of the 'fundamentally alien' Umwelt of the bat, cannot ever be satisfactorily answered. Though we can understand the science of echo-location in objective, third-person terms, know, as Nagel writes, that 'most bats (the microchiroptera, to be precise) perceive the external world primarily by sonar, or echolocation, detecting the reflections, from objects within range, of their own rapid, subtly modulated, high-frequency shrieks', this knowledge can only get us so far in our attempts understand bat consciousness.[16] 'Bat sonar', Nagel concludes,

> though clearly a form of perception, is not similar in its operation to any sense that we possess, and there is no reason to suppose that it is subjectively like anything we can experience or imagine. This appears to create difficulties for the notion of what it is like to be a bat.[17]

Our application of objective knowledge of bat phenomenology as an abstraction is useless when it comes to truly knowing bat experiences, which would involve replicating these experiences within our own consciousness. 'Reflection on what it is like to be a bat', therefore, leads to the conclusion 'that there are facts that do not consist in the truth of propositions expressible in a human language.'[18] This is not to say that we will *never* be able to experience bat consciousness, argues Nagel, for eventually technological advances might well provide us with ways of having such experiences. But the logical possibility of such replication cannot be taken, on its own, as evidence for the non-existence of qualia.

What is true of bats, Nagel argues, is true of all other minds whatever. 'The subjective character of the experience of a person deaf and blind from birth is', he says, 'not accessible to me, for example, nor is mine to him.'[19] We do, however, know what it is like to be us, and 'while we do not possess the vocabulary to describe it adequately', knowledge of the mind's 'subjective character is highly specific, and in some respects describable in terms that can be understood only by creatures like us.'[20] According to Nagel, then, there is a difference between understanding the cognitive capabilities of other organisms in a scientific or literary sense and knowing what it is like for those organisms to experience the world as they do. It is only through familiarity with shared experiences expressed in public language (understandable 'only by creatures like us') that the illusion of the 'shareability' of consciousness emerges. Any attempt to enter another organism's unfamiliar Umwelt, either through the discourses of science or of literature, is according to Nagel doomed to come up against the problem of qualia, and thus to fail.

Presented in this way, the problem of qualia asserts itself as one concerned with communicability and with the role and availability of public languages. Nagel's answer (or lack of answer) to the question of what it might be like to be a bat challenged reductively physicalist accounts of cognition and dramatised the problems inherent in attempts to encode the kind of knowledge associated with sense-experience in language. To pose a challenge to physicalism – the thesis that mind can be understood solely in terms of physical process which can be articulated without loss – 'what-is-it-like-ness' should not be interpreted as seeking to draw figurative comparisons between bat and human experiences, something which would suggest that we *can* know what a particular experience is like by comparing it to some other, known, experience. As Peter Hacker summarises:

> It is important to note that the phrase 'there is something *which it is like* for a subject to have experience E' does *not* indicate *a comparison*. Nagel does not claim that to have a given conscious experience *resembles* something (e.g. some other experience), but rather that there is something which it is like *for the subject* to have it, i.e. 'what it is like' is intended to signify 'how it is for the subject himself.'[21]

The slipperiness of the formulation suggests one reason so many critics have failed to recognise the challenge Nagel's formulation poses to literary descriptions of sensation. 'What-is-it-like-ness' in Nagel's sense is not a figurative comparison, but describes an ontologically discrete property of consciousness itself.

Many critics have commented on the similarities between the thought experiment as a philosophical tool and pro-qualia arguments such as Nagel's, and it is striking that the question of what it might be like to be another mind is asked again and again in many modernist novels. It is a question that is asked implicitly, through the formal strategies associated with modernist literary aesthetics, and explicitly, as a question asked by characters within those novels themselves. In *Flush* Virginia Woolf wrote an entire novel from the perspective of a dog, dramatising what she termed 'the widest gulf that can separate one being from another. She spoke. He was dumb. She was a woman; he was a dog. Thus closely united, thus immensely divided, they gazed at each other.'[22] In a manuscript draft of *The Years,* she asked Nagel's question in regards to the consciousness of a baby: 'He's still asleep. Fast asleep. That's why I fell asleep, looking at him, thinking, whats [sic] it like being a baby? What d'you think its [sic] like, being a baby?'[23]

David Herman has argued that much of Woolf's fiction 'emerges from a rejection of Cartesian dualism', and that it thus constitutes an engagement with the notion of the 'extended mind' that has been popularised by philosophers such as Antonio Damasio. 'If there is no dichotomy between the mind in here and the world out there', Herman writes,

> if minds are not closed-off, inner spaces but rather lodged in and partly constituted by the social and material structures that scaffold people's encounters with one another and the world; then access to what Kate Hamburger called the I-originarity of another is no longer uniquely enabled by engagement with fictional narratives.[24]

Nagel's argument, however, draws attention to the fact that there *does* seem to be an ontologically significant dualism at play between mind and world. Access to Kate Hamburger's 'I-originarity' is, if qualia exist, equally *inaccessible* no matter what modes of discourse you employ. Under this understanding, genre distinctions – between the novel and the thought experiment, between fiction and scientific treatise – become philosophically insignificant not because *all* discourse can potentially grant access to the mind, but because *none* can.

As a form the novel is often held to be a mode of literature which seeks to encode qualia in language and to pass it on to other minds. In David Lodge's *Thinks . . .* , the connection between the novel and Nagel's thought experiment becomes a central feature of the plot when Helen Reed, a lecturer in English, encounters the qualiaphile philosopher Ralph Messenger. Messenger explains Nagel's thought experiment to her, and she then uses it as the basis of a creative writing exercise for her students. One of them answers Nagel's question by producing a pastiche of Beckett:

> Where? When? Why? Squeak. I am in the dark. I am always in the dark. It was not always so. Once there were periods of light, or shades of darkness. Squeak. There would be a faint luminosity from the mouth of the cave. When it faded I knew it would soon be time to leave the cave, with the others, to go flittering through the dusk. Squeak. Now it is always dark, uniformly dark. Whether at any given moment it is dark outside my head as well as inside, I do not know.[25]

As Andrew Gaedkte has argued, in her exegesis of the passage Reed – and consequently arguably Lodge himself – interprets Nagel's category of 'what-is-it-like-ness' as merely a function of style and language. 'For Helen', writes

Gaedkte, 'the fact that this endo-psychic, Beckettian world can be convincingly inhabited by the student writer suggests that something like literary qualia – style – can be shared and circulated with little loss.'[26] But that 'something like' begs the ontological question at issue in much the same way that, as we have seen, the idea of 'rendering' sensations does in many critical discussions of cognitive realism. A style can be inhabited, parodied and replicated. A first-person consciousness cannot. It is this very poverty of language, I will suggest, that Joyce was interested in dramatising within *Ulysses*, a novel that has often been read as an exemplary modernist enquiry into what it might be like to inhabit another mind.[27]

BLOOM AND THE BAT

Ulysses can be read as an experimental novel in one of two ways: as an exercise in style, a novelistic experiment in form, or as a sort of epistemological laboratory which experiments *on* its readers. These two interpretations are themselves fictionalised within the novel, which on one level represents a sort of compendium of epistemological thought experiments. In 'Proteus', for instance, Stephen walks upon the beach and engages in a bout of extended sensory introspection:

> Ineluctable modality of the visible: at least that if no more, thought through my eyes. Signatures of all things I am here to read, seaspawn and seawrack, the nearing tide, that rusty boot. Snotgreen, bluesilver, rust: coloured signs.[28]

This famous passage is, ultimately, a meditation on qualia; on the 'ineluctable modality of the visible' and the ineffable and infallible nature of the world you 'damn well have to see'.[29] Sara Danius interprets the scene as a 'practical experiment in apperception' which 'stages the question of how sight and hearing mediate his knowledge and experience of the physical world, that is, how they read sense data.'[30] In his extended meditation Stephen trips from Aristotelian interpretations of perception, through Bishop Berkley's Idealism and the epistemological thesis outlined in Jacob Böhme's *The Signature of All Things*. Descartes' argument from illusion – an observation from his fourth meditation in which he notices that the image of a stick which appears broken when placed in a glass of water is contradicted by the act of touching it – might lie behind Stephen's next observation: 'If you can put your five fingers through it, it is a gate, if not a door. Shut your eyes and see.'[31]

The scene is justly celebrated as an evocation of Stephen's precocious learning. In Proteus he brings his classical knowledge to bear on the scene presented to his senses, but which cannot exist for his readers. This is epistemological enquiry *as* fiction: the qualia of the seascape – those ineluctable starting-points of perceptual experience – are there to be 'read' by the young scholar, and thus placed in an interpretive framework, just as we must read his own analysis of the scene in our turn. The role of public language in making accessible sensory phenomena that generally are occluded because forever unnamed lies behind the notion of a 'snotgreen' sea, which, as we are told in 'Telemachus', is a 'new art colour for our Irish poets', and suggests the apocryphal nineteenth-century notion that Homer's 'wine-dark' descriptor was employed not due to a poverty of language, but of perception.[32] 'Open your eyes now', Stephen continues, 'I will. One moment. Has all vanished since? If I open and am for ever in the black adiaphane. *Basta!* I will see if I can see.'[33] Blind readers that we are, 'Proteus' sets up an interpretive schema that recurs throughout *Ulysses*, and which Nagel endorsed in his thought experiment. It asks what the world is like for a character by engaging with the epistemological assumptions they bring to their own interpretations of the world, all the while challenging the very possibility of answering that question satisfactorily at all.

Throughout *Ulysses* Leopold Bloom ponders the consciousnesses of other beings in ways which bear striking resemblances to Nagel's question. He frequently tries to imagine himself into the consciousnesses of others, both human and animal, in a way that contrasts with Stephen's more cerebral cogitations. But his attempts, too, are all failures. Again and again he fails to provide an altogether convincing answer to the question of what it might be like to inhabit another mind. In 'Calypso', as he prepares his breakfast of mutton kidney, Bloom's cat becomes the subject for analysis:

> They call them stupid. They understand what we say better than we understand them. She understands all she wants to. Vindictive too. Cruel. Her nature. Curious mice never squeal. Seem to like it. Wonder what I look like to her. Height of a tower? No, she can jump me.[34]

A few pages later he thinks about his cat's whiskers, and what it might be like to use them to navigate the world:

> He watched the bristles shining wirily in the weak light as she tipped three times and licked lightly. Wonder is it true if you clip them they can't mouse after. Why? They shine in the dark, perhaps, the tips. Or kind of feelers in the dark, perhaps.[35]

This shift from first-person to third-person narration, from Bloom speculating about the cat's point of view (asking 'wonder what I look like to her'), to us speculating about Bloom watching the cat ('he watched the bristles shining wirily in the weak light'), forces us to confront the ontological limits of subjective focalisation as a literary technique. Are we really any closer to knowing what it is like to be Leopold Bloom – if that means experiencing Bloom's Umwelt – when we are offered his thoughts 'directly', through techniques associated with the stream-of-consciousness method and free indirect discourse, than he is to experiencing his cat's when he wonders what he looks like to her? I would suggest that Joyce's manipulation of what Gérard Genette called 'internal focalisation' and Franz Stanzel termed 'figural narration' here is not an attempt to *portray* the mind at all, but rather a way of dramatising and interrogating the limits of knowledge, and of literature's ability to convey conscious experience to readers.[36]

Later, in 'Nausicaa', as he cleans himself up on the beach after his fleeting encounter – whether real or imagined – with Gerty MacDowell, Bloom looks up and sees something flying about in the evening air. 'Ba', he thinks:

> What is that flying about? Swallow? Bat probably. Thinks I'm a tree, so blind. Have birds no smell? . . . Ba. There he goes. Funny little beggar. Wonder where he lives. Belfry up there. Very likely. Hanging by his heels in the odour of sanctity. Bell scared him out, I suppose . . . Ba. Again. Wonder why they come out at night like mice. They're a mixed breed. Birds are like hopping mice. What frightens them, light or noise? Better sit still. All instinct like the bird in drouth got water out of the end of a jar by throwing pebbles. Like a little man in a cloak he is with tiny hands. Weeny bones. Almost see them shimmering, kind of a bluey white . . . Ba. Who knows what they're always flying for. Insects?[37]

The bat, each sweep of whose flight is announced by the interruption of a phonetic identifier, 'Ba', flies through Bloom's mind as a metaphor for thought itself. But at the level of his *articulated* thoughts it represents a fundamentally alien form of life: an epistemological 'other' prompting another stream of Nagelian speculation. Are bats blind? Do they, like birds, lack a sense of smell? Why do they come out at night? Are animals even conscious, or are they 'all instinct', merely displaying autonomous and mechanical problem-solving behaviour, like the bird in drouth, with no accompanying qualia? Is there really *anything* that it is like to be a bat?

'Nausicaa' is often read as an exploration of the peculiarities of focalisation and narrative perspective. A single event – an encounter during which, as an 'irritated' Joyce told Arthur Power, 'nothing happened between them . . . It all took place in Bloom's imagination' – is presented as being shared between Gerty and Bloom, and is then interpreted and presented to us in two very different ways.[38] Whether Gerty's cliché-ridden narrative is the product of her own consciousness or of Bloom's misogynistic attempts to imagine what it might be like to be *her* isn't particularly important, for both perspectives are, ultimately, the product of Joyce's own imagination. Whether Joyce or Bloom is doing the imagining, in both cases Gerty's narrative mind stream is the product of a man imagining what it might be like to be a young romantic woman: employing the language of women's magazines to construct an Umwelt fundamentally alien to his own. What's so remarkable about the episode, and about *Ulysses* in general, however, is the way in which it can accommodate these competing readings while never collapsing into any single one of them.

Ulysses is full of representations of what is a peculiarly modern anxiety: the possibility of a reductive science of brain and mind capable of providing a faithful account of interiority in language. Throughout the novel Bloom is presented as an amateur scientist of perception, experimenting on himself and those around him by engaging with the material world in all its sensory manifestations, mapping the ineluctable modality of all sensory modes onto their physical correlates. He is an astute reader of odours: he confronts the olfactory assaults of contemporary Dublin, sitting 'calm above' his own 'rising smell', thinking about piss-reeking kidney and comparing 'potted herrings gone stale' to female menstruation, as well as experiencing the seductive delights of Gerty MacDowell's heliotrope perfume and Molly's Peau d'Espagne.[39] He conducts furtive haptic experiments on himself too, stroking his stomach to ascertain whether he can feel colour with his fingertips.[40] He ponders the fact that fish which swim in the sea don't taste salty, and confidently misinterprets the science of optical illusions, investigating the notion of 'parallax' in pop-scientific terms.[41]

Bloom's speculations often involve the creation of an environmentally mediated conception of sensation in which the signatures of the world are 'read', rather than experienced, in all their sensory manifestations. As he speculates about the blind stripling in 'Lestrygonians':

> Poor young fellow! How on earth did he know that van was there? Must have felt it. See things in their forehead perhaps: kind of sense of volume. Weight or size of it, something blacker than the dark. Wonder would he feel it if something was removed. Feel a gap. Queer idea of Dublin he must have, tapping his way round by the stones. Could he walk in a beeline if he hadn't that cane? . . . Look at all the things they can learn to do. Read with their fingers. Tune pianos. Or we are surprised they have any brains.[42]

Again and again Bloom tries to imagine himself into the consciousnesses of others, both human and animal, in this way, and again and again he fails to provide an altogether convincing answer to the question of what it might be like to inhabit another mind. Here he translates the ineffable 'what-is-it-like-ness' of blindness into terms he can understand – a 'kind of sense of volume' – but these attempts to describe blindness are essentially metaphorical, getting Bloom (and consequently us) no closer to experiencing the inner life of a blind stripling than any other technique might. Bloom's speculations on the minds of others fuse the proto- or pseudo-scientific with the anecdotal, singularly failing to grant us access to these other minds: we are 'surprised they have any brains' because the brain, as a physical organ, is all we can ever access.

As he watches the blind stripling tap his way down Molesworth Street, Bloom offers him help to cross the road:

> – Do you want to cross? Mr Bloom asked.
> The blind stripling did not answer. His wall face frowned weakly. He moved his head uncertainly.
> – You're in Dawson street, Mr Bloom said. Molesworth street is opposite. Do you want to cross? There's nothing in the way.
> The cane moved out trembling to the left. Mr Bloom's eye followed its line and saw again the dyeworks' van drawn up before Drago's. Where I saw his brilliantined hair just when I was. Horse droppings. Driver in John Long's. Slaking his drouth.
> – There's a van there, Mr Bloom said, but it's not moving. I'll see you across. Do you want to go to Molesworth street?
> – Yes, the stripling answered. South Frederick street.
> – Come, Mr Bloom said.[43]

In *A Foray into the Worlds of Animals and Humans*, Jakob von Uexküll had described an imaginary blind man's Umwelt, suggesting that such a person's

> environment is very limited; he knows it only insofar as he can feel out his path with his cane and feet. The street through which he strolls is for him plunged into darkness, but his dog is supposed to lead him home via a certain path.[44]

This symbiotic map of the city Uexküll called the blind man's 'familiar path'. In *Ulysses*, Joyce's description of Bloom leading the blind stripling is a kind of literary familiar path, offered as much for our benefit as it is for his. Joyce famously told Frank Budgen that with *Ulysses* he wanted 'to give a picture of Dublin so complete that if the city one day suddenly disappeared from the earth it could be reconstructed out of my book', and there is a sense in which all of the novel is a map, not just of Dublin, but of the minds of the characters within it.[45] And, as a map, we must be wary of mistaking it for the territory. The imaginative cartography of *Ulysses* always implies a critical distance. As readers, we too are blind to Bloom's Dublin, receiving it only through the map of the text, which itself constitutes a set of instructions issued against a background of white noise.

Sara Danius has said that in *Ulysses* Joyce 'aligns himself with a modernist aesthetic that aims to render what is perceived rather than what is known'.[46] But as we have seen the question of the representability of perception, and the apparent tension between empirical and sensory knowledge, goes to the heart of the problem of qualia. Thus Danius's identification of *Ulysses* as a novel engaged with what she calls 'an aesthetics of immediacy', in which 'the everyday has to be named anew, and continually, in order to retain its desired immediacy, and this is why, in Joyce, the imperative to make you *see* is so often an aesthetic end in itself' is not the whole story.[47] Taking as her example the description of the journey to Paddy Dignam's funeral in 'Hades', in which Bloom travels through Dublin, watching the city through the frame of a carriage window, Danius argues that the carriage is figured as a kind of cinematograph so that the 'proper content of the passage . . . is the mourner's processing of a number of sense data, as though the implicit narrator endeavours to report what they actually see, not what they know is there.'[48] But as we saw in Chapter 2, it is difficult to maintain a distinction between a character's description of a scene and their knowledge of the 'sense data' of that scene which they are presented as perceiving. From the reader's perspective the two are identical.

In the above passage Bloom maps Dublin's spaces for *us* as well as for the stripling. The knowingness with which Joyce manipulates both his focalisers and his readers in this way is evoked too in 'Proteus' when Stephen asks 'who watches me here? Who ever anywhere will read these written words? Signs on a white field', to which the answer, obviously, is us: the readers of *Ulysses*.[49] In recreating the Umwelt of Joyce's characters, we are inevitably forced to read over their shoulders, and we are imperfect readers. 'The *absolute* is synonymous with *perfection*', wrote Henri Bergson in *An Introduction to Metaphysics*. 'Were all the photographs of a town, taken from all possible points of view, to go on indefinitely completing one another, they would never be equivalent to the solid town in which we walk about.'[50] To mistake the map Dublin for the territory is to ignore one of the lessons of reading Joyce provided us with in *Ulysses*.

The Epic of the Human Body

A critical tendency to insist upon the epistemologically transcendental status of Joycean literature has asserted itself at least since Samuel Beckett wrote, of *Finnegans Wake*, that:

> It is not written at all. It is not to be read – or rather, it is not only to be read. It is to be looked at and listened to. His writing is not *about* something, *it is that something itself*.[51]

Beckett's acclamation has often been interpreted as raising *Finnegans Wake* to the status of a literary *Gesamtkunstwerk*, suggesting that by virtue of its complexity as a literary artefact it takes on material and experiential properties – that it is somehow able to convey to us what it is like to look at and listen to the world. John Rodker identified *Finnegans Wake*'s most fundamental question as that of sensory communication: 'With this . . . work some enquiry into the symbols that govern the communication through writing of thought and emotion becomes imperative . . . How do men then, through literature, communicate with each other and what is it they succeed in conveying.'[52]

For Rodker, the *Wake* was successful at breaking down the barriers between subject and object; between reader and text, allowing us to access what it is like to inhabit another mind. As he continued, Joyce 'brings to fruition . . . the possibility of a complete symbiosis of reader and writer.'[53] Like *Finnegans Wake*, almost from its inception *Ulysses* too was read as a work of cognitive realism. Guided by Joyce's various schemata for the novel, which (though they did not always agree) suggested associations between various episodes and various sensory organs, critics have for a long time interpreted *Ulysses* as what Joyce told Frank Budgen it was, an 'epic of the human body'.[54] Many critics have taken this to mean that *Ulysses* was mimetic of the body: of its processes and of its experiences and rhythms.

It is undoubtedly the case that *Ulysses* is scandalously corporeal. What unites many of Bloom's investigations into alien Umwelten is their focus on the under-represented senses, especially on the proximate senses of taste and smell. Just as in Uexküll's thesis and Nagel's thought experiment, it is our underused (and often ignored) senses that provide the biggest challenges to literary representations of sensation. Yet a theoretical conflation of body and mind should not be interpreted as equivalent to a material conflation of language and world. Clearly, we are as divorced from the corporeal phenomenological experiences of literary characters – from the qualia of fictional individuals – from what it is like to truly *be* them, as Bloom is when he considers what it might be like to be Gerty, a blind stripling, a cat, or a bat. The problem of qualia, at least as it is elucidated by Nagel, is, like so much else, *fictionalised* within *Ulysses*, hinted at obliquely and encoded in the very fabric of the novel. It is a philosophical conundrum that is consumed metafictionally, with Bloom's musings offering a self-referential commentary on the limits of literature itself. They arguably get us no closer to knowing what it might be like to be a bat, or a cat, or a blind stripling, but they do give us a literary understanding of what it might be like to think – if not to feel – like Leopold Bloom. This is Hugh Kenner's 'Uncle Charles principle' writ large, exemplifying the limitations of fiction while coercing us with a vivid account of a man's *articulated* thoughts. The behaviourist question that remains is one that haunted the development of the novel-form in the period: is knowing another person any different from knowing a fictional character?

In light of this, is it true to suggest, as does David Lodge in *Consciousness and the Novel*, that:

> Joyce's representation of consciousness was a quite new combination of third-person and first person discourse. The third-person narrative is impersonal and objective – there is no trace of an authorial persona, a confiding, commenting, ruminating authorial 'I' such as Fielding's or Dickens' or George Eliot's. [Joyce] came as close to representing the phenomenon of consciousness as perhaps any writer has ever done in the history of literature.[55]

As I argued in Chapter 1, if qualia exist than it makes little sense to refer to narrative fiction in terms of a hierarchy of cognitive fidelity in this way. If they exist it is a category error to claim that Joyce came closer to 'representing the phenomenon of consciousness' than any other writer has done previously. Certainly there is an enormous (and enormously important) difference between reading a scientific, third-person description of a sense-experience and reading a more nuanced narrative of the same experience, but does this really mean that we are any closer to experiencing the 'phenomenon' of another person's consciousness in the latter case?

Just how 'new' Joyce's 'combination of third-person and first-person discourse' was is likewise a matter of some debate. Clearly, as David Herman summarises, it is difficult to ascertain 'how much of a shift in accent, a departure from the practices of nineteenth-century realism ... these modernist methods actually entail[ed].'[56] Indeed Wyndham Lewis's early critique of Joyce's 'interior' method, as articulated in *The Art of Being Ruled*, was that it did not seem all that different to Dickens's method of characterisation in *The Pickwick Papers*. As evidence Lewis quoted an extract from *Ulysses* where Stephen's observations become entangled with his feelings towards the Provost, knitting quotation, perception and articulated thought together in one synthesised whole:

> Provost's house. The reverend Dr Salmon: tinned salmon. Well tinned in there. Like a mortuary chapel. Wouldn't live in it if they paid me. Hope they have liver and bacon today. Nature abhors a vacuum ... There he is: the brother. Image of him. Haunting face. Now that's a coincidence.[57]

In *The Pickwick Papers*, argued Lewis (slightly misquoting Dickens), Mr Jingle is introduced in a very similar manner:

> Rather short in the waist, ain't it? . . . Like a general postman's coat – , queer coats those – , made by contract – , no measuring – , mysterious dispensations of Providence – , all the short men get the long coats – , all the long men short ones.[58]

In *The Art of Being Ruled* Lewis railed against what he saw as the fundamental artificiality of such methods, arguing that in *Ulysses,* Joyce

> had to pretend that we were really surprising the private thought of a real and average human creature, Mr. Bloom. But the fact is that Mr. Bloom was abnormally *wordy*. He *thought in words*, not images, for our benefit, in a fashion as unreal, from the point of view of the strictest naturalist dogma, as a Hamlet soliloquy.[59]

In 'showing' us the content of his characters' minds, Lewis said, Joyce was inevitably engaged in a process of translation, transforming mental states into literary utterances, and like all authors was forced to use words as his tools. For Lewis the results were degenerative: 'so by the devious route of a fashionable naturalist device', he concluded, 'that usually described as "presenting the character from the *inside*" . . . Mr. Joyce reaches the half-demented crack figure of traditional english [sic] humour.'[60] Whether we agree with Lewis's aesthetic assessment or not, his philosophical objection is surely correct.

Vike Plock has suggested that 'it could be argued that Joyce's literary experimentation and neurophysiology as an academic science are equally significant manifestations of modernity.'[61] Concentrating on 'Eumaeus', Plock argues that Joyce develops this 'associative relationship' by 'reproducing vocabulary relating to thought processes, brain activity, and neuroscientific manifestations'.[62] She goes on to read the episode as mimetic of the cognitive dissonance associated by contemporary medicine with nervous agitation and with ergography, the study of nervous exhaustion. I will explore the implications of a burgeoning neurology for the novel-form and the question of qualia in Chapter 4, but for now it is worth noting that Joyce himself was largely uninterested in whether or not *Ulysses* could be read in terms of what I have called cognitive realism. Richard Ellmann records that

> when Joyce was told that the representational validity of the internal monologue had been questioned by critics, he replied, 'From my point of view, it hardly matters whether the technique is "veracious" or not; it has served me as a bridge over which to march my eighteen episodes, and once I have got the troops across, the opposing forces can, for all I care, blow the bridge sky high.'[63]

Instead of reading *Ulysses* in search of a portrayal of what it is like to be another mind, therefore, I believe it is important to read it as a radical interrogation of any such claims. We probably know more about Leopold Bloom than we do about any other figure in the western literary canon. We know what he likes for breakfast; we know his opinion on various political and aesthetic questions; we know what he reads, and what he thinks about while on the toilet, his sexual proclivities, and on and on. And yet, despite all this, we can't know and will never know what it feels like to *be* him (not least because he never existed). In *Ulysses* Joyce's radical and encyclopaedic cataloguing of cognitive processes alongside the matter of twentieth-century Dublin draws attention to the void between mind and world rather than closing it. Indeed the radical polyphony of his novel should force us to be very careful when defining any sort of hierarchy of style within it. As we shall see in Chapter 5, the tension between an episode like 'Ithaca', in which the exhaustive description of certain types of information functions to interrogate the apparent attempts at psychological verisimilitude of many of the other episodes, immediately serves to undermine any straightforwardly cognitive realist interpretation of the novel.

Instead I would contend that we feel that certain parts of *Ulysses* are a more immediate or realistic record of human consciousness than, say, a scientific paper about the operations of neurons, largely because we live in its and in modernism's wake. *Ulysses*, and modernist aesthetics more broadly, can be seen to have set the terms of the debate, providing a model of consciousness which remains influential to this day. In an important sense Joyce's method created, rather than recorded, modern conceptions of the mental. It is little wonder that Daniel Dennett, the most hostile qualiaphobic philosopher of our time, calls his materialist model of consciousness the 'Joycean Machine'.[64] In asking what it is like to be Leopold Bloom, therefore, we must beware of mistaking the richness of Joyce's prose for that of the richness of the mind itself. For it is surely in realism's failures, in the gaps between mind and world, that Bloom continues to live.

Notes

1. In *The Open Man and Animal* Giorgio Agamben notes that Uexküll's investigations were 'contemporary with both quantum physics and the artistic avant-gardes. And like them, they express the unreserved abandonment of every anthropocentric perspective in the life sciences and the radical dehumanization of the image of nature'. Giorgio Agamben, *The Open Man and Animal*, trans. by Kevin Attell (Stanford, CA: Stanford University Press, 2004), p. 39. Anne Harrington has traced the political dimensions of what she calls Uexküll's 'anti-mechanistic science of life and behavior' in *Reenchanted Science Holism in German Culture from Wilhelm II to Hitler* (Princeton, NJ: Princeton University Press, 1996), pp. 34–68. More recently, David Herman has used the concept of the Umwelt to examine what he calls the 'ecologies of experience' represented in Virginia Wool's animal narrative *Flush*. See

David Herman 'Modernist Life Writing and Nonhuman Lives: Ecologies of Experience in Virginia Woolf's Flush', *Modern Fiction Studies*, 59.3 (2013), 547–568.
2. Evan Thompson, *Mind in Life: Biology, Phenomenology, and the Sciences of Mind* (Cambridge, MA: Harvard University Press, 2007), p. 59.
3. Jakob von Uexküll, *A Foray into the Worlds of Animals and Humans: with A Theory of Meaning*, trans. by Joseph D. O'Neill (Minneapolis, MN: University of Minnesota Press), p. 69.
4. Uexküll, *A Foray*, p. 70.
5. Uexküll, *A Foray*, p. 53.
6. Uexküll, *A Foray*, p. 50.
7. Uexküll, *A Foray*, p. 51. Joseph D. O'Neill translates 'Umwelt' as 'environment', but for the sake of clarity I have retained Uexküll's terminology.
8. Uexküll, *A Foray*, p. 53.
9. Uexküll, *A Foray*, p. 43.
10. Uexküll, *A Foray*, p. 84.
11. There is a suggestion of Max Nordau's conception of 'degeneration' in this. Synaesthesia, in Nordau's words, represented a desire 'to designate as progress the return from the consciousness of man to that of the oyster'. See Max Nordau, *Degeneration* (London: William Heinemann 1913), p. 142. It is an image echoed in the numerous allusions to 'oyster eyes' in *Ulysses*. See, for instance, Joe Menton's 'oyster eyes' noticed several times by Bloom in 'Hades'; James Joyce, *Ulysses*, ed. by Hans Walter Gabler (London: The Bodley Head, 1986), 6.1031, 8.322; or Blazes Boylan's 'winebig oyster eyes' described in 'Wandering Rocks', *Ulysses*, 10.1230. All references to James Joyce's *Ulysses* are to the Gabler synoptic edition, and are given in the form [episode number.line number].
12. Thomas Nagel, 'What is it Like to be a Bat?', *The Philosophical Review*, 83.4 (1974), 435–450 (p. 435).
13. Nagel, 'What is it Like to be a Bat?', p. 436.
14. Nagel cites a roster of functionalist reductive arguments here, including: J. C. C. Smart, *Philosophy and Scientific Realism* (London: Routledge & Kegan Paul, 1963); Hilary Putnam's 'Psychological Predicates', in *Art, Mind, and Religion*, ed. by W. H. Capitan and D. D. Merrill (Pittsburgh, PA: University of Pittsburgh Press, 1967); David M. Rosenthal, *Materialism and the Mind–Body Problem* (Englewood Cliffs, NJ and London: Prentice-Hall, 1971); and D. M. Armstrong, *A Materialist Theory of Mind* (London: Routledge & Kegan Paul, 1968). To which list could be added the prominent voice of Daniel Dennett. I will explore the implications of modernism's reductive impulses in the following chapter.
15. Nagel, 'What is it Like to be a Bat?', p. 438.
16. As we saw in Chapter 1, quite what is meant by 'third-person' in this context is difficult to define. Frequently the term is invoked in discussions about consciousness in order to draw a distinction between 'subjective' (and therefore more 'literary') accounts of a mental phenomena and 'objective' descriptions of the same phenomena. In terms of qualia, however, our relationship with a piece of writing is always in the 'third person': the use of the first-person pronoun does nothing to alter the ontology of that which is described. Nagel, 'What is it Like to be a Bat?', p. 438.

17. Nagel, 'What is it Like to be a Bat?', p. 438.
18. Nagel, 'What is it Like to be a Bat?', p. 441.
19. Nagel, 'What is it Like to be a Bat?', p. 440.
20. Nagel, 'What is it Like to be a Bat?', p. 440.
21. M. R. Bennet and P. M. S. Hacker, *The Philosophical Foundations of Neuroscience* (Oxford: Blackwell Publishing, 2003), p. 273.
22. Virginia Woolf, *Flush* (London: The Hogarth Press, 1933), p. 27.
23. New York Public Library, Berg Coll., MSS Woolf, *The Pargiters*, M42, vol. v, pp. 2–3.
24. Herman, 'Modernist Life Writing', p. 553.
25. David Lodge, *Thinks. . .* (London: Secker & Warburg, 2001), p. 95.
26. Andrew Gaedtke, 'Cognitive Investigations: The Problems of Qualia and Style in the Contemporary Neuronovel', *Novel: A Forum on Fiction*, 45.2 (2012), 184–201 (p. 193).
27. Samuel Beckett, *Three Novels: Molloy, Malone Dies, The Unnameable* (New York: Grove Press, 2009), p. 11.
28. Joyce, *Ulysses*, 3.1–3.
29. Joyce, *Ulysses*, 3.9.
30. Sara Danius, *The Senses of Modernism: Technology, Perception, and Aesthetics* (Ithaca, NY and London: Cornell University Press, 2002), p. 171.
31. Joyce, *Ulysses*, 3.8.
32. Joyce, *Ulysses*, 1.73; see R. Rutherfurd-Dyer in 'Homer's Wine-dark Sea', *Greece & Rome Second Series*, 30.2 (1983) pp. 125–128.
33. Joyce, *Ulysses*, 3.25–26.
34. Joyce, *Ulysses*, 4.26–29.
35. Joyce, *Ulysses*, 4.39–42.
36. See Gérard Genette, *Narrative Discourse: An Essay in Method*, trans. by Jane E. Lewin (Ithaca, NY: Cornell University Press, 1980), pp 189–194; and F. K. Stanzel, *A Theory of Narrative* (Cambridge: Cambridge University Press, 1984).
37. Joyce, *Ulysses*, 13.1117–1143.
38. Arthur Power, *Conversations with James Joyce*, ed. by Clive Hart (London: Millington, 1974), p. 32.
39. Joyce, *Ulysses*, 4.4, 13.1009, 18.865.
40. Joyce, *Ulysses*, 8.1140–1142.
41. Joyce, *Ulysses*, 8.110–113.
42. Joyce, *Ulysses*, 8.1107–1111
43. Joyce, *Ulysses*, 8.1077–1089.
44. Uexküll, *A Foray*, pp. 99–100.
45. Frank Budgen, *James Joyce and the Making of Ulysses* (Bloomington, IN: Indiana University Press, 1960), pp. 67–68.
46. Danius, *The Senses of Modernism*, p. 156.
47. Danius, *The Senses of Modernism*, p. 164.
48. Danius, *The Senses of Modernism*, p. 164.
49. Joyce, *Ulysses*, 3.414–415.
50. Henri Bergson, *An Introduction to Metaphysics*, trans. by T. E. Hulme (London: Macmillan and Co., Ltd, 1913), p. 4.

51. Samuel Beckett, 'Dante ... Bruno. Vico ... Joyce', in Samuel Beckett, ed, *Our Exagmination Round His Factification for Incamination of Work in Progress* (Paris: Shakespeare and Company, 1929), p. 14 (emphases in original).
52. Rodker, 'Joyce's Dynamic', *Our Exagmination*, p. 143.
53. Rodker, 'Joyce's Dynamic', *Our Exagmination*, p. 143.
54. Budgen, *James Joyce and the Making of Ulysses*, p. 21.
55. David Lodge, *Consciousness and the Novel: Connected Essays* (London: Secker & Warburg, 2002), p. 55.
56. David Herman, 'Re-minding Modernism', in *The Emergence of Mind: Representations of Consciousness in Narrative Discourse in English*, ed. by David Herman (Lincoln, NE and London: University of Nebraska Press, 2011), p. 248.
57. Qtd in Wyndham Lewis, *The Art of Being Ruled*, ed. by Reed Way Dasenbrock (Santa Rosa, CA: Black Sparrow Press, 1989), p. 347.
58. Qtd in Lewis, *The Art of Being Ruled*, p. 348.
59. Lewis, *The Art of Being Ruled,* pp. 346–347.
60. Lewis, *The Art of Being Ruled*, p. 348.
61. Vike Martina Plock, *Joyce, Medicine, and Modernity* (Gainesville, FL: University Press of Florida, 2010), p. 90.
62. Plock, *Joyce*, pp. 90–91.
63. Richard Ellmann, *Ulysses on the Liffey* (London: Faber, 1972), p. 109.
64. Daniel C. Dennett, *Consciousness Explained* (London: Allen Lane, The Penguin Press, 1992), p. 275.

4

NEUROMODERNISM AND THE EXPLANATORY GAP

But is there nothing new under the sun? It remains to be seen. What! My head has been X-rayed. I have seen, while I live, my own cranium, and that would be nothing new?
                        Guillaume Apollinaire, 'The New Spirit and the Poets'

Neuromodernism

In Chapters 2 and 3 we saw how, during the early twentieth century, developments in science and philosophy influenced the various forms of knowledge that literature in general, and the novel in particular, was thought capable of containing. During the period enormous upheavals within the physical sciences led to a profound renegotiation of the relationship between mind and world, giving rise to the representational abstractions associated with modernism, and to the metaphysical uncertainties which led to the definition of qualia. The abstract nature of advanced physics caused an epistemological crisis as profound as that previously associated with Cartesian doubt, forcing philosophers to settle on the nebulous certainties offered by sense-data as a foundation for the new physics.

These abstractions were not the only kinds of new knowledge being popularised during the modernist moment, however. Anxieties over what it might be like to be another mind were accompanied by huge advances in the fields of medicine, neurology and brain science. The relationship between the mind and the brain as it was understood within clinical medicine came to represent another fault line in modernity's battles over knowledge, and it is this fault line that most characterises contemporary debates over literature's ability to represent consciousness. What was the relationship between mind and brain when understood in the context of neuroscience? 'It must be frankly confessed', wrote William James, defining the 'stream of consciousness':

> that in no fundamental sense do we know where our successive fields of consciousness come from, or why they have the precise inner constitution which they do have. They certainly follow or accompany our brain states . . . But, if we ask just *how* the brain conditions them, we have not the remotest inkling of an answer to give.[1]

This chapter will consider some of the ways in which inklings of answers to this question were formulated during the modernist period, and how these answers continue to influence critical interpretations of modernist fiction and the problem of qualia. From the late nineteenth to the mid-twentieth centuries, a fevered 'neuromodernism' sought to reconcile the insides of people with the outsides – their brain states with their mind states – in terms of neurological function. But in doing so it often ended up reinforcing the neo-Cartesian binaries it sought to annihilate.

'To speak of neurology *and* modernity', argue Laura Salisbury and Andrew Shail in *Neurology and Modernity*, 'is to describe a relationship of mutual constitution.'[2] During the late nineteenth and early twentieth centuries, technological and diagnostic revolutions cast neuroscience as the dominant paradigm according to which consciousness would have to be explained, enshrining the nervous system at the heart of contemporary models of consciousness, and the neuron as the basic physical unit of cognition. Once discovered, however, the neuron became more than a physiological entity: a new scientific object requiring measurement and a functional 'explanation'. The practice of neurology gave rise to new pathologies and to new anxieties, while neurological theories provided rich new metaphors for the nature of the self and for consciousness more generally. Like the atom, the wave and, later, the gene – objects of science whose properties and significances underwent profound intellectual shifts during the period – the neuron, as Shail and Salisbury contend, should be interpreted as constitutive of modernity itself.

One of the earliest ways in which the new neurology manifested its influence was in the cultural arena, where it provided a new language of cognition. In *The Life of Sir Humphrey Davy* John Paris records an admirer who, puzzled by Coleridge's attendance of Davy's lectures on chemistry, asked the poet 'what attractions he could find in a study so unconnected with his known pursuits. "I attend Davy's lectures", Coleridge replied, "to increase my stock of metaphors."'[3] In this chapter I will consider the ways in which the discovery and invention of the neuron increased modernity's common stock of metaphors, and redefined the limits of enquiries into the nature of the mind. I shall therefore employ Kirsten Shepherd-Barr's notion of 'neuromodernism', described by her as the 'use of science by scholars in the humanities trying to understand modernist writings and mechanisms', not in an attempt to *explain* modernist aesthetics in scientific terms – as somehow anticipating or mirroring the discoveries of contemporary neuroscience – but to show how many of modernist fiction's epistemological and philosophical preoccupations were contingent upon modernity's material and technological contexts, contexts which continue to create problems for critical approaches to literature broadly defined as 'neuro-aesthetic'.[4] Such questions relate directly to the question of qualia as properties of conscious states which are resistant to conceptual reductions of the kind most often associated with neurology.

The development of mnemonic technologies able to store and transmit the data of sense were accompanied by the development of introspective technologies able to image the brain as never before, producing a relationship between nerve and world that can best be described as a dialogue. Under the new paradigm sensations became essentially relative and context-specific, dependent for their quality on the particular nerves they agitated. In *Discourse Networks 1800/1900*, Friedrich Kittler argued that the burgeoning neurology of the period led to the triumph of information over matter, and that the processes which governed this victory were essentially reductive.[5] 'The modern spirit is vivisective', Stephen Dedalus remarks somewhat wearily to Cranly in *Stephen Hero*; 'vivisection itself is the most modern process one can conceive'.[6]

Neuromodernism was undoubtedly a product of this vivisective spirit: of a desire to analyse, measure and categorise material and mental objects and in the process reduce them to something else. The inward turn associated with modernist narrative was therefore accompanied in the psychological disciplines by a thorough re-evaluation of the status of the body-in-perception, and in medicine by an analysis of the gross matter of the sense organs. The language of such analysis quickly entered literary discourse. Thus the locus of interaction between literature and psychological case study was decidedly two-way. As Mark S. Micale summarises:

> Before the final quarter of the nineteenth century, psychiatric cases published in medical textbooks and monographs tended to be short and mechanical recitations of hereditary background, symptom profile, diagnosis and prognosis. Dynamic models of mental functioning, however, were centrally concerned with the *consciousness* and the inner mental life of that patient; accordingly, a new aim of psychiatric case histories beginning around 1890 became the representation of individual emotional experience and intrapsychic subjectivity.[7]

Attempts to map this 'intrapsychic subjectivity' onto physical brain states became the dominant methodology of contemporary neuropsychology, which represented the most sustained attempt to trace correlative connections between these two apparently separate realms. As Kittler summarises, such approaches tended to annex theoretical or theological objections: murdering the flesh in order to dissect the mind.

The first move of these strains of psychological behaviourism – which in their most extreme forms denied the existence of interiority and qualia completely – was to concentrate neurology on the study of reflexes. The mysteries of consciousness that remained after the neuronal system had been isolated and described were gleefully appropriated both by progenitors of the 'stream of consciousness' as a psychological metaphor or principle, and by novelists. For some writers, the promise of subjective fragmentation inculcated by the materialist paradigm of neurological reduction was to be welcomed. As F. T. Marinetti declared in his 'Technical Manifesto of Futurist Literature', in light of such discoveries the aim of the Futurist should be to:

> *Destroy the 'I' in literature* – that is, all psychology. Man, utterly ruined by libraries and museums, ruled by a fearful logic and wisdom, is of absolutely no more interest. So abolish him in literature. Replace him with matter, whose essence must be grasped by flashes of intuition, something physicists and chemists can never do.
>
> Auscultate, through things in freedom and capricious engines, the breath, the sensibility, and the instincts of metal, stone, wood, etc. Replace the psychology of man, now spent, with a *Lyrical Obsession with matter*.[8]

Others felt that the physical fragmentation of the brain brought about by the new neurology threatened the unity of the human person, creating space for the role of the novelist as a unifier of newly atomised subjects. As D. H. Lawrence lamented in 1925, the reductive methodologies of neuroscience seemed to foretell the death of the subject:

> To the scientist, I am dead. He puts under the microscope a bit of dead me, and calls it me. He takes me to pieces, and says first one piece, and then another piece, is me. My heart, my liver, my stomach have all been scientifically me, according to the scientist; and nowadays I am either a brain, or nerves, or glands, or something more up-to-date in the tissue line. Now I flatly deny that I am a soul, or a body, or a mind, or an intelligence, or a brain, or a nervous system, or a bunch of glands, or any of the rest of these bits of me. The whole is greater than the part . . . For this reason I am a novelist.[9]

For Lawrence the novel-form promised to save the subject from this conceptual fragmentation by giving voice to those emergent properties of the mind that transcend the material conditions of the body. The scientist dissects the body, Lawrence argues, seeking the sovereign 'I' in ever smaller pieces of matter. But novelists can address the whole person at once, through the body. Neuromodernism had destroyed the unity of the subject, and it was the job of the novelist to reassemble it into the first-person pronoun.

But abandoning the notion of spirit-as-substance in favour of the apparent immateriality of 'information' – a model bolstered by the newly vital technology of electricity – meant that the impression, the sense-datum and the 'given' in experience were seen as occupying an increasingly uncertain ontological position. Such phenomena were not quite physical, but neither were they quite mental. 'Are sense-data physical or mental? Asked H. H. Price in his *Perception* 'or are they vital, in the sense in which breathing and digestion are vital?'[10] The invocation of an abstract notion of 'vitality', so typical of aesthetic manifestoes of the period, suggests that Price was unable to provide a fully satisfactory answer to his own question. In one respect the neuron could be seen as supplying the other term in this debate, as the material analogue to the sensation, sense-content or 'given' in experience.

As Salisbury, Shail and George Rousseau have shown, though the idea that the brain is the seat of the mind goes back at least to the time of Hippocrates, the thesis that the mind could be *fully* identified with the brain, and explained solely in terms of a localising study of nerve fibres, was largely a product of modern medicine.[11] In the early nineteenth century the Galenic theory of the nerves, which held that neurons were the conduits of pneumatic 'animal spirits' – analogous to the other bodily fluids or humours, and thus fundamentally mechanistic in nature – was abandoned in favour of a neurological model based on 'nervous energy': apparently insubstantial, or at any rate materially paradoxical, electro-chemical impulses. In 1837, when Johannes Müller's multivolume *Elements of Physiology* was published in London, he noted that the 'new orthodoxy that there is no nervous fluid' was already well established.[12]

This transition from analysis of substance to analysis of system had its origins, argues Michael Foucault, in the eighteenth century, during which period

> the image . . . of animal spirits in the channels of the nerves . . . with all its mechanical and metaphysical implications, . . . was frequently replaced by the image, more strictly physical but of an even more symbolic value, of a tension to which nerves, vessels, and the entire system of organic fibers were subject.[13]

This trend towards a gradual de-materialising the contents of the nervous system – even as that system itself was coming into ever-sharper focus as a mappable physical entity – continued during the nineteenth century. Cartographic or modal studies of the brain, such as Franz Joseph Gall's much-maligned theory of phrenology (which held that mental faculties could be mapped onto the physical attributes of brain and skull), and Paul Broca's seminal 1861 study of language production in the left frontal gyrus, began to dominate interpretations of the mind–brain dichotomy.[14] Experimental psychology and the burgeoning cognitive sciences were thus seen primarily as cartographic endeavours: quests for correlative relations that had no qualms deferring the causal or ontological questions associated with qualia such approaches inevitably brought to the fore.

The conceptual and technological breakthrough which allowed modernity to engage with the notion of the individual nerve-cell can be traced to 1873, when Camillo Golgi developed his silver-chromate staining technique. The Golgi method allowed individual neurons to be isolated visually and conceptually, eventually proving conclusively the existence of the synaptic gap, and consequently calling into question cohesive and unitary models of the self. The neuroscientist Santiago Ramón y Cajal, who shared the Nobel Prize for the discovery with Golgi in 1906, described the experience of seeing individual nerve-cells for the first time as a moment of aesthetic as well as conceptual revelation:

> What an unexpected sight! Sparse, smooth and thin black filaments, or thorny, thick, triangular, stellate, or fusiform black cells could be seen against a perfectly translucent yellow background. One might almost liken the images to Chinese ink drawings on transparent Japanese paper.[15]

Thus modernism's 'inward turn' was accompanied by a vivisective or diagnostic impulse which used the visual codes of neurology to throw light on the interiors of subjects. The quest was to pin down feelings and thoughts in physical space. 'If I can imagine that, while I am having sensations, I myself or someone else could observe my brain with all the necessary physical and chemical appliances' wrote Ernst Mach in his *The Analysis of the Sensations*, 'it would then be possible to ascertain with what processes of the organism sensations of a particular kind are connected.'[16] Mach's correlative and localising methodology – which, as we have seen, was built on the work of Hermann von Helmholtz and sought a solution to the Cartesian impasse in the increasingly visible nexus of nerve fibres and brain functions that were seen to dominate the structures of consciousness – had a huge influence both on the introspective psychologies of the analytical and phenomenological traditions, and on the psycho-physical manifestos released in a stream during the early years of the twentieth century.[17]

While some philosophers and psychologists appropriated the techniques associated with the 'inward turn' in literature to investigate the phenomena of consciousness, other theoretical interventions rejected interiority, treating the human subject as a machine and ignoring qualia in favour of measuring reaction times and reading abilities solely as mechanical manifestations of behavioural impulses. 'Following the procedure of Helmholtz, who built device after device to measure reaction-time thresholds', notes Friedrich Kittler, 'the psychophysics of the [eighteen] nineties went to work measuring reading with kymographs, tachistoscopes, horopterscopes, and chronographs.'[18] Behaviourism of this kind denied that introspection was a legitimate psychological technique at all (and, in its most extreme forms, denied that there were such things as internal mental states at all). 'Psychophysics', Kittler continues, citing F. T. Marinetti, investigated 'only the movements of matter, which are not subject to the laws of intelligence and for that reason are much more significant.'[19]

Golgi's method was, above all, a technology of visualisation. Much like the Röntgen rays, which swept fashionable society in the late nineteenth century as an after-dinner party trick before they became a diagnostic tool, the beauty of the images produced by the Golgi method was as striking as any scientific 'truth' they might uncover.[20] As such the method contributed to narratives of legibility of the human body more generally: to the modernist interest in looking 'inside' the self in different and often contradictory ways. Turning the brain inside out in this way, 'as if', as T. S. Eliot wrote in 'The Love Song of J. Alfred Prufrock', 'a magic lantern threw the nerves in patterns on a screen',[21] exposed what David Herman has termed the 'Cartesian geographies' of the modern brain as never before.[22] Such processes and technologies, as Vike Plock notes, gave a new urgency to the philosophical problems associated with subjectivity, epistemology and the problem of qualia. Neuroscience, as she notes in *Joyce, Medicine and Modernity*, 'literally turned the subject inside out and made the individual's innermost and intimate physiological mechanisms the object of medical scrutiny.'[23]

Neuromodernism was thus primarily concerned with 'reading' or analysing the inner worlds of its subjects, a process that drew attention to the metaphysical gaps that emerged between differing accounts of the same phenomena. It is for this reason that 'neurology and modernity', as Salisbury and Shail note, 'worked together to create narratives of legibility for previously occluded experiences and structures, registering as "data" occurrences that had previously been either unnoticed or unavailable'.[24] But in doing so neuromodernism quickly demonstrated how these different narratives often seemed incompatible. Almost as soon as Golgi's method threw the nerves in patterns on a screen the metaphysical implications, and limitations, of the new boundaries of science were felt. By turning the human subject inside out, cognitive scientists and neurologists were forced to radically alter their conception of traditional notions of the executive consciousness, the self, and the brain as a 'Cartesian theatre': a complex yet fundamentally mechanistic organ in which or through which a material body somehow became connected with an immaterial mind.

MODERNIST FICTION AND THE EXPLANATORY GAP

Midway through John Middleton Murry's 1916 novel *Still Life*, a doctor, during a lecture on the workings of the optic nerve, breaks from his notes to speculate on the limits of knowledge. Dennis Beauchamp is a disappointed physician facing a romantic crisis, and is beginning to feel constrained by the 'mathematical regularity' of his life, a regularity deemed 'appropriate to the utter remoteness of the matter of his analysis.'[25] In many ways *Still Life* is a rather crudely drawn caricature of the sympathetic awakening of a coldly objective man of science, yet it provides a case-study for the kinds of anxieties over neurological explanations of sensation that are typical of literature of the period. Dr Beauchamp comprehensively fails to connect. He frets about his alienation from society at large and his inability to appreciate aesthetic pleasure, yet he clothes these aporia in the cold language of science.

During the lecture he surveys the crowd of medical students in front of him and a 'puff of anger and disgust' sweeps over him.[26] Struck by the absurdly limited purview of science, with its claims to 'explain' the workings of the senses, he begins wilfully to undermine the authority of his own lecture. He goes off the record, remarking that 'it would be more correct and more honest if I were to acknowledge here and now that this approach, the normal medical approach, to psychology is only a *pis-aller*.'[27] To explain the workings of visual perception only in scientific terms is, Dr Beauchamp suggests, to ignore the real problem that is raised by conceiving of sensations solely in terms of brain processes. 'We explain and explain', he tells his students:

> We speak of a sensation being communicated along a nerve fibre. We point out these nerve fibres on a chart, and follow them out in the dissecting-room. We imagine we have said something of account concerning them. What is the fact of the matter? By our use of the word sensation we have begged the whole question. What is a sensation but something which has been present to our consciousness? How can this something be communicated along a nerve-fibre? ... At one end of the nerve-fibre is some material stimulus, at the other end a sensation, painful or pleasant. And what is a sensation? Something at any rate of which we are conscious, for otherwise it could not be. A miracle has occurred. Material shock has been communicated, and it ends in consciousness of material shock. Between these two things is an abyss. Physiology is so lucid concerning the mechanism of sensation only because it takes account of nothing but mechanism. In other words, it ignores entirely the abyss between stimulus and consciousness of stimulus. What kind of an explanation can that be where there is no conception of the thing to be explained? It is a delusion.[28]

In drawing attention to the distinction between the objective knowledge of sensory processes provided by science and the experiential knowledge of sensory consciousness as it is experienced – to qualia – the passage articulates the epistemological limits of modern scientific accounts of the senses founded on a neurological understanding of consciousness. Despite the fact that we *can* ascertain that certain brain states (optic nerves firing) are associated with certain mental states (visual perception), the latter do not seem to be reducible to the former. When it comes to accounting for sensation, neuroscientific knowledge appears only to address half the problem.

In *Still Life* these questions are framed in terms of the technological advances of modernity, anticipating what Joseph Levine has termed 'the explanatory gap' between brains and minds. In his essay 'Materialism and Qualia: The Explanatory Gap' Levine reacts to the discovery that sensations of pain are always accompanied by the firing of certain specific nerve fibres (called 'c-fibres'), by asking whether such knowledge will ever allow us to provide an 'explanation' of pain: will ever allow us to reduce the former to the latter. Does the discovery that c-fibres fire whenever we are in pain mean that such mechanisms are *sufficient* to account for pain experiences? Or are they merely *necessary* conditions for the feeling of pain? According to Levine, although mapping neuronal activity might allow us to explain with greater clarity certain correlative relations between brain states and mental states, it gets us no closer to solving what David Chalmers calls the 'hard problem' of consciousness associated with the existence of qualia: precisely *how it is* that brains can cause conscious sensory experiences. As Levine comments:

> What is explained by learning that pain is the firing of C-fibers? Well, one might say that in fact quite a bit is explained. If we believe that part of the concept expressed by the term 'pain' is that of a state which plays a certain causal role in our interaction with the environment (e.g. it warns us of damage, it causes us to attempt to avoid situations we believe will result in it, etc.), [then such a conception] explains the mechanisms underlying the performance of these functions ... However, there is more to our concept of pain than its causal role, there is its qualitative character, how it feels; and what is left unexplained by the discovery of C-fiber firing is *why pain should feel the way it does!*[29]

The qualia of pain are inevitably ignored by functionalist and other reductive accounts of sensory experience founded on neurology, argues Levine, because qualia seem impossible to explain in terms of neuronal activity.

By defining neuromodernism as a cultural-historical process, I wish to draw attention to the myriad interpretative approaches that immediately spring up in response to the problem of identifying brain states with their mental correlates.

In describing the relationship between knowledge of brain states and introspective knowledge of sensory states in terms of an 'explanatory gap', Levine was attacking various doctrines of physical monism, which denies any form of dualism, including that associated with qualia. A particular target of his analysis was the 'identity thesis' of consciousness conceived by E. G. Boring, which holds that, as Ted Honderich summarises, 'mental events are (that is, are identical with) physical-biological processes in the brain.'[30] Identity physicalism is intertheoretically reductive, claiming that mental events simply *are* brain events, analogous to claims such as 'temperature *is* mean kinetic molecular energy', 'light *is* electromagnetic radiation' and so on. And yet the nature of the phenomena under discussion – mental states, including sensations – is, as we saw in Chapter 1, different in kind to things like temperature and radiation as physical phenomena. As both Murry and Levine suggest, to hold that brain events are *identical* with mental events seems instinctively unsatisfactory. 'Psycho-physical identity statements' Levine concludes, 'leave a significant *explanatory gap*, and, as a corollary, . . . we don't have any way of determining exactly which psycho-physical identity statements are true.'[31]

E. G. Boring's *The Physical Dimensions of Consciousness* was an early and influential philosophical response to the new paradigms provided by neuroscience, and did much to develop the identity theory of mind, as well as summarising the recent history of experimental psychology's attempts to pin down consciousness as a biological phenomenon. To do so Boring was ultimately forced to question the existence of qualia (though he didn't use the term directly, framing his objections in terms of 'the given' in experience). As U. T. Place notes, Boring was not the first material monist – a position which 'is at least as old as our earliest records of speculation on such matters' – but he was 'undoubtedly the first to formulate this position in terms of the relation of identity.'[32] Boring's reductive theory of consciousness was explicitly modelled on the classical sciences. He argued that during the first quarter of the twentieth century psychologists had been 'inspired by the chemists' successes in filling in Mendeléyev's table' and in imitation were engaged in attempts to 'seek . . . new kinds of mental elements'.[33] Such elements he associated with the entities uncovered by the narratives of perceiving subjects, and with the quest for a scientific basis for 'sense data', 'sense-contents', 'impressions' and 'the given' in experience. The discovery of the neuron provided a physical analogue to those properties named by the 'elemental' sciences of the mind, and a methodology for cognitive science, conducted explicitly along the lines of the classical sciences, seemed complete. Neurology had found an object that promised to provide a basic physical correlative to psychical states.

One problem that presented itself forcefully to the vivisectionists of the nervous system and proponents of type-identity theory like Boring, however, was that the newly discovered properties of the neuronal brain seemed in no way similar to those of the mind we are familiar with through introspection. As H. H. Price summarised in his *Perception*: 'To say that when a man looks at a tomato he is acquainted with a reddened portion of his own brain, or with a sounding tract of it when he hears a noise, is very singular.'[34]

This disparity – between qualia as they are experienced and their existence as electro-chemical activity in the brain – led Price to attack Machian 'descriptionist' accounts of science, which, he felt, were limited by the fact that they sought similarities between two irreconcilable sets of data, and as such tended to commit category mistakes. What we might term the mimetic theory of sense-perception – the argument that the qualia of a representation of a mental must be like the qualia of that which it is purporting to represent – is a problem of resemblances, and as such is threatened by Leibniz's law. As Price continued:

> It has been held that sense-data are related to material things merely by a relation of indirect causal dependence (sometimes resemblance has been added); and that perceptual consciousness either is, or at any rate ought to be, and argument from effects to causes. This theory has of course been attacked, almost from the beginning . . . and its hold upon educated opinion has been further weakened of late years by the spread of the 'descriptive' view of Science.[35]

Instead of differentiating between the physical and psychical properties of cognition as mutually oppositional, Price invoked the notion of a Bergsonian 'vitality' as a unifying concept to explain away the contradictions, establishing a position that has come to be termed 'the double aspect theory' of psycho-physical correspondence[36]:

> It might be said that the total process going on in the brain at any one time has both its physico-chemical 'aspect' and its vital 'aspect', and that sense-data belong to the vital 'aspect'; the total process, one would insist, includes both of them together, and cannot be fully understood in physico-chemical or in vital (*inter alia* sensuous) terms. In so far as cerebral processes have this sensuous aspect, the brain, one would say, is also the *sensorium*: if so, the thesis is that it is the sensorium which is sonorous when we hear a bell, and red when we see a tomato. Or one might use the language of the Emergent Theory, and hold that sensuous qualities like red and loud emergently qualify certain physico-chemical processes in the brain when these reach a certain degree of complexity.[37]

More recently the neuroscientist V. S. Ramachandran and philosopher William Hirstein have re-formulated the 'double aspect theory' of consciousness as one of competing discourses, arguing that the barrier between knowledge of neuronal activity and knowledge of qualia 'is only apparent and that it arises due to *language*'.[38]

What is so striking about all of these theories is the way in which they diagnose the problem of qualia as emerging from language itself. Far from representing a form of sensory immediacy, for Ramachandran and Hirstein language alienates us from qualia. They go on to propose a technological solution to the problem of other minds, noting that qualia are

> only private *so long as* [one] *uses spoken language* as an intermediary. If you, the colour blind superscientist, avoid that and take a cable made of neurons from X's area V4 . . . and connect it directly to the same area in your brain, then perhaps you'll see colour after all.[39]

But in relation to the question of representing consciousness within literature such moves beg the entire question. No one doubts that technology can provide ways of encoding and transmitting sense-data; rather the problem of qualia as it relates to literature hinges on what precisely the representational codes of public language refer to. The discovery of the neuron, therefore, directly gave rise to the notion of an explanatory gap between the having of an experience and the mapping of that experience into scientific or literary language. Objections to neuronal 'readings' of consciousness thus tended to privilege the individual over the general: the specific experience with its apparent ineffability over the potential public 'meaning' of such an experience.

The limitations of the reductive brain/mind identity project during the modernist moment were acknowledged by contemporary experimental psychologists, who noted that it made little sense to seek self-contained and atomistic units of 'sensation' that could be identified with the excitation of distinguishable types of nerve fibres in this way. One objection was that to endorse such a conception was to ignore or deny the 'phenomenological field': the fact that the visual sensation of seeing a stick, for instance, inevitably takes place against a background (both literal, as a part of the gestalt visual field, and psychological: the object 'stick' is recognised as such and brings with it all sorts of associations and meanings) of some sort. Contrast seems a necessary precondition for the recognition of objects.

But, taken to extremes, proponents of identity physicality were forced to deny the very data which their model of cognition was concerned to interpret. E. G. Boring's belated response to the apparent contradictions exposed by the new neurology was to deny that individual sensations actually existed at all. 'The reign of the attribute was, however, short-lived', he confidently asserted in his history of experimental psychology, 'the phenomenology of Gestalt psychology has in the last decade been making great headway. It doomed elementarism and with it the sensations.'[40] Boring's solution to the impasse was to deny that there was any such thing as 'the given' in experience whatsoever. Despite the fact that 'every sensation can be said to have an attribute of *quality*, which designates it as red or yellow or bitter or cold or C#', he argued, there are in fact no instances in which the beguiling and rhetorically slippery phenomenon of 'experiencing pure sensation' – of being aware only of a pre-linguistic category of 'sense data' – actually occurs. 'Even in the simplest case', he continued,

> as when an observer notes the presence of a tone, he is not merely catching a fleeting phenomenon and fixing it in a report. He is making an interpretive judgement under the influence of a particular intent ... In all experimental observation, physical or introspective, one is working with realities by way of their symbols. One never comes directly to grips with that in which one is primarily interested.[41]

Boring believed that as creatures with language we were doomed to dwell in a world of symbols. Rather than indulge in misguided attempts to get back to 'things in themselves' – either through scientific reduction or the arts – we should be content to employ the abstracted categories culture has provided us with to describe the world. Boring's faith in the explanatory power of brain science thus allowed him to confidently conclude that 'nowadays the gaps are being filled', with none of the messy nomological danglers associated with qualia left over. 'Mystery remains', Boring concluded, only 'so long as we hold that consciousness is direct experience.'[42]

The Aesthetics of the Reflex Arc

Boring's version of eliminative materialism (the belief that materialist accounts of psychological phenomena would inevitably replace, and therefore 'eliminate', our folk psychological terms for those same phenomena) was not the only proposed solution to the mind–brain impasse which emerged from advances in neurology, just as the neuron was not the only unit of study that emerged from the impulse to apply the discoveries of the classical sciences to the cerebral realm. As Melissa Littlefield has shown, the 'psychon' or 'psychone' was an equally attractive potential scientific object that promised to close the explanatory gap in the first decades of the twentieth century.[43] The psychon found initial support by appealing to the scientific metanarratives of the period. 'Ethereal protons and electrons we know as the constituents of matter' noted one proponent of the psychon, Henry Lane Eno, in his book *Activism* in 1920, 'as the basis of the "immaterial substance" we may postulate a second order of "ons" which are, like protons and electrons, fashioned out of the ether. Let us call these "ons" by the name "psychons".'[44] The psychon stood as a cipher for an apparently immaterial object – mind – which could interact with the physical nervous system through the mysterious mechanisms of the synaptic gap.[45] As we have seen, the precise status of the senses – and the question of whether they were material or not – was an ongoing field of debate for philosophers and physicians in the period. The emergence of the 'psychon' can thus be read, as Littlefield does, as an attempt to ease the explanatory difficulties associated with the neuron, relocating the Cartesian solution to the problem of mental causation – which held that the pineal gland was the principal seat of the soul – to the individual synapses themselves.

Indeed at first the psychon was explicitly conceived as a conceptual unit, a way of drawing attention to the explanatory gap, and as such it resisted full integration into cognitive discourse. Early adopters of the term were generally wary of fully endorsing the psychon as 'real'. Littlefield notes that for August Forel, who coined the term 'psychome', the concept referred not to a 'material object; it [was] a hypothetical term – a conceptual placeholder – introduced for "brevity's sake" from which Forel spun his larger theories about mind, brain and matter.'[46] While Forel was tentative in his definition, William Marston, a later champion of the psychon, was far more enthusiastic about the explanatory potential of the new concept. 'Psychology's proper object of study is consciousness' he wrote in 1927, asserting that 'consciousness is to be identified with synaptic energy.'[47] According to Marston, the psychon was a manifestation of 'the totality of energy generated within the junctional tissue between any two neurons.'[48] 'In short', Littlefield summarises, 'the psychon was a way to describe the energy transferred between neurons – energy that, in its ultimate translation, is equal to consciousness itself.'[49] Yet one limitation of the psychon as what we might term a 'phenomenon of the gaps' was that it could not be observed by scientific instruments. It existed solely as an endlessly deferred hypothetical unit (somewhat like qualia), waiting to be explained away, similar in function to the notion of 'luminiferous aether', the theoretical medium for the propagation of light that had been proposed by nineteenth century physicists, or the Bergsonian notion of 'vitality'.

Compared to the ephemerality of the psychon, the neuron was soon accepted as a robust and – once made visible through the silver chromate staining technique – strangely beautiful object. Almost as soon as it was discovered, the visual power of the Golgi method stimulated imaginary models of brain–mind relations, as the nerve was quickly appropriated as a cultural metaphor. Most frequently commentators were interested in the nervous system as a model of communication, an image which seemed to mesh with that other technology of modernity: the telegraph. One of the most striking properties of the new nervous system was its ability to translate various competing sensory stimuli into a common language of impulse and response. 'The nervous fiber', Foucault would later note, 'is endowed with remarkable properties, which permit it to integrate the most heterogeneous elements. Is it not astonishing that, responsible for transmitting the most diverse impressions, the nerves should be of the same nature everywhere, and in every organ?'[50]

Interpreting the nervous system as a telegraph system or telephone exchange, able to convert whatever material stimulus it received into pure and neutral *information*, became a popular figurative strategy. By the time that Karl Pearson illustrated his theory of cognition by 'comparing the brain to the central office of a telephone exchange, from which wires radiate to the subscribers A, B, C, D, E, F, &c., who are senders, and to W, X, Y, Z, &c., who are receivers of messages' in 1897, he was already invoking something of an explanatory cliché. As Cornelius Borck notes, citing Wilhelm Wundt, by the late nineteenth century scientists 'had already begun to lament "this frequently used metaphor", which depended on 'speaking of the cable network as the "nervous system of the state" – or vice versa of the body's "telegraph system".'[51] The appropriation and biologisation of the images of a telephonic system of 'listening', and a cinematic system of 'seeing', became well established in the popular scientific press also, with the brain schematised as a machine. Under the machine gaze of neuromodernism, the nervous system became a cage from which it was impossible to escape. Karl Pearson noted that we 'are accustomed to talk of the "external world", of the "reality" outside us', and yet this external world is only available to us with the aid of those sensory nerves themselves – if we lose them, then the world ceases to exist:

> How close can we then actually get to this supposed world outside ourselves? Just as near but no nearer than the brain terminals of the sensory nerves. We are like the clerk in the telephone exchange who cannot get nearer to his customers than his end of the telephone wires.[52]

Neuromodernism's sustained focus on automatic processes, both as pathology and as an aesthetic trope, was therefore explicitly associated with the systems uncovered by the new neurology. Sara Danius's identification of the 'autonomy of the eye and ear' as central to Joyce's concerns in *Ulysses* in which, she claims, 'eyes claim autonomy for themselves, not just from the other senses and the human body at large but also from the central processing instance, the hermeneutic switchboard called the brain' is therefore the almost inevitable outcome of a physiology which stressed the division, fragmentation and isolation of the component parts of the nervous system.[53] As Friedrich Kittler has argued, the striking thing about the new orthodoxy was that intellect as well as labour were subsumed by machine functionality. During the period machines

> [took] over functions of the central nervous system and no longer, as in times past, merely those of muscles. And with this differentiation – and not with steam engines and railroads – a clear division occurs between matter and information, the real and the symbolic . . . So-called man is split up into physiology and information technology.[54]

This division had repercussions for the status of consciousness itself, recasting it as an emergent and not particularly important by-product of the nervous system that was at root automatic, reflex-driven and senseless. Under such a paradigm, argues Kittler:

> Thought is replaced by a Boolean algebra, and consciousness by the unconscious, which (at least since Lacan's reading) makes of Poe's 'Purloined Letter' a Markoff chain. And that the symbolic is called the world of the machine undermines Man's delusion of possessing a 'quality' called 'consciousness', which identifies him as something other and better than a 'calculating machine'.[55]

The French materialist philosopher Pierre Cabanis believed that the brain secretes thought as the liver secretes bile: neuromodernism often tended to deny that there was anything to secrete in the first place.

Analyses of this paradigm – based on an understanding of what might be termed the 'material unconscious' – in the period were in many cases developments of Marshall Hall's notion of the 'reflex arc', outlined in a paper in 1832, which provided an atomised, rhizomatic model for the human sensorium, suggesting a level of neurological sensuous autonomy not available to models of the Cartesian executive consciousness. Throughout the late nineteenth and early twentieth centuries it became apparent that groups of such arcs could account for complex networks of action, and so the neuron itself promised to federalise the body, dividing its labour between a series of independent self-governing systems. By 1930 E. G. Boring was able confidently to assert that a 'true reflex is supposed to be fixed, automatic and unconscious, involving few neurons . . . However, the reflex arc may be very long and complicated indeed, and now-a-days psychologists speak of variable, learned, conscious reflexes as *conditioned reflexes.*'[56] Freud's associationism located this automatism in the subconscious. Errors and mistakes – Freudian slips – were the results of the 'relaxation' of the attention of an executive consciousness, allowing the automatic processes of the body to take over and that 'uninhibited stream of associations' to 'come . . . into action.'[57]

Thus by the beginning of the twentieth century it had been established that even apparently sophisticated behavioural processes could, as Karl Pearson argued in *The Grammar of Science*, be wholly and comprehensively explained in mechanistic terms according to neurological theories, especially if memory was included within the psycho-physical repertoire:

> Everything up to the receipt of the sense-impression by the brain is what we are accustomed to term physical or mechanical, it is a legitimate inference to suppose that what from the psychical aspect we term

> memory, has also a physical side, that the brain takes for every memory a physical impress, whether by change in the molecular constitution or in the elementary motions of the brain-substance, and that such physical impress is our stored sense-impress.[58]

The impact of such models was wide ranging. Pearson went on to describe several different responses to the stimulus of banging his knee on a table. In the first scenario he rubs his knee 'involuntarily': the

> whole process may be so rapid, I may be so absorbed in my work, that I never realized the message from the sensory nerve at all. I do not even say to myself, 'I have knocked my knee and rubbed it.' Only a spectator, perhaps, has been conscious of the whole process.[59]

From this possibility it seems clear, concludes Pearson, that one 'can receive a sense-impression without recognizing it, or a sense-impression does not involve consciousness.'[60] It is only when he turns the experience into a narrative – a description of events with ascribed motives, interpretations and the positing of another character (the spectator) – that the full paradox of consciousness emerges. 'Thus what we term consciousness', he concludes, 'is largely, if not wholly, the stock of stored sense-impressions, and to the manner in which these condition the messages given them by the motor nerves when a sensory nerve has conveyed a message to the brain.'[61]

This internalisation of automatic processes led quite directly to what David Trotter has identified as modernism's generalised 'will-to-automatism'. But it is worth noting how directly Hall's discovery influenced everything from philosophy to literary criticism in the period, leading to a conception of a neurological unconscious that was for a time as attractive to investigators as the psychoanalytical unconscious that would eventually replace it. Equipped with autonomous behavioural systems, the body was increasingly seen as divided, as divorced from the self or the ego and even at war with its other impulses. As Laura Salisbury summarises, Hall's identification of the diastaltic nervous system meant that nerves were not 'the mere messengers of sensation or voluntary action between nerve endings and the brain; instead, nerves themselves undertook a kind of intellection, interpreting stimuli independently of the brain.'[62]

Thus the previously occluded experiences of the neuron contributed to an understanding of the human subject as fragmented and to the self as a distributed, and often self-deceiving, system of impulse and reflex, leading to the identification of all sorts of modern maladies, neuroses and nerve-ailments that were understood to be caused by the disconnect between self and organism, or between nervous system and world. 'Trauma', Lawrence Rainey reminds us, 'was thought by early psychologists to be characterized by a dissociative process of the self or the ego, which undergoes a process of dissociation (*desagregation*) that generates multiple strands of independent selves functioning automatically.'[63]

The theoretical assault on conceptions of a stable executive consciousness of this kind was the direct result of the dissolving of unified brain systems as physiological realities. Neurons were specialised, associated with certain perceptual functions, and as such would be conceptualised as functioning independently of each other and of a central consciousness or ego. In his 1925 work *Mind and Its Place in Nature*, C. D. Broad outlined what he termed the 'argument from the nervous system' to question the very existence of a classical conception of a stable mind:

> Now we know the nervous structure which is used in such acts as these. A stimulus is given to the outer end of an afferent nerve; some change or other runs up this nerve, crosses a synapse between this and an afferent nerve, travels down the latter to a muscle, causes the muscle to contract, and so produces a bodily movement. There seems no reason to believe that the mind plays any essential part in this process.[64]

Later, Broad turned his objection into a critique of the neurological metaphor of the telephone exchange, writing, in terms strikingly similar to Joseph Levine's:

> They think of the mind as sitting somewhere in a hole in the brain, surrounded by telephones. And they think of the afferent disturbance as coming to an end at one of these telephones and there affecting the mind. The mind is then supposed to respond by sending an afferent impulse down another of these telephones. As no such hole, with afferent nerves stopping at its walls and afferent nerves starting from them, can be found, they conclude that the mind can play no part in the transaction. But another alternative is that this picture of how the mind must act if it acts at all is wrong. To put it shortly, the mistake is to confuse a gap in an explanation with a spatio-temporal gap, and to argue from the absence of the latter to the absence of the former.[65]

'It is admitted', Broad concluded,

> that the mind has nothing to do with the causation of purely reflex actions. But the nervous structure and the nervous processes involved in deliberate action do not differ in kind from those involved in reflex action; they differ only in degree of complexity . . . So it is unreasonable to suppose that the mind has any more to do with causing deliberate actions than it has to do with causing reflex actions.[66]

In his *Principles of Literary Criticism*, I. A. Richards had endorsed a neuromodernist view of literary criticism, incorporating the notion of an egoless or mindless response to literature into his critical project by outlining a theory of the 'impulse' as 'the basic unit of conscious experience.'[67] Richards' 'impulse' was the affective equivalent of the reflex arc, and was 'loosely understood as a unit, or packet, of nervous activity whose combination with others of its kind composes our conscious experience.'[68] Richards held that 'impulses' were distinct from sensations or perceptions, and that they were 'the essential and fundamental things in any experience. All else, whether intellectual or emotional, arises as a consequence of their activity.'[69] Misreadings of literature, arising from Pater's insistence that the critic's job was to discern her own impression of objects seen, meant that, according to Richards, too much importance had been:

> attached to the sensory qualities of images. What gives an image efficacy is less its vividness as an image than its character as a mental event peculiarly connected with sensation. It is, in a way which no one yet knows how to explain, a relict of sensation and our intellectual and emotional response to it depends far more upon its being, through this fact, a representative of sensation, than upon its sensory resemblance to one. An image may lose almost all its sensory nature to the point of becoming scarcely an image at all, a mere skeleton, and yet represent a sensation quite as adequately as if it were flaring with hallucinatory vividity. In other words, what matters is not the sensory *resemblance* of an image to the sensation which is its prototype, but some other relation, at present hidden from us in the jungles of neurology.[70]

In *A Philosophy of Rhetoric*, Richards questioned whether the 'impulse' was identical with certain neurophysiological conditions, remarking that

> I will only say that I hold that . . . an identification of Thought with an activity of the nervous system is to me an acceptable hypothesis, but too large to have interesting applications. It may be left until more is known about both; when possibly it may be developed to a point at which it might become useful.[71]

'Today', argues Edward Jayne, 'Richards' neurological paradigm seems best appreciated as metaphor, as in fact his notion of impulse may also be granted metaphoric value in depicting conscious dynamics otherwise resistant to analysis.'[72] Nevertheless, Richards's use of the notion of the 'impulse' demonstrates the degree to which paradigms provided by neuroscience were adopted and adapted by critics to serve the anti-mimetic ends of modernism.

The reflex arc quickly garnered support as a metaphor for aesthetic experience itself therefore: for the immediate and unconscious reception of the significant form of a painting, piece of music, or poem, unimpeded by the interruptions of the higher cognitive faculties. Gertrude Stein, who studied automatic writing with Leon M. Solomon under William James, concluded one of her experiments (which involved a subject slowly reciting a dull story while transcribing another narrative read to her by an experimenter – usually very successfully) noting: 'we may sum up the experiment by saying that a large number of acts ordinarily called intelligent, such as reading, writing, etc., can go on quite automatically in ordinary people.'[73] By 1953 Clement Greenberg, a fierce defender of atomistic conceptions of an art designed for 'eyesight alone', was able to declare that aesthetic judgements are 'immediate, intuitive, undeliberate, and involuntary.'[74]

Much modernist literary experimentation was therefore concerned – or was understood by critics to have been concerned – with capturing this reflexive autonomy, applying it to the production of literary texts and thus bypassing the controlling intervention of the executive consciousness. On this reading, spiritualism and the practices of automatic writing were both attempts to render the will-to-automatism associated with incorporating the neuronal reflex into critical discourse performative. Indeed, as Lawrence Rainey argues, the notion of the spiritualist medium as a conduit of some transcendent source of knowledge was intimately associated in the period with the technological matrices of modernity, and of the nerves as providing a basis of knowledge of the world. The medium was often figured as a wireless or telegraph receiver, complicating the imagery of this pseudo-spiritual/mechanical endeavour.[75]

Thus neuromodernism appropriated the language of neuroscience and fused it with images of the machine, finding common ground and points of comparison that were themselves fed into novels and poetry of the period. Futurism's obsession with the nerve-jangling affects of velocity, Virginia Woolf's meticulous descriptions of the state of her nerves (and her fierce suspicion of neurologists like Sir William Bradshaw in *Mrs. Dalloway*), and Gertrude Stein's endeavours to produce linguistic and neuronal 'maps' of utterances all represent an impulse to consume and re-appropriate the discourses of brain science within the literary realm. One of the central questions facing both neurological accounts of mind and modernist fictional representations of consciousness in the period was, as we have seen, whether consciousness could be written. Yet rather than providing an answer to this question, it might be more profitable to read modernist narrative fiction as interested in asking a more speculative question: what kind of written explanation of consciousness could be ever satisfy us as being complete?

This is a question that is addressed directly in Joyce's *Ulysses*, in 'Eumaeus' (an episode associated in the Linati schema with 'the nerves'), as Stephen and

Bloom – blended together as 'Stoom' and 'Blephen' – argue at cross-purposes about the nature of the soul.[76] 'You, as a good catholic', observes Bloom,

> talking of body and soul, believe in the soul. Or do you mean the intelligence, the brainpower as such, as distinct from any outside object, the table, let us say, that cup. I believe in that myself because it has been explained by competent men as the convolutions of the grey matter. Otherwise we would never have such inventions as X rays, for instance. Do you?[77]

In answer Stephen invokes Aquinas and the notion of the simple substance, indivisible (in the *Summa Theologica* Aquinas asserted that 'the intellectual principle we call the human soul is incorruptible') and constant.[78] The dialectic places the schoolman in conflict with the modern materialistic intellect, but ultimately both are shown to be preposterous. They are 'poles apart' in their thinking, but they are both equally wrong.[79] Whereas Stephen idly considers the lessons of the schoolmen, Bloom places his faith in the *symbols* of modern science rather than in the knowledge it has produced: Röntgen rays and the 'Sherlockholmesing' of the medical method, concluding that thought 'has been explained by competent men as the convolutions of the grey matter'.[80]

Despite Bloom's certainty, an anxiety over the rhetoric of such reductions – over the threats such methodologies might pose to the explanatory power of the arts – emerged in parallel with these very processes, leading to the creation of a host of competing narratives of reduction in the period. In the modern moment the 'competent men' singularly *failed* to reduce the mind to 'convolutions of the grey matter', and this failure, too, soon became grist to the novelist's mill.

Notes

1. William James, 'The Stream of Consciousness', in *Writings 1878–1899* (New York: Library of America, 1992), p. 722.
2. Laura Salisbury and Andrew Shail, 'Introduction: Neurology and Modernity', in *Neurology and Modernity*, ed. by Laura Salisbury and Andrew Shail (Basingstoke: Palgrave Macmillan, 2010), p. 1.
3. John Ayrton Paris, *The Life of Sir Humphrey Davy*, 2 vols (London: Colburn & Bentley, 1831), vol. I, p. 138.
4. See Kirsten Shepherd-Barr and Gordon M. Shepherd, 'Madeleines and Neuromodernism: Reassessing Mechanisms of Autobiographical Memory in Proust', *Auto/Biography Studies*, 13.1 (1998), 39–60. Shepherd-Barr and Shepherd cite Bruce E. Fleming as one of the originators of the term: see Bruce E. Fleming, 'The Smell of Success: A Reassessment of Patrick Süskind's '"Das Parfum"', *South Atlantic Review*, 56.4 (1991), 71–86.
5. See Friedrich A. Kittler, *Discourse Networks 1800–1900*, trans. by Michael Metteer and Chris Cullens (Stanford, CA: Stanford University Press, 1990), p. 328.

6. James Joyce, *Stephen Hero: Part of the first draft of 'A Portrait of the Artist as a Young Man'*, ed. by Theodore Spencer (London: Jonathan Cape, 1960), p. 190.
7. Mark S. Micale, 'The Modernist Mind: A Map', in *The Mind of Modernism: Medicine, Psychology and the Cultural Arts in Europe and America, 1880–1940*, ed. by Mark S. Micale (Stanford, CA: Stanford University Press, 2004), p. 6.
8. Filippo Tommaso Marinetti, 'Technical Manifesto of Futurist Literature', in Selected Poems and Related Prose, trans. by Elizabeth R. Napier and Barbara R. Studholme (New Haven, CT and London: Yale University Press, 2002), p. 79 (emphasis in original).
9. D. H. Lawrence, 'Why the Novel Matters', in *Study of Thomas Hardy and Other Essays*, ed. by Bruce Steele (Cambridge: Cambridge University Press, 1985), p. 195.
10. H. H. Price, *Perception* (London: Methuen & Co. Ltd, 1932), p. 127.
11. See Salisbury and Shail (eds), *Neurology and Modernity*; Micale, *The Mind of Modernism*, and George S. Rousseau, *Nervous Acts: Essays on Literature, Culture and Sensibility* (Basingstoke: Palgrave Macmillan, 2004).
12. Johannes Müller, *Elements of Physiology*, trans. by William Baly, 4 vols (Bristol: Thoemmes, 2000), vol. I, p. 12.
13. Michel Foucault, *Madness and Civilization: A History of Insanity in the Age of Reason*, trans. by Richard Howard (London and New York: Routledge, 1989), p. 119–120.
14. See Salisbury and Shail, *Neurology and Modernity*, pp. 41–46.
15. Santiago Ramon y Cajal, *Histology of the Nervous System of Man and Vertebrates*, trans. by L. Azoulay, Neely Swanson and Larry W. Swanson, 2 vols (New York and Oxford: Oxford University Press, 1995), vol. I, p. 26.
16. Ernst Mach, *The Analysis of Sensations and the Relation of the Physical to the Psychical*, trans. by C. M. Williams (Chicago, IL and London: The Open Court Publishing Company, 1914), p. 242.
17. I will examine some of these in greater detail below, but the principle exhibits that we have encountered previously are Mach's *Analysis of the Sensations*, Karl Pearson's *The Grammar of Science* (London: Walter Scott, 1892), E. G. Boring's *The Physical Dimensions of Consciousness* (New York and London: The Century Co., 1933), and C. I. Lewis's *Mind and the World Order* (New York: Dover Publications, Inc., 1929).
18. Kittler, *Discourse Networks*, p. 222.
19. Kittler, *Discourse Networks*, p. 224.
20. See, for instance, Sara Danius's reading of the use of X-rays in Thomas Mann's *The Magic Mountain*, in Sara Danius, *The Senses of Modernism: Technology, Perception, and Aesthetics* (Ithaca, NY and London: Cornell University Press, 2002), pp. 72–79; or Leopold Bloom's speculative account of the movement of food round the body, James Joyce, *Ulysses*, ed. by Hans Walter Gabler (London: The Bodley Head, 1986), 8.1030. All references to James Joyce's *Ulysses* are to the Gabler synoptic edition, and are given in the form [episode number.line number].
21. T. S. Eliot, 'The Love Song of J. Alfred Prufrock', in *The Poems of T. S. Eliot Volume I: Collected and Uncollected Poems*, ed. by Christopher Ricks and Jim McCue (London: Faber & Faber, 2015), p, 105.

22. David Herman, 'Re-minding Modernism', in *The Emergence of Mind: Representations of Consciousness in Narrative Discourse in English*, ed. by David Herman (Lincoln, NE and London: University of Nebraska Press, 2011), p. 260.
23. Vike Martina Plock, *Joyce, Medicine, and Modernity* (Gainesville, FL: University Press of Florida, 2010), p. 88.
24. Salisbury and Shail, *Neurology and Modernity*, p. 8.
25. John Middleton Murry, *Still Life* (London: Constable and Company Ltd, 1918), p. 138.
26. Murry, *Still Life*, p. 139.
27. Murry, *Still Life*, p. 139.
28. Murry, *Still Life*, pp. 139–140.
29. Joseph Levine, 'Materialism and Qualia: The Explanatory Gap', *Pacific Philosophical Quarterly*, 64.4 (1983), 354–361 (emphasis in original).
30. Ted Honderich, *The Oxford Companion to Philosophy* (Oxford: Oxford University Press, 1995), p. 392.
31. Levine, 'Materialism and Qualia', p. 354.
32. U. T. Place, 'E. G. Boring and the Mind–Brain Identity Theory', *British Psychological Society, History and Philosophy of Science Newsletter*, 11 (1990), 20–31 (p. 20).
33. E. G. Boring, *Physical Dimensions*, p. 18.
34. H. H. Price, *Perception*, p. 127.
35. H. H. Price, *Perception*, p. v.
36. See Raymond Tallis, *Aping Mankind: Neuromania, Darwinitis and the Misrepresentation of Humanity* (Durham: Acumen Publishing Ltd, 2011).
37. H. H. Price, *Perception*, p. 128.
38. V. S. Ramachandran and William Hirstein, 'Three Laws of Qualia: What Neurology Tells Us about the Biological Functions of Consciousness, Qualia and the Self', *Journal of Consciousness Studies*, 4.5–6 (1997), 429–457 (p. 432).
39. Ramachandran and Hirstein, 'Three Laws of Qualia', p. 432.
40. Boring, *Physical Dimensions*, p. 21.
41. Boring, *Physical Dimensions*, p. 11.
42. Boring, *Physical Dimensions*, p. 13.
43. See Melissa M. Littlefield, 'Matter for Thought: The Psychon in Neurology, Psychology and American Culture', in *Neurology and Modernity*, ed. by Laura Salisbury and Andrew Shail (Basingstoke: Palgrave Macmillan, 2010), p. 267–286.
44. Henry Lane Eno, *Activism* (Princeton, NJ: Princeton University Press, 1920), p. 22.
45. In the 1990s Sir John Eccles reanimated the 'psychon' as a unit of consciousness in his neo-dualist tract *How the Self Controls Its Brain* (Berlin and London: Springer-Verlag, 1994).
46. Littlefield, 'Matter for Thought', p. 273.
47. William Martson, C. D. King and E. H. Marston, *Integrative Psychology; A Study of Unit Response* (London: Harcourt, Brace & World, 1931), p. 46.
48. Marston, King and Marston, *Integrative Psychology*, p. 52.
49. Littlefield, 'Matter for Thought', p. 273.
50. Foucault, *Madness*, p. 143.

51. Cornelius Borck, 'Communicating the Modern Body: Fritz Kahn's Popular Images of Human Physiology as an Industrialized World', *Canadian Journal of Communication*, 32.3–4 (2007), 495–520 (p. 511).
52. Pearson, *The Grammar of Science*, p. 74.
53. Danius, *The Senses of Modernism,* p. 160.
54. Friedrich A. Kittler, *Gramophone, Film, Typewriter*, trans. by Geoffrey Winthrop-Young and Michael Wutz (Stanford, CA: Stanford University Press, 1999), p. 16.
55. Kittler, *Gramophone, Film, Typewriter*, p. 16.
56. Boring, *The Physical Dimensions of Consciousness*, p. 38 (emphasis in original).
57. Sigmund Freud, *The Psychopathology of Everyday Life*, trans. by A. A. Brill (London: T. Fisher Unwin, 1914), p. 61.
58. Pearson, *The Grammar of Science*, p. 51.
59. Pearson, *The Grammar of Science*, p. 52.
60. Pearson, *The Grammar of Science*, pp. 52–53.
61. Pearson, *The Grammar of Science*, p. 53.
62. Salisbury and Shail, *Neurology and Modernity,* p. 19.
63. Rainey, 'Shock Effects', p. 206.
64. C. D. Broad, *The Mind and Its Place in Nature* (London: Kegan Paul, Trench, Trubner & Co., Ltd, 1937), pp. 109–110.
65. Broad, *The Mind and Its Place in Nature*, p. 111.
66. Broad, *The Mind and Its Place in Nature*, p. 110.
67. I. A. Richards, *Principles of Literary Criticism* (London: Kegan Paul, Trench, Trubner & Co. Ltd, 1925), p. 8.
68. Richards, *Principles of Literary Criticism*, p. 125.
69. Richards, *Principles of Literary Criticism*, p. 125.
70. Richards, *Principles of Literary Criticism*, pp. 119–120.
71. I. A. Richards, *The Philosophy of Rhetoric* (New York and London: Oxford University Press, 1936), p. 13.
72. Edward Jayne, 'I. A. Richards: Theory of Metaphor, Theory as Metaphoric Variation Affective Criticism: Theories of Emotion and Synaesthesis in the Experience of Literature' (Dissertation, SUNY at Buffalo, 1970), p. 9.
73. Leon M. Solomons and Gertrude Stein, 'Normal Motor Automatism', *Psychological Review*, 3.5 (1896), 492–512 (p. 492).
74. Clement Greenberg, 'Complaints of an Art Critic', in *Artforum*, 6.2 (October 1967), 38–39.
75. Rainey, 'Shock Effects', p. 197.
76. Joyce, Ulysses, 17.549–551.
77. Joyce, *Ulysses,*16.748–753.
78. St Thomas Aquinas, *Summa Theologica*, 22 vols (London: Burns, Oates & Washburne, 1918–1928), vol. II, p. 80.
79. Joyce, *Ulysses*, 16.774.
80. Joyce, *Ulysses*, 16.751–752.

5

SAMUEL BECKETT AND MODERNISM'S NARRATIVES OF REDUCTION

> For between the poet and the public, in fact, the same kind of relations exist as between two old friends. They can speak to each other with a half-word, a gesture, a wink.
> F. T. Marinetti, *Destruction of Syntax – Wireless Imagination – Words-in-Freedom*

Modernism and the Spectre of Reductionism

As we saw in Chapter 4, a suspicion of science's explanatory power as it related to consciousness emerged in parallel with the identification of the neuron and the reflex arc, discoveries which promised to solve the mind–body problem by providing ever more efficient models of cognition. Novelists were quick to affirm that what they offered differed from these new narratives of the self, while being equally quick to incorporate reflexive models of aesthetic response into their works. Despite the fundamentally localising nature of his psycho-aesthetic project, for instance, which sought to draw frequently fanciful inferences from various psycho-bodily correspondences, D. H. Lawrence was particularly wary of the threats posed by the reductive strategies of modern medicine, especially those associated with neuromodernism. In 'Why the Novel Matters' Lawrence expanded on ideas he'd first articulated in *Fantasia of the Unconscious*, noting that the tendency to 'think of ourselves as a body with a spirit in it, or a body with a soul in it, or a body with a mind in it' seems to run counter to observation. 'It is a funny sort of superstition', he notes:

> Why should I look at my hand, as it so cleverly writes these words, and decide that it is a mere nothing compared to the mind that directs it? Is there really any huge difference between my hand and my brain? Or my mind? My hand is alive, it flickers with a life of its own. It meets all the strange universe in touch, and learns a vast number of things, and knows a vast number of things. My hand, as it writes these words, slips gaily along, jumps like a grasshopper to dot an i, feels the table rather cold, gets a little bored if I write too long, has its own rudiments of thought, and is just as much *me* as is my brain, my mind, or my soul. Why should I imagine that there is a *me* which is more *me* than my hand is? Since my hand is absolutely alive, me alive.[1]

Lawrence's notion of the 'blood consciousness' functioned as a means of complicating the conceptual straitjacketing of the executive cogito: the homunculus which, according to Descartes, dwelt in the pineal gland, taking in the data of the body, pondering it, and sending out commands via the nerves in response. Instead, Lawrence argued, the whole body was involved in all forms of cognition. Just as an individual nerve cell doesn't 'have' but simply *is* a sensation (despite the fact that *how* it might be so defies explanation), so for Lawrence was the entire body called upon to participate in the process of thinking, and living.[2] Lawrence's fear was that the scientist, in reducing the person to 'either a brain, or nerves, or glands, or something more up-to-date in the tissue line', would pronounce the human subject dead.[3] Reducing mind to body, or even just to nerve cell, threatened to leave out the very thing that, he believed, was most essential about personhood. In this reading, reduction – in a broad sense which includes medical as well as philosophical understandings of the term – becomes a methodological threat to the idea of the person itself.

By the mid-twentieth century Lawrence's fear had become widespread. In his 1947 essay 'The Meaning of a Literary Idea' Lionel Trilling identified a reductive 'spectre' that, he felt, 'haunts our culture'. 'It is', he wrote:

> that people will eventually be unable to say, 'They fell in love and married,' let alone understand the language of Romeo and Juliet, but will as a matter of course say 'Their libidinal impulses being reciprocal, they activated their individual erotic drives and integrated them within the same frame of reference' . . . There can be no doubt whatever that [such language] constitutes a threat to the emotions and thus to life itself.[4]

Though Trilling's spectre was psychoanalytic rather than neurological, his underlying anxiety was the same as Lawrence's. Where Virginia Woolf had argued, in 'On Being Ill', that a rigorous language of science could be productive, giving voice to hitherto unspeakable pains and shivers, Trilling felt that scientific or pseudo-scientific discourse threatened to usurp literary language and replace it with a colder discourse that would in turn reduce personhood to mechanism.

Though Trilling's anxiety now seems unfounded (the terminology of psychoanalysis has singularly *failed* to replace our folk or literary registers when describing love, or any other emotional state), its form is typical of anxieties over both the power and the insufficiency of the reductive discourses associated with modernity. Trilling traced his 'truism of contemporary thought' to the eighteenth century, arguing that it expresses horror 'at the prospect of life being intellectualized out of all spontaneity and reality', but in the first half of this chapter I will suggest that with modernism emerged another, more specific form of this fear: that of one register or discourse (the scientific) replacing the explanatory claims of another (the literary) in terms of its ability to contain or convey qualia. In the second half of the chapter I will consider how modernism's narratives of reduction, both philosophical and aesthetic, are particularly illuminating when mapped on to a specific sense modality – that of hearing. This mapping is particularly relevant to the work of Samuel Beckett, an author whose position within the modernist canon is unstable, but whose work can be read as responding directly both to the maximalist claims made by some critics on behalf of high modernism, and to ongoing theoretical debates over the literary reducibility of sound, music and noise.

Neurological and Philosophical Reductions

In Chapter 4 we saw how the discovery of the neuron prompted a fundamental reappraisal of the sites and objects of consciousness conceived as a reified, material phenomenon. Here I wish to extend the discussion to consider more broadly the ways in which modernism's narratives of reduction asserted themselves in the period, both theoretically – through debates over the possibility of reductive models of brain science to psychology – and aesthetically, in the commitment to an efficiency of description at the level of the sentence that is discernible within some strains of modernism. These narratives of reduction often pulled against each other. Though some of modernism's aesthetic ideologies (particularly those associated with poetry and the visual arts) were motivated by a desire to condense or distil, seeking ever more efficient means of articulation, in fiction they often resulted in works which were expansive and encyclopaedic in scope. Thus while on the one hand many of the most polemical modernists endorsed an aesthetics of reduction that sought to make literary language functionally equivalent to the formula or the equation, others worried that reducing the world to representation was inherently impoverishing. This tension was accompanied by developments within neuroscience and analytical philosophy which sought to find logical structures for narratives of reduction, movements which were themselves often vehemently attacked by literary critics, but which have subsequently been enshrine within the various critical projects oriented towards a 'neuroaesthetic' or 'cognitive' approach to literature.

Many critiques of scientific discourses relating to consciousness during the first half of the twentieth century expressed a fear of science's attempts to reduce the complexities of our mental lives to other phenomena: to psychoanalytical metanarratives, to the firing of neurons, or to genetically predisposed behavioural tendencies. Contemporary literary criticism continues to be both beguiled and appalled – in almost equal measure – by what Raymond Tallis terms a reductive 'neuromania': the propensity to accept neuronal descriptions of behaviours as sufficient explanations for those behaviours themselves.[5] Francis Crick's polemical statement, in *The Astonishing Hypothesis*, that 'you, your joys and sorrows, your memories and your ambitions, your sense of personal identity and free will, are in fact no more than the behaviour of a vast assembly of nerve cells and their associated molecules', is typical of these arguments.[6] Crick's brand of reductionism is both ontological – holding that one entity (consciousness) is no more than a structure of other kinds of entity (nerve cells and associated molecules) – and explanatory, in that he argues that reductionism 'is the main theoretical method that has driven the development of physics, chemistry and molecular biology.'[7] But often approaches to neurology and the problem of qualia tend to conflate these two forms of reduction. In *The Philosophical Foundations of Neuroscience*, M. R. Bennett and Peter Hacker define reductionism 'in the broadest sense' as:

> the commitment to a single unifying explanation of a type of phenomenon. In this sense, Marxism advocates a reductive theory of history, and psychoanalysis defends a reductive explanation of human behaviour . . . The idea of 'unified science', advocated by the Vienna Circle positivists in the 1920s and 1930s and adopted by the logical empiricists in the 1950s, was committed to what has been called 'classical reductionism'.[8]

It is this notion of 'classical reduction' that posed such a threat to Trilling's interpretation of humanism.

In order to understand what precisely is at issue in debates over neuroscience's ability to 'reduce' mental states to brain states and thus close the explanatory gap, it is worth briefly assessing contemporary philosophical formulations of what Patricia Churchland has defined as 'intertheoretic reduction'.[9] 'Reductionism', notes Churchland, 'has come in some quarters to be used as a general term of insult and abuse':

> Sometimes it is used as a synonym for 'behaviorism' (which is a case of the vague hounding the vague), or as a synonym for such diverse sins as 'materialism,' 'bourgeois capitalism,' 'experimentalism,' 'vivisectionism,' 'communism,' 'militarism,' 'socio-biology,' and 'atheism.' In the sense of

'reduction' that is relevant here, reduction is first and foremost a relation between theories. Most simply, one theory, the *reduced* theory Tr, stands in a certain relation . . . to another more basic theory Tb. Statements that a phenomenon Pr reduces to another phenomenon Pb are derivative upon the more basic claim that the *theory* that characterizes the first reduces to the *theory* that characterizes the second.[10]

Churchland here describes intertheoretic reduction as not concerned with the reduction of mental states, including perceptions and sensations, to brain states. It describes 'a relation between theories' rather than a relation between phenomena themselves. But what exactly do we deny when we deny the possibility of reducing mental states to brain states, while allowing that other phenomena (temperature, for instance) can be reduced (to mean kinetic energy)? Churchland extrapolates two central questions. These can be paraphrased as:

1. Can our 'folk-intuitions' about states of consciousness, our belief in entities such as feelings, desires, beliefs themselves, and so on, ever be described more efficiently in other terms?
2. Can those experiences themselves be contained within their descriptive discourses, or is something always and inevitably lost in translation?

Clearly, Churchland's analysis of intertheoretic reduction, which functions so well as an analysis of the development of scientific concepts, doesn't address the problems inherent to any attempt to provide an explanation of qualia based on brain science (partly because she doesn't accept that qualia exist). This difficulty is caused by the misattribution of historical examples of scientific reduction to the case of consciousness. During the eighteenth century, Churchland continues:

> it would have been true to say that temperature did not reduce, inasmuch as thermodynamics was still an autonomous science. This did not entail that it never would reduce to a more basic theory or that temperature is an emergent property. Indeed, by the late nineteenth century thermodynamics was the beneficiary of a triumphant reduction to statistical mechanics, at which time it was evident that temperature (of gases) is not emergent but is identical with mean molecular kinetic energy.[11]

But is this really the case? Certainly in the scenario Churchland describes above one set of pointer-readings (to borrow Arthur Eddington's terminology) was replaced with a set of more finely grained pointer-readings, and so in one sense 'temperature is identical with mean molecular kinetic energy'.[12] But experiencing the affect of temperature on the body – what the qualiaphile philosopher seeks to 'explain' when the notion of 'temperature' is invoked – is still far from complete in the second formulation. For Churchland here 'temperature' refers to a phenomenon in exactly the same way that 'high kinetic energy' refers to that same phenomenon. And yet the phenomenon itself – the feeling of heat – is left unexplained. In this example 'temperature' is to 'the feeling of temperature' as 'kinetic energy' is to 'the feeling of temperature': neither term nor explanation is sufficient.

Of course, Churchland is right to object, as she does, that we seem to expect a higher explanatory capability from theories of consciousness than we do from theories of other scientific phenomena. We should no more expect that a full understanding of a completed scientific model of photosynthesis would cause the brain to start breaking down carbon dioxide and producing food than we should that a perfect model of visual perception should cause visual perceptions to occur, for instance. 'Just as the obstetrician does not become pregnant by knowing all about pregnancy', argues Churchland, 'so [the perceiving subject] does not have the sensation of redness by knowing all about the neurophysiology of perceiving and experiencing red.'[13] Yet, as we have seen, many literary critics who subscribe to the cognitive realist thesis argue precisely this: that, in some sense, literature *is* able to reduce sensory phenomena to symbolic language, and thus share qualia with other minds.

Where do the origins of this tension lie? In *The Logical Structure of the World* Rudolf Carnap announced confidently that 'it is in principle possible to reduce all concepts to the immediately given.'[14] 'The main problem' that logical positivism sought to overcome, he continued, 'concerns the possibility of the rational reconstruction of the concepts of all fields of knowledge on the basis of concepts that refer to the immediately given.'[15] This was a more formal philosophical instantiation of the Helmholtzian and Machian projects, and it was also more comprehensive, and more audacious. Carnap's project sought to create a system that would place Mach's mental 'elements' in relation to one another by deploying the formal rules of logic. 'I should now consider', he wrote:

> for use as basic elements, not elementary experiences . . . but something similar to Mach's elements, e.g., concrete sense data, as, for example, 'a red of a certain type at a certain visual field at a certain place at a certain time.' I would then choose as basic concepts some of the relations between such elements, for example '*x* is earlier than *y*', the relation of spatial proximity in the visual field and in other sensory fields, and the relation of qualitative similarity, e.g., color similarity.[16]

W. V. O. Quine's influential 1951 paper 'Two Dogmas of Empiricism' characterised Carnap's project as one of 'radical reductionism', and in doing so attacked the central premises of logical positivism. The first 'dogma' Quine attacked was the distinction Carnap had made between analytic and synthetic statements. The second dogma was that of 'reductionism' itself, defined by Quine as 'the belief that each meaningful statement is equivalent to some logical construct upon terms which refer to immediate experience.'[17] Radical reductionism, Quine summarised, held that 'every meaningful statement is ... translatable into a statement (true or false) about immediate experience'.[18] Such 'radical reductionism', he concluded, 'set itself the task of specifying a sense-datum language and showing how to translate the rest of significant discourse, statement by statement, into it.'[19] In *The Logical Structure of the World*, Carnap had attempted to map sensory qualities onto mathematical principles. And yet, Quine continued:

> Carnap did not seem to recognize ... that his treatment of physical objects fell short of reduction not merely through sketchiness, but in principle. Statements of the form 'Quality q is at point-instant $x; y; z; t$' were, according to his canons, to be apportioned truth values in such a way as to maximize and minimize certain over-all features, and with growth of experience the truth values were to be progressively revised in the same spirit.[20]

Just as William James had argued that 'no one ever had a sensation on its own', and the phenomenological tradition rejected the possibility of experiencing a 'sensation' in isolation, so Quine argued that 'our statements about the external world face the tribunal of sense experience not individually but only as a corporate body.'[21] The reductive, localising project of neurology and the new physics was on uncertain ground when faced with the challenge of mapping the body as a living, cohesive whole.

How do these issues manifest themselves not in science, which seeks general structural rules for such interpretations, but in the novel, a form which is particularly concerned both to ask epistemological questions and to relate these questions to more general conceptual schemata? In the next part of this chapter I will consider the ways in which a range of modernist novelists, culminating in the contested modernism of Samuel Beckett, engaged with the question of 'radical reduction' in their appropriation of metaphors of notation and reproduction derived not only from science, but from music.

Modernism's Ideologies of Reduction

As well as becoming the dominant methodology within the sciences, during the modernist moment reductionism provided models for a new kind of literary value. As Evelyn Cobley argues in *Modernism and the Culture of Efficiency*, modernity was often characterised by narratives of 'efficiency', a concept which was mechanical and economic in origin but which soon extended to encompass all forms of human endeavour.[22] In *The Mantra of Efficiency: From Waterwheel to Social Control*, Jennifer Karns Alexander describes the metaphorical appropriation of 'efficiency' as a sociological concept directly derived from the cult of the machine.[23] Initially a technical term describing the increase of output through the minimisation of waste in a closed system – usually in mechanised systems such as steam engines – 'efficiency' became a *de facto* measure of value: a way of evaluating the input-output relationships of a wide variety of systems and social phenomena, including the literary, during the period.

Cobley considers representations of efficiency as an explicit theme in the work of D. H. Lawrence, E. M. Forster, Joseph Conrad and H. G. Wells, and the principles of efficiency she describes could equally apply to some modernist writers, not simply as a theme but as aesthetic principle. As we saw in Chapter 3, Joyce's most radical innovations, especially those associated with *Ulysses*, were encyclopaedic, expansive and concerned to extend the form of the novel itself in terms of its ability to contain multifarious forms of knowledge. Describing his own work as a reaction against Joyce's method, Samuel Beckett argued that Joyce's innovations signalled the end of the novel's propensity to expand. 'I realised', Beckett recalled,

> that Joyce had gone as far as one could in the direction of knowing more, [being] in control of one's material. He was always adding to it; you only have to look at his proofs to see that. I realised that my own way was an impoverishment, in lack of knowledge and in taking away, in subtracting rather than in adding.[24]

What implication does this tension between maximalism and reduction have for the cognitive realist thesis? In 'The Ideology of Modernism' George Lukács argued that 'modernism leads not only to the destruction of traditional literary forms; it leads to the destruction of literature as such.'[25] According to Lukács, classical realism's status as a safe and somewhat staid harbour of literary artifice was directly challenged by modernism's assaults on its formal structures. He viewed stream-of-consciousness narration, in particular, not as the articulation of the essential nature of the mind, but as the 'reduction of reality to nightmare', and thus as indicative of an utter rejection of realism.[26] Yet, as we have seen, many critics have been keen to interpret modernism's formal experimentalism as a continuation of the realist project. Such readings tend to argue that, rather than rejecting realism, modernism redefined the 'real' so as to include mental events within its remit. Of course in one sense to describe the world is necessarily to reduce it to representation. If it is accepted that modernist literature was interested in conveying the object of consciousness as a distinct thing or phenomenon rather than as a set of qualities or capacities, then is such a project doomed from the beginning?

Modernism's ambivalent relationship with reduction is therefore partly the result of a certain slippage between two interpretative possibilities. While many modernist authors and artists explicitly endorsed the notion of a kind of descriptive reducibility, building it into the very fabric of their work, this did not often result in a any reduction in the length or substance of the works themselves. Though a formally reductive impulse is certainly present in certain aesthetic movements – in Imagism, and in the minimalism of much modernist architecture – it's equally true that in the realm of fiction many writers added rather than took away. In *Quantum Poetics* Daniel Albright argues that modernism 'is famous for its stripped-down, streamlined look', and that 'Modernist art – or one aspect of it – alarms us through sheer absence of elaboration', but one can think of countless examples of the opposite tendency.[27]

However one might characterise the formal properties of modernist literature, it is clear that much modernist literature was has been interpreted precisely for its ability to reduce mind to representation. Virginia Woolf's attack on the 'materialists' Wells, Bennett and Galsworthy in 'Mr Bennett and Mrs Brown' was partly founded on the charge that these authors tried to cram too much stuff into their novels. In describing Mrs Brown, as Woolf argued in another essay, 'Character in Fiction', Arnold Bennett:

> would keep his eyes in the carriage. He, indeed, would observe every detail with immense care. He would notice the advertisements; the pictures of Swanage and Portsmouth; the way in which the cushion bulged between the buttons; how Mrs. Brown wore a brooch which had cost three-and-ten at Whitworth's bazaar; and had mended both gloves – indeed the thumb of the left-hand glove had been replaced. And he would observe, at length, how this was the non-stop train from Windsor which calls at Richmond for the convenience of middle-class residents, who can afford to go to the theatre but have not reached the social rank which can afford motor-cars, though it is true, there are occasions (he would tell us what), when they hire them from a company (he would tell us which). And so he would gradually sidle sedately towards Mrs. Brown, and would remark how she had been left a little copyhold, not freehold, property at Datchet, which, however, was mortgaged to Mr. Bungay the solicitor . . . One line of insight would have done more than all those lines of description.[28]

After this skewering of Bennett's meticulous detailing of his characters' material conditions – with their every social and environmental property being recorded and catalogued – Woolf moves on to outline her conception of how character *should* be evoked in fiction: through the use of a single striking phrase or word, through the use of 'one line of insight'. Similarly in *Jacob's Room*, after offering a limited account of Jacob's physiognomy, Woolf retreats from what she sees as the formulaic and fossilising habit of describing physical characteristics as a means of evoking character: 'then his mouth – but surely, of all futile occupations this of cataloguing features is the worst. One word is sufficient. But if one cannot find it?'[29] Woolf's desire here for the 'one word' capable of truly conveying character in place of endless plodding materialist description is shared by Bernard in *The Waves*, when he calls for 'some little language such as lovers use, broken words, inarticulate words, like the shuffling of feet on the pavement' that would allow him to 'record impressions with words of one syllable'.[30]

All of which is not to say that Woolf's proposed descriptive compression was significantly different, ultimately, from the methods of the 'materialists' whom she so often attacked. As Anne Fernihough has argued, rather than reducing the amount of 'matter' in her novels, Woolf can be seen to have merely replaced one kind of stuff – world-stuff – with another kind of stuff – mind-stuff – in the process transmuting 'physical into psychological clutter, into superabundancy of impressions and memories.'[31] If the interiors of Woolf's houses are the architectural equivalents of the minds of her characters, then they are just as stuffy as those of the Edwardian novelists she attacked.

There is a tension here, of course. Just as one strand of modernism, particularly within music and the visual arts, sought to do away with what it saw as extraneous, so did others add things to artworks and literature (to the novel in particular) until they almost collapsed under the weight. Nevertheless, despite the sheer prodigality of Joyce and Woolf, within the novel the experimental developments associated with modernist narrative, especially with the stream-of-consciousness technique, have often been commended by critics primarily for their reductive *efficiency*: their ability to compress meaning or significance into ever slighter and thus more polished and meaningful utterances.

One question raised by modernism's engagement with the ideologies of reduction is therefore: who decides what is extraneous to a piece of writing, the author or the reader? Even apparently irrelevant linguistic details will inevitably always mean *something*, to someone, at some point. Albright is surely right to interpret the reductive impulses of modernist poetry as an example of poets applying metaphors culled from science to the writing of poetry. And yet during the same period science was undergoing its own eruptions and self-doubts concerning the reducibility of world to representation, especially, as we have seen, in the case of the reduction of sensations to language.

What Gillian Beer has called 'descriptive neutrality' – the ideal of a discourse stripped of all rhetorical flourishes – seduced modernist aesthetics and contemporary science through its appeals to declarative authority. As Beer has argued, scientific discourse most fully embraces the ideals of neutrality in description that we have encountered previously. As we have seen, Ernst Mach's explicitly descriptionist scientific project was founded on the notion that science's value lay in its ability to provide ever more efficient pictures of a world in flux, leading to what he called 'the economy of thought'.[32] As Michael Whitworth summarises 'the Machian school of science rejected the idea that science *explained* the universe, preferring instead the more modest claim that it provided economic descriptions.'[33] Thus descriptionist reduction was mechanistic, having much in common with the Helmholtzian quest for a science founded on the 'elemental' qualities of perception, and sharing with scientific narrative more generally a faith in an economics of efficiency. Such models derived, as Whitworth shows, from thermodynamic and Darwinist ideas which often justified economy of description in terms of biological efficiency.[34] The better the system of compression employed – the more efficient the language of description – the greater the value that system possessed.

In literature it was the reader whose labour was thought to be spared by the new efficiencies of these kinds of modernist reduction. Melvin Friedman's assessment of the achievements of the innovations associated with stream-of-consciousness narrative is typical in its application of the principles of reduction to the interpretation of fiction: 'The novel of narration, attempting communication by means of conventional syntax, is troublesome and exhaustive; the stream of consciousness novel, on the contrary, carries on uninterruptedly without difficulty, with reminiscences and anticipations.'[35]

Yet despite this both the scientific descriptionist project and literary modernism largely *failed* to provide the unified and compressed language of sensation their strongest proponents felt they inevitably would. Friedman's assertion that modernist fiction can be read 'uninterruptedly without difficulty' rings particularly false in this regard: the fruits of modernism, despite some claims to the contrary, do not seem to be any more eidetic or immediate or straightforward than more conventional forms of literature. Indeed much modernist literature is characterised by the difficulties it poses to interpretation: the work involved in deciding precisely what is meant.[36]

The paradigms provided by reproductive mnemonic technologies complicate this critical narrative. With the advent of such technologies, sense-data could be reduced, without loss of clarity, to a groove on a record, to an electrical impulse and, eventually, to a collection of 1s and 0s registered in any abstract medium. A tendency towards an aesthetics of reduction associated with certain branches of modernism was therefore accompanied in the mid-twentieth century by theoretical approaches to information that formalised the rules of compression and transmission, reducing the mind to a set of reflexive neuronal responses. According to N. Katherine Hayles this was particularly noticeable in the domain of the ear. During the late 1940s and early 1950s, she finds, mainly through the work of Claude Shannon, information became 'a more fundamental entity in the world than either matter or energy', coming to denote 'a rigorously defined quantity that [could] be measured with scientific instruments and expressed by mathematical equations.'[37] Friedrich Kittler argues that the 'discourse networks' of the late nineteenth and early twentieth centuries made of the body a machine for the transfer of information; by the mid-twentieth century, Hayles shows, information theory had formalised the rules by which such a body could operate.

The opening chapter of Robert Musil's *The Man Without Qualities* offers a consummation and synopsis of many of the oppositional dualisms associated with modernism's narratives of reduction as they relate to the senses and the qualia debate. In it Musil describes the weather in Vienna with minute attention, using the specialised language of meteorology and astronomy to estrange us from what would, if written in other words, be almost a cliché of scene-setting:

> the isotherms and isotheres were functioning as they should. The air temperature was appropriate relative to the annual mean temperature and to the aperiodic monthly fluctuations of the temperature. The rising and setting of the sun, the moon, the phases of Venus, of the rings of Saturn, and many other significant phenomena were all in accordance with the forecasts in the astronomical yearbooks . . . In a word that characterizes the facts fairly accurately, even if it is a bit old-fashioned: It was a fine day in August 1913.[38]

The playful juxtaposition of registers and the deflationary bathos of the final clause brings to mind distinctions between our 'folk' intuitions about the world – indiscriminate yet largely accurate assumptions about physical or mental phenomena – and the specialised, more strictly accurate languages of maths and science. Throughout *The Man Without Qualities* these different levels of interpretation are played off against each other. Ulrich, the protagonist of the novel, a mathematician who finds it difficult to perceive the world except in terms of numbers, is a walking embodiment of the problem of qualia as it manifests itself within modernism.

Musil, who trained as a philosopher before becoming a novelist, wrote his PhD thesis on the work of Ernst Mach, and his mathematical definition of redness in terms of measurement clearly owes much to Mach's *Analysis of Sensations*.[39] In an essay on 'Mind in Experience', Musil came down firmly on the side of the mathematicians on the question of knowledge, writing 'Mathematical subjects . . . have the advantage over others in that they allow us to distinguish between real knowledge and the imitative fluency that belletristic minds can so quickly establish in any field.'[40]

Here the hierarchical organisation of different forms of knowledge that is so typical of modernist epistemological anxieties is stressed. Maths, Musil suggests, acquaints us with primary qualities, which are more valuable than knowledge of qualia: truer and therefore less open to misinterpretation than the subjective 'belletristic' judgments of the senses.

In a letter written in 1921, James Joyce had described the process of writing the 'Ithaca' episode of *Ulysses* in similar terms. 'I am writing *Ithaca* in the form of a mathematical catechism', he wrote:

> All events are resolved into their cosmic, physical, psychical etc. equivalents, e.g. Bloom jumping down the area, drawing water from the tap, the micturating in the garden, the cone of incense, lighted candle and statue so that the reader will know everything and know it in the baldest and coldest way, but Bloom and Stephen thereby become heavenly bodies, wanderers like the stars at which they gaze.[41]

'Ithaca', like much of *The Man Without Qualities,* is an episode almost overburdened with information: dense with descriptions of physical processes, with interiors and objects and definitions and causal phenomena. It pays painstaking attention to things seen and heard, but makes little attempt to clothe those experiences in any naturalistic sensory or psychological context. As we have seen, in *Ulysses* Joyce often fictionalised the kinds of epistemological enquiries that contemporary popular science and philosophy were spreading abroad. But he always did so playfully. More than any other episode in the novel, 'Ithaca' draws attention to the different levels of description that so complicate the reductionist project when applied to the writing of fiction. It leaves the question of reducibility tantalisingly unresolved.

One representational code that promised to provide a model for the kind of sensory reductions modernism sometimes aspired to was that of musical notation. Language, considered as a system of notation, seems to be more attuned to the ear than to the eye: we are born equipped lungs and vocal chords, with the technologies of aural reproduction, and are therefore able to recreate sounds from written language in a way that is impossible for other sense modalities. And yet, as Eric Prieto argues in *Listening In: Music and Mind in Modernist Narrative*, during the nineteenth and twentieth centuries the novel generally ceased to be associated with sound and music. Though, as Prieto points out, 'like the musical score, the literary text determines a sequence of sounds ordered in time', the novel has since then increasingly denied or obfuscated its status as a bearer of noise instead preferring to consider itself a storehouse of information.[42]

Prieto traces the break between poetry and the novel and their relationship to music to the Renaissance, when the rediscovery of Aristotelian aesthetics prompted a reappraisal of the mimetic functions of art. Denying the platonic notion of harmony, music increasingly came to be interpreted as mimetic of emotions and, ultimately, of the mind itself.[43] The rise of Opera, and the relationship between Wagnerianism and Symbolism, Prieto argues, were symptomatic of the identification of music with the mental realm. As he concludes 'by the end of the nineteenth century voice was no longer a necessary element of the relationship between music and literature: a new link between the two had been found, and that link was thought.'[44] It is little wonder, therefore, that the 'crisis of sensation' that critics like Sara Danius identify as being typical of various strands of modernism should manifest itself particularly strongly in the domain of the ear.[45]

In the 'Sirens' episode of *Ulysses*, Bloom, that amateur scientist of perception, subjects his hearing to rigorous analysis, pondering what he terms the 'musemathmatics' of music: the counterintuitive way in which simple vibrations in the air give can rise to the apparently epiphenomenal experience of sound. 'It's in the silence you feel you hear', he observes, 'vibrations. Now silent air . . . Numbers it is', he thinks:

> All music when you come to think. Two multiplied by two divided by half is twice one. Vibrations: chords those are. One plus two plus six is seven . . . Musemathmatics. And you think you're listening to the ethereal. But suppose you said it like: Martha, seven times nine minus x is thirtyfive thousand. Fall quite flat. It's on account of the sounds it is.[46]

Here Bloom, the reductive materialist, is beguiled by the emergent properties of sensory experience, by the emergence of qualia from their material causes, and by his inability to fully account for them – or to share them with other minds – in objective, mathematical terms. Translating sounds into symbols doesn't let you share their sensuous reality with others. Indeed an algebraic approach to hearing sounds would 'fall quite flat'. The question that emerges in Bloom's attempt to 'read' sound mathematically is one which haunts reductive accounts of consciousness, as well as modernist literary aesthetics more generally. How can mechanical encounters with colourless, odourless and soundless matter make us experience sensations, make us feel that we are 'listening to the ethereal'? The horrific circularity of Bloom's conclusion, that it is only 'on account of the sounds' that sounds sound the *way* that they sound, is one which motivated a whole host of competing epistemological theories and aesthetic strategies throughout the twentieth century, ultimately exploding the confident dictats of the reductive methodologies associated with science and leading directly to the conceptualisation of qualia.

More than most forms of art, music is emergent: it must be performed before it can be experienced. The musical score is a symbol of potential experience rather than an experience in itself, but it contains within it sufficient information to be translated into specific sounds when appropriate technology – a musical instrument; a voice – is employed by a skilled musician. As such the musical paradigm is often invoked in discussions over the reducibility of sensation, or qualia, to symbolic representation. Treating written language as though it engages with the senses in a similar manner to musical notation was of course one of the declared aims of many modernist authors who followed

Walter Pater in their belief that 'all art constantly aspires to the condition of music.'[47] The prevalence of onomatopoeic experiment within modernism supported the idea that symbolic language was able to replace matter with information. But in engaging with the phonic properties of language literature must inevitably undergo its own reductions, encoding sound only as speech. 'What good are the poetic mnemonic techniques of rhyme and meter when wax rolls can store not only substance and tone but real sounds?' asks Friedrich Kittler.[48] Mnemonic technologies such as the gramophone freed sense-data from language, from what Kittler terms the 'bottleneck of the signifier'. But in doing so they showed that sound could be stored in material form, and musical notation continued to provide a beguiling metaphor for the ways in which sensory experience could be represented in language.

As I have suggested, Joyce's method in *Ulysses* can be seen to have pre-emptively challenged this aural reductive thesis. In the Linati scheme, the technique of 'Sirens' is identified as music, and the frequent descriptions of sounds and melody in the episode, as well as the interpolated scraps of notation into the matter of the text, are all testament to Joyce's taking 'quite seriously', as Jeri Johnson suggests, the problem of how to represent music in language.[49] With its 'proliferation of onomatopoeic noises', Johnson continues, Joyce asks 'how words might perform like the tonal sounds of music'.[50] But the episode ultimately illustrates that such endeavours are impossible. In his second Futurist Manifesto, F. T. Marinetti had argued, in terms similar to Johnson's, that:

> Our growing love for matter, the will to penetrate it and know its vibrations, the physical sympathy that links us to motors, push us to the *use of onomatopoeia*. Since noise is the result of rubbing or striking rapidly moving solids, liquids, or gases, onomatopoeia, which reproduces noise, is necessarily one of the most dynamic elements of poetry.[51]

Yet the questions raised by 'Sirens' seem to undermine such claims. Does onomatopoeia really 'reproduce' – or even aspire to reproduce – noise? Despite its best efforts to represent the non-standard pronunciation of words or the naturalistic aurality of the world of abstract noise, the technique often functions, especially in Joyce's writing, as a signpost to silence rather than as a means of mechanically encoding sonorous experiences. Indeed, *Ulysses* often challenges us directly with its very muteness, presenting mere words on the page and forcing us to ask why it is that, despite the almost encyclopaedic amount of information we are given to decode them, they remain silent.

Nevertheless, music does provide a compelling paradigm for the potential of language to encode qualia, precisely because notation provides a model of a kind of reductive reproduction unavailable to the other sense modalities. The relationship between visual language, encoded and standardised by the printing press, and spoken or heard language was a huge source of both conflict and innovation within modernism.[52] As Hugh Kenner has argued, the rise of the printing press and mass literacy forced authors to consider the relationship between readers and words on the page as never before, leading to what Joyce called in *Finnegans Wake* the 'earsighted view' of modernism.[53] Much of the sense of Ulysses depends on this interplay between sound, sight and meaning – the reader, like 'Bald deaf Pat' in *Ulysses*, 'seehears lipspeech'.[54] But imagining the sounding out of words isn't the same as sounding them out. Things that can be read often can't be heard. Visual puns litter *Ulysses*, and the tension between the orthographic and sonic properties of language was something that, in Joyce's wake, many Irish authors became preoccupied with. Samuel Beckett and Flann O'Brien, in particular, were obsessed with the relationship between author and editor; between sound and sense, and with the difficulties presented by the pluralities of interpretation offered by the visual pun. Joyce's art suggested ways in which dialogue could register something of the characteristics of the speaker, and *Ulysses* was profoundly concerned with these subtle compressions of character, which were carried over into the very fabric of language. As Hugh Kenner observes, these preoccupations are manifested on the textual level in *Ulysses*:

> Misspelled words once served like details of musical notation, to cue a storyteller's change of voice. And James Joyce's most radical, for that matter his most un-Irish act, was dispensing with the story-teller. He forces us to confront printed pages, and make what we can of them.[55]

In Kenner's reading, *Ulysses* operates in that limbo between voice and idea. As a novel it is dense with metadata, containing an interpretative scaffolding which constantly works to thicken the novel's potential meanings.

Nowhere was the desire to try to listen to language rather than read it more consistently questioned than in the work of Samuel Beckett, an author who was uniquely interested in the reconfigurations of the literary brought about by technical innovations of reduction and information theory. Beckett is often read as the reductionist's reductionist. In *The Ideal Real* Paul Davies points out that experiments 'in reducing language to its barest elements have been the topic of countless studies of Samuel Beckett', and while it is true that Beckett's experimental reductions have been well-studied, the relationship between these experiments and the material conditions which gave rise to them remains relatively underexplored.[56] In the final part of this chapter, I wish to react to Beckett's narratives of reduction by connecting them to larger critical concerns over the idea of encoding sound in language, and the consequent dualism between 'information' and 'noise', which parallels that between brains and minds, that such a dialogue engenders.

Beckett's Radical Reductions

Beckett's representation of the ear and of listening more generally was intimately bound up with subjectivity and of the functions of consciousness. In *The Unnameable* he defined the subject as a sort of all-encompassing ear:

> perhaps that's what I am, the thing that divides the world in two, on the one side the outside, on the other the inside, that can be as thin as foil, I'm neither one side nor the other, I'm in the middle, I'm the partition, I've two surfaces and no thickness, perhaps that's what I feel, myself vibrating, I'm the tympanum, on the one hand the mind, on the other the world.[57]

As a technique, the internal monologue was often conceived of in distinctly aural terms – as Wyndham Lewis asserted, Leopold Bloom's internal narrative, however disjointed, is that of a man talking to himself – and within the paradigm it provided auditory influences on the human subject were not limited to the sounds that one hears. 'To represent subjectivity', writes Angela Frattarola, modernist novelists therefore had 'not only had to think about how we listen to the world and are shaped by the sounds we hear, but they also had to get a feel for the sound of "inner speech"': the modernist subject had to listen to herself as much as to the external world.[58] Though Beckett's Molloy states that he 'liked thinking in monologue', during which his 'lips moved visibly', for most other subjects of the internal monologue thought was rarely manifested in behaviour in such direct ways.[59]

This tension – between technological reproducibility and the natural voice, between sound and silence – is one that has underpinned critical accounts of the mind in Beckett's work in a number of ways. For early critics it seemed clear that he was an author who subscribed by and large to a Cartesian conception of consciousness. John Fletcher was able confidently to assert that substance dualism 'underlies the whole of Beckett's work', as is made evident by the many direct references to Descartes throughout it, and by the proliferation of tools and prosthetic attachments which, especially in Beckett's novels, characters depend upon as props.[60] Hugh Kenner too has argued for an understanding of Beckett's characters based on their Cartesian inheritance, and sees the bicycle as a recurring symbol of this ability of mind to transcend the material.[61]

Certainly it is true that material bodies in Beckett are frequently fickle and unreliable. They decay, dissipate in space, or disobey the instructions of the mind, all while the voice rambles on. Malone's body, for instance, is 'impotent. There is virtually nothing it can do.'[62] Yet at other times the Cartesian tradition is suggested more subtly within Beckett's work. Critics have described many of his plays as 'skullscapes' or 'soulscapes' and such definitions suggest a dichotomy of mind and world which conforms to the principles of the Cartesian theatre. Similarly, the curious chapter in *Murphy* where 'a justification of the expression "Murphy's mind" has to be attempted' is laced with the rhetoric of dualism:

> Happily we need not concern ourselves with this apparatus as it really was – that would be an extravagance and an impertinence – but solely with what it felt and pictured itself to be. Murphy's mind is after all the gravamen of these informations.[63]

Murphy's mind, the circuitous centre of the novel, cannot be approached directly. Instead the metaphors Beckett employs to express or reify it here are themselves derived from the Cartesian tradition. It (not 'he') 'pictured itself as a large hollow sphere, hermetically closed to the universe without'[64] (hints of Leibniz's monads here) so that as a being Murphy

> felt himself split in two, a body and a mind. They had intercourse apparently, otherwise he could not have known that they had anything in common. But he felt his mind to be bodytight and did not understand through what channel the intercourse was effected nor how the two experiences came to overlap.[65]

Though he viewed it as fundamentally impossible, Beckett persistently sought to represent the closed world of the mind in his fiction and drama, therefore. Though rooms provide compelling models for epistemological enquiry in the work of, among others, Virginia Woolf, it is in Beckett's novels that the full impact of the trope of the room as an isolating space and a model for the mind is imagined. A plethora of isolated and monadic rooms is scattered throughout Beckett's fiction: in the depressing bedsits of *Murphy* or the lunatic asylums and padded cells in the trilogy, providing further isolation for the already isolated minds of his characters. Murphy's garret, for instance, is: 'windowless, like a monad, except for the shuttered judas in the door, at which a sane eye appeared, or was employed to appear, at frequent and regular intervals throughout the twenty-four hours.'[66]

The presence of all these rooms in Beckett's work suggests the Cartesian theatre as a model for consciousness, and Beckett's protagonists are often obsessively focused on analysing the sense-data which they are supplied with, either from their immediate environments or from the world beyond the rooms in which they're trapped. This sense-data, as befits an author so interested in the artistic potential of radio broadcasting, is more often than not made up of noise.

The complicated matrix of music, silence and technology was a fertile field of exploration for both authors and musicians of the period, as it has been for contemporary critics of modernity. Jacques Derrida, in particular, showed how both the gramophone and the telephone threatened the closely woven association between voice and presence within modernism, associating the gramophone in modernity, as Leopold Bloom does in *Ulysses*, with death and absence.[67] As Yoshiki Tajiri has argued, Derrida's observations regarding *Ulysses* in 'Ulysses Gramophone' could equally apply to Beckett.[68] By allowing us to hear disembodied voices, recording technologies capture our old or non-existent selves, letting us hear the past in a quite literal way, and in a way which Beckett was to explore most famously in *Krapp's Last Tape*. But the absence of sound, too, is explored in Beckett's work, something which connects him with musicians in the period. For both Schoenberg and his pupil John Cage silence was taken to be an important feature of all music, and came in their compositions to be explored for its own sake. As N. Katherine Hayles has shown, radio broadcasting also drew attention to the fact that the semantic content of a sound consisted in large part of the gaps between noises, so that silence came increasingly to be seen as integral to meaning. Eventually, after Claude Shannon published his seminal paper 'A Mathematical Theory of Communication' in 1948, information began to be conceived of as a binary stream of 1s and 0s: interpolated presence and absence.

Much of Beckett's writing, like Joyce's before it, was explicitly concerned with the reductive tensions that exist between the way words sound in the ear and the way they look on the page. Throughout *Murphy*, for instance, we are directly addressed as readers rather than as 'hearers'. The novel is full of visual puns typical of the type of orthographic textual play that both Joyce and Flann O'Brien were also fond of:

> 'Why did the barmaid champagne?' he said. 'Do you give up?'
> 'Yes,' said Celia.
> 'Because the stout porter bitter,' said Murphy.[69]

This joke does not amuse Celia, Beckett continues, for 'far from being adapted to her, it was not addressed to her' but, presumably, to us: the readers of *Murphy*, who are forced to sound out the pun for ourselves.[70] After *Murphy* Beckett abandoned altogether the use of typographic markers for speech, and in these later works both reader and printer are addressed again and again as potential editors. In *Watt* Beckett muses metatextually on the status of the book *as* book, telling us that much 'valuable space has been saved, in this work, that would otherwise have been lost, by avoidance of the plethoric reflexive pronoun after *say*.'[71] Here a modernist commitment to reduction asserts itself again as an inefficient orthographic marker is removed. Yet by drawing attention to the intervention Beckett gently ironises the self-same impulse – the 'valuable space' is filled with a justification of the reductive practice.

Occasionally Beckett addresses both editor and compositor directly in this manner: 'M.M.M. stood suddenly for Music, MUSIC, MUSIC, in brilliant, brevier and canon, or some such typographical scream, if the gentle compositor would be so friendly.'[72]

Are these interventions to be read as notes to composition that should be deleted after their instructions are followed? If so, why are they still present in the novel? Self-reflexive commentaries like these occur in the radio plays also, drawing attention to the very medium in which they're presented, as when Maddy Rooney in *All That Fall* states 'I do not exist. The fact is well known', and asks 'Am I then invisible, Miss Flitt?'[73] She doesn't exist, we may respond; she is invisible. That is the whole point.

The passivity of hearing, and the way in which meaning is made up from reduced sensory instructions, which require decoding, is, then, a central predilection throughout Beckett's work, manifesting its influence in the stark featurelessness of the landscapes 'described' in the early novels (which are generally dominated by the speaking voice), and in his interest in recording and broadcasting technologies in the radio plays. No modernist author engaged with the theoretical questions relating to the reduction of sound and sense as provocatively as did Beckett. In both the radio plays (which, as Marjorie Perloff has noted, are deeply concerned with exploring the role of abstract sound as a bearer of meaning) and in his novels, mnemonic and broadcasting technologies are often used as metaphors for memory, or to challenge our association of sensation with meaning.[74]

As Perloff has observed, Beckett's interest in the emerging field of recorded sound may well have had an autobiographical precedent. While Beckett was hiding out from occupying forces in France from 1942 to 1945 'the radio transmitter' became for him '*the* crucial information conduit for Resistance groups, and the BBC, which was to commission *All That Fall* (1956) and *Embers* (1959), its main source.'[75] N. Katherine Hayles has argued that war was central to the conceptual revolution of information that occurred in the mid-twentieth century, with Alan Turing cracking the Enigma code, and radio operators becoming as important as foot soldiers to the war effort. Information, Hayles argues, particularly of the kind that could be conveyed over the radio, became in an important sense more *real* in the period, altering the outcome of battles and saving or condemning lives.[76]

After the war the radio play became one of Beckett's most fruitful outlets. The form of the radio play proved incredibly stimulating for an author who had already demonstrated a fascination as much with the ways in which meaning is transferred via sound, as with interpreting meaning itself. Beckett's radio plays often play with this dynamic, forcing us to acknowledge the fundamental tension between the qualia of sound – its phenomenological reality – and its status as a bearer of meaning. What does it mean to treat the sounds of the radio plays – once enacted, recorded and listened to – as meaningful? What does it mean when 'noise' becomes 'information' in this way: gaining significance through the symbolic tasks it is asked to perform? Though the soundscapes of Beckett's radio plays are often written about in terms of their ability to conjure up imaginary yet specific topographies, they are also frequently interpreted in terms of the mimetic function of these symbolic correspondences. Attempts to 'read' the radio plays in this way often ignore some of the unique properties of aural representation, properties that were increasingly being explored by both philosophers engaged in questioning how sensations might be reduced to brain states, and to mathematicians and musicians who were asking how diagrams, scores, or equations might be translated into sounds.

Hayles proposes that Beckett's radio plays should be interpreted as engaged in a theoretical as well as an aesthetic intervention, therefore, one that was ultimately founded on the aesthetics of reduction. According to Hayles the plays represent and contribute to an oppositional dualism between the categories of 'information' and 'noise'. Throughout Beckett's fiction, she shows, intelligible language is described as breaking down into meaningless sound, or as receding into silence. In *The Calmative* for instance we are told that: 'I marshalled the words and opened my mouth, thinking I would hear them. But all I heard was a kind of rattle, unintelligible even to me who knew what was intended.'[77]

Here the human subject is imagined as a sort of Turing machine, oblivious to his or her own utterances, or to their intended meaning. As Christopher Ricks has shown, words often die in Beckett's work in this way, becoming devoid of meaning and present only as sense-data to the characters who experience them.[78] Devices or animals capable of mimicking noises without understanding their meanings are prominent within his work. Beckett would eventually employ technologically mediated sound to represent and explore memory functions, but in his early works parrots are a recurring image of the production of sonic qualia stripped of sense; for the idiotic babble of technologically reproducible sound. In *Murphy*, for instance, Celia is described as having 'Not the slightest idea . . . of what her words mean. No more insight into their implications than a parrot into its profanities.'[79] Watt, too, sometimes speaks 'as one speaking to dictation, or reciting, parrot-like, a text, by long repetition become familiar'.[80] Elsewhere we are introduced to another parrot, of which the eponymous Molloy notes: 'I understood him better than his mistress. I don't mean I understood him better than she understood him, I mean I understood him better than I understood her.'[81] *The Unnameable* describes the semantic challenge presented by his captors in similar terms: 'A parrot, that's what they're up against, a parrot.'[82] It is in *Malone Dies* that the most significant act of parroting in Beckett's oeuvre takes place.[83] When Jackson tries to teach his bird to say 'Nihil in intellectu, etc.' we are told that '[t]hese first three words the bird managed well enough, but the celebrated restriction was too much for it, all you heard was a series of squawks.'[84] Here the quotation enacts its own reductive impossibility. The phrase Jackson is attempting to teach the parrot to regurgitate is 'nihil in intellectu nisi prius in sensu' ('nothing in the intellect unless first in sense'): the guiding first principle of empiricism. The squawks, meaningless in semantic terms but present to the senses as sounds – as qualia – are a significant coda to the expression. So is the 'etc.' (itself a contraction: a reduction), for in reducing the length of the quotation it denies us knowledge of whether Jackson (and Beckett) intended to include the Leibnizian appendage 'nisi intellectus ipse' ('except the intellect itself') to the 'celebrated restriction', establishing an epistemological precedent which enacts its own recurrence throughout his work.

In many of Beckett's novels, therefore, meaningful and abstract sounds – qualia and their symbolic associations – are brought into conflict with one another. Sometimes sounds are represented to be enjoyed purely for their own sake, and at other times we are urged to parse them for their significance. The type of knowledge that is carried by noise or ambient sound in the novels and radio plays is at times fundamentally opposed to that which is contained in linguistic utterances. Watt is perhaps Beckett's most experimental linguist, and comes to his own conclusions over the semantic content of utterances:

> This further modification Watt carried through with all his usual discretion and sense of what was acceptable to the ear, and aesthetic judgement. Nevertheless to one, such as me, desirous above all of information, the change was not a little disconcerting.[85]

We of course are identified with 'me'; a reader, desirous above all of information, deriving little from the experience of the text, set painfully to puzzle out the content of sentences. Watt's often tortuous experiments in the encoding of concepts in language, where he runs through all the possible manipulations of the parts of speech again suggest the dichotomy between sound and sense in this way:

> The following is an example of Watt's manner, at this period:
> *Ot bro, lap rulb, krad klub. Ot murd, wol fup, wol fup. Ot niks, sorg sam, sorg sam. Ot lems, lats lems, lats lems. Ot gnut, trat stews, trat stews.*
> These were sounds that at first, though we walked breast to breast, made little or no sense to me.
> Nor did Watt follow me. Geb nodrap, he said, geb nodrap, nodrap.
> Thus I missed I suppose much I presume of great interest touching I suspect the second stage of the second or closing period of Watt's stay in Mr. Knott's house.[86]

As Richard Coe and others have suggested, the extreme fragmentation of language which occurs in Part 3 of *Watt* suggests at least a passing interest in linguistic theory, notably the disconnect between 'langue' and 'parole' that is a feature of Saussurean linguistics. Coe argues that in the sections of linguistic experimentation in *Watt* Beckett exhausted his interest in writing in English and became more and more interested in the notion of translation, and that by separating language and thought from sensation, Beckett left us 'a style *in vacuo*'.[87]

The dying of words that occurs here certainly has much in common with the preceding shuffling of statements and parts of speech – exhaustive in its completeness – that was becoming an important cultural metaphor through the development of the logic of the computer. But it also highlights the primary meaning of the 'sense' of words. However meaningless Watt's 'utters' or 'effs' are, we can still attempt – indeed are compelled – to sound them out for ourselves: they possess syntactic content even as they lack semantic meaning. The qualia of their sounded-out performance persists even if these utterances are utterly devoid of meaning: they are sounds even if they are not words. Watt's demand, expressed later on, for 'semantic succour' derives from precisely this in-built human desire to name and thus to understand the sensations of which experience is composed: 'he would set to trying names on things, and on himself, almost as a woman hats.'[88]

As listeners, if not as readers, therefore, we exist in relation to the imagined topographies of Beckett's skullscapes and soundscapes as does Malone as he lies in bed naming the sounds he hears, like an Adam of aurality. This is a moment of Proustian mnemonic association, but is also one that suggests the difficulties of categorising abstract sounds using the straitjacket of language:

> When I stop, as just now, the noises begin again, strangely loud, those whose turn it is. So that I seem to have again the hearing of my boyhood. Then in my bed, in the dark, on stormy nights, I could tell from one another, in the outcry without, the leaves, the boughs, the groaning trunks, even the grasses and the house that sheltered me. Each tree had its own cry, just as no two whispered alike, when the air was still. I heard afar the iron gates clashing and dragging at their posts and the wind rushing between their bars. There was nothing, even the sand on the paths, that did not utter its cry.[89]

In Malone's world everything emits a sound, and everything can be identified from the sound that it makes. But though Malone could as a child easily discriminate between the different sounds he heard, as he ages the clarity of his hearing, and his ability to isolate and name the sounds he experiences, diminishes:

> What I mean to say is possibly this, that the noises of the world, so various in themselves and which I used to be so clever at distinguishing from one another, had been dinning at me for so long, always the same old noises, as gradually to have merged into a single noise, so that all I heard was

one vast continuous buzzing. The volume of sound perceived remained no doubt the same, I have simply lost the faculty of decomposing it.[90]

Malone has lost the 'faculty of decomposing it', and his inability to discriminate between the various sonic events that he can hear means that the world around him retreats into noise. It ceases to carry any information. This is not straightforward deafness, but a linguistic failure: a growing inability to dress the qualia of sound in descriptive language. It's a failure that recurs in much of Beckett's work, which has often been read as an articulation of a sort of will-to-silence. In *Malone Dies*, as in much of the experimental music that was contemporaneous with it, sounds that could formerly be associated quite clearly with external objects (one thinks of *All That Fall* and *Embers*: aural landscapes that were evoked by the bleating of sheep or the crashing of the sea) become instead abstract noises, themselves unnameable, the white noise of what Beckett earlier calls 'the so-called silence.'[91]

Thus Beckett's early novels, and many of his radio plays, can be read as engaging in a fruitful if open-ended dialogue with contemporary theories of meaning, sensation and qualia. His work consummates many of the tentative modernist impulses to separate the world between its primary and secondary qualities, reducing the latter to the former. In the final chapter of this book I will read the novels of Wyndham Lewis alongside what David Trotter has termed modernism's 'will-to-automatism' as reacting to similar expressionist concerns, asking what happens when a literature designed not for people but for machines meets a theory of consciousness which suggests that people are nothing *more* than machines.

NOTES

1. D. H. Lawrence, 'Why the Novel Matters', *Study of Thomas Hardy and Other Essays*, ed. by Bruce Steele (Cambridge: Cambridge University Press, 1985), p. 193.
2. Lawrence, 'Why the Novel Matters', p. 194.
3. Lawrence, 'Why the Novel Matters', p. 195.
4. Lionel Trilling, 'The Meaning of a Literary Idea', in *The Liberal Imagination: Essays on Literature and Society* (London: Secker and Warburg, 1951), p. 285.
5. See Raymond Tallis, *Aping Mankind: Neuromania, Darwinitis, and the Misrepresentation of Humanity* (Durham: Acumen Publishing Ltd, 2011).
6. Francis Crick, *The Astonishing Hypothesis: The Scientific Search for the Soul* (New York: Charles Scribner's Sons, 1994), p. 3.
7. Crick, *The Astonishing Hypothesis*, p. 8.
8. M. R. Bennett and P. M. S. Hacker, *Philosophical Foundations of Neuroscience* (Malden, MA; Oxford: Blackwell, 2003), p. 357.
9. Patricia Smith Churchland, *Neurophilosophy: Toward a Unified Science of the Mind–Brain* (Cambridge, MA and London: The MIT Press, 1986), p. 278.
10. Churchland, *Neurophilosophy*, p. 278.
11. Churchland, *Neurophilosophy*, p. 326–7.

12. See Arthur Eddington, *The Nature of The Physical World* (Cambridge: Cambridge University Press, 1928), pp. 247–273.
13. Churchland, *Neurophilosophy*, p. 332.
14. Rudolf Carnap, *The Logical Structure of the World: Pseudoproblems in Philosophy*, trans. by Rolf A. George (London: Routledge & Kegan Paul, 1967), p. vi.
15. Carnap, *The Logical Structure of the World*, p. v.
16. Carnap, *The Logical Structure of the World*, p. vii.
17. Willard Van Orman Quine, *From a Logical Point of View: 9 Logico-Philosophical Essays* (Cambridge, MA: Harvard University Press, 1953), p. 20.
18. Quine, *From a Logical Point of View*, p. 38.
19. Quine, *From a Logical Point of View*, p. 39.
20. Quine, *From a Logical Point of View*, p. 40.
21. Quine, *From a Logical Point of View*, p. 41.
22. Evelyn Cobley, *Modernism and the Culture of Efficiency: Ideology and Fiction* (Toronto and London: University of Toronto Press, 2009), pp. 5–6.
23. Jennifer Karns Alexander, *The Mantra of Efficiency: from Waterwheel to Social Control* (Baltimore, MD: The Johns Hopkins University Press, 2008), p. 3.
24. Samuel Beckett, qtd in James Knowlson, *Damned to Fame: The Life of Samuel Beckett* (London: Bloomsbury, 1996), p. 352.
25. Georg Lukács, 'The Ideology of Modernism', in *Realism in Our Time: Literature and the Class Struggle* (New York: Harper Torchbooks, 1971), p. 45.
26. Lukács, 'The Ideology of Modernism', p. 31.
27. Daniel Albright, *Quantum Poetics: Yeats, Pound, Eliot and the Science of Modernism* (Cambridge: Cambridge University Press, 1997), p. 111.
28. Virginia Woolf, 'Character in Fiction', in *The Essays of Virginia Woolf Volume III: 1919–1924*, ed. by Andrew McNeillie (London: The Hogarth Press, 1988), p. 428.
29. Virginia Woolf, *Jacob's Room* (London: The Hogarth Press, 1922), p. 114.
30. Virginia Woolf, *The Waves* (London: The Hogarth Press, 1931), p. 323.
31. Anne Fernihough, 'Consciousness as a Stream', in *The Cambridge Companion to the Modernist Novel*, ed. by Morag Shiach (Cambridge: Cambridge University Press, 2007), p. 71.
32. Ernst Mach, 'The Economical Nature of Physical Enquiry', in *Popular Scientific Lectures,* trans. by Thomas J. McCormack (Chicago, IL: The Open Court Publishing Company, 1898), pp. 186–213.
33. Michael H. Whitworth, *Einstein's Wake: Relativity, Metaphor, and Modernist Literature* (Oxford: Oxford University Press, 2001), p. 86.
34. Whitworth, *Einstein's Wake*, p. 85.
35. Melvin Friedman, *Stream of Consciousness: A Study in Literary Method* (New Haven, CT: Yale University Press, 1955), p. 4.
36. See George Steiner, 'On Difficulty', in *On Difficulty and Other Essays* (Oxford: Oxford University Press, 1978).
37. N. Katherine Hayles, 'Information or Noise? Economy of Explanation in Barthes's *S/Z* and Shannon's information Theory', in *One Culture: Essays in Science and Literature*, ed. by George Levine (Madison, WI: The University of Wisconsin Press, 1987), p. 120.

38. Robert Musil, *The Man Without Qualities*, trans. by. Sophie Wilkins, 2 vols (London: Picador, 1995), vol. I, p. 3.
39. Musil's thesis has been published as *On Mach's Theories*, trans. by Kevin Mulligan (Washington, DC: Catholic University of America Press, 1882). A good account of the influence of Mach on Musil's thought is provided by Thomas Sebastian, *The Intersection of Science and Literature in Musil's The Man Without Qualities* (Rochester, NY: Camden House, 2005).
40. Robert Musil, *Precision and Soul: Essays and Addresses,* ed. and trans. by Burton Pike and David S. Luft (Chicago, IL and London: University of Chicago Press, 1990), p. 134.
41. James Joyce, *Letters of James Joyce*, ed. by Stuart Gilbert, 3 vols (London: Faber and Faber/Viking, 1957), vol. I, pp. 159–160 (emphasis in original).
42. Eric Prieto, *Listening In: Music, Mind and the Modernist Narrative* (Lincoln, NE and London: University of Nebraska Press, 2002), p. 25.
43. See Prieto, *Listening In,* pp. 5–10.
44. Prieto, *Listening In*, p. 10.
45. See Sara Danius, *The Senses of Modernism: Technology, Perception, and Aesthetics* (Ithaca, NY and London: Cornell University Press, 2002), p. 3.
46. James Joyce, *Ulysses*, ed. by Hans Walter Gabler (London: The Bodley Head, 1986),11.830–837. All references to James Joyce's *Ulysses* are to the Gabler synoptic edition, and are given in the form [episode number.line number].
47. Walter Pater, *The Renaissance Studies in Art and Poetry*, ed. by Adam Phillips (Oxford: Oxford University Press, 1986), p. 86.
48. Friedrich A. Kittler, *Discourse Networks 1800–1900*, trans. by Michael Metteer and Chris Cullens (Stanford, CA: Stanford University Press, 1990), p. 236.
49. Jeri Johnson, explanatory notes to James Joyce, *Ulysses*, ed. by Jeri Johnson (Oxford: Oxford University Press, 1993), p. 875.
50. Johnson, explanatory notes to *Ulysses*, ed. by Johnson, p. 875.
51. F. T. Marinetti, 'Geometric and Mechanical Splendor and the Numerical Sensibility', in *Let's Murder the Moonshine: Selected Writings*, ed. by R. W. Flint, trans. by R.W. Flint and Arthur A. Coppotelli (Los Angeles, CA: Sun and Moon Press, 1991), p. 109 (emphasis in original).
52. See Walter J. Ong, *Orality and Literacy: The Technologizing of the Word* (London: Methuen, 1982).
53. James Joyce, *Finnegans Wake* (London: Faber & Faber, 1939), 143.9–10.
54. Joyce, *Ulysses*, 11.1003.
55. Hugh Kenner, *The Mechanic Muse* (New York and Oxford: Oxford University Press 1987), p. 69.
56. Paul Davies, *The Ideal Real: Beckett's Fiction and Imagination* (London: Associated University Presses, 1994), p. 131.
57. Samuel Beckett, *Three Novels: Molloy, Malone Dies, The Unnameable* (New York: Grove Press, 2009), p. 376.
58. Angela Frattarola, 'Developing an Ear for the Modernist Novel: Virginia Woolf, Dorothy Richardson, and James Joyce', *Journal of Modern Literature*, 33.1 (2009), 132–153 (p. 138).

59. Beckett, *Three Novels*, p. 90.
60. See John Fletcher, 'Samuel Beckett and the Philosophers', *Comparative Literature*, 17 (1965), 43–56.
61. See Hugh Kenner, 'The Cartesian Centaur', in *Samuel Beckett: A Critical Study* (New York: Grove Press, 1961).
62. Beckett, *Three Novels*, p. 180.
63. Samuel Beckett, *Murphy* (London: George Routledge & Sons Ltd, 1938), p. 107.
64. Beckett, *Murphy*, p. 107.
65. Beckett, *Murphy*, p. 109.
66. Beckett, *Murphy*, p. 181.
67. See Yoshiki Tajiri, *Samuel Beckett and the Prosthetic Body: The Organs and Senses in Modernism* (Basingstoke: Palgrave Macmillan, 2007), p. 141.
68. See Tajiri, *Beckett and the Prosthetic Body*, p. 141.
69. Beckett, *Murphy*, p. 139.
70. Beckett, *Murphy*, p. 139.
71. Samuel Beckett, *Watt* (London: John Calder, 1976), p. 6.
72. Beckett, *Murphy*, p. 236.
73. Samuel Beckett, *Collected Shorter Plays* (London: Faber & Faber, 1984), pp. 19, 22.
74. Marjorie Perloff, 'The Silence that is not Silence: Acoustic Art in Samuel Beckett's *Embers*', in *Samuel Beckett and the Visual Arts: Music, Visual Arts, and Non-Print Media*, ed. by Lois Oppenheim (New York: Garland, 1998, pp. 247–268).
75. Perloff, 'Silence', p. 247.
76. Hayles, 'Information or Noise ?', p. 122.
77. Samuel Beckett, *The Expelled; The Calmative; The End; with First Love*, ed. by Christopher Ricks (London: Faber & Faber, 2009), p. 24.
78. See Christopher Ricks, *Beckett's Dying Words* (Oxford: Clarendon Press, 1993).
79. Beckett, *Murphy*, p. 39.
80. Beckett, *Watt*, p. 154.
81. Beckett, *Three Novels*, p. 33.
82. Beckett, *Three Novels*, p. 329.
83. Both Ulrike Maude and Laura Salisbury have discussed Beckett's interest in 'parroting' in terms of his complicated relationship with behaviorist psychology and animal narratives. See Ulrike Maude, 'Pavlov's Dogs and Other Animals in Beckett', in *Beckett and Animals*, ed. by Mary Bryden (Cambridge: Cambridge University Press, 2013), pp. 82–94; and Laura Salisbury, *Samuel Beckett Laughing Matters, Comic Timing* (Edinburgh: Edinburgh University Press, 2012), pp. 104–111.
84. Beckett, *Three Novels*, p. 212.
85. Beckett, *Watt*, p. 163.
86. Beckett, *Watt*, p. 163.
87. Richard N. Coe, 'Beckett's English', in *Samuel Beckett: Humanistic Perspectives*, ed. by Morris Beja, S. E. Gontarski and Pierre Astier (Columbus, OH: Ohio State University Press, 1983), p. 53.
88. Beckett, *Watt*, pp. 79–80.
89. Beckett, *Three Novels*, p. 200.
90. Beckett, *Three Novels*, p. 201.
91. Beckett, *Three Novels*, p. 200.

6

HOLLOW MEN AND CHINESE ROOMS: WYNDHAM LEWIS AND THE WILL-TO-AUTOMATISM

> Creatures of Fronts we are – designed to bustle
> Down paths lit by our eyes, on stilts of clockwork muscle –
> 							Wyndham Lewis, 'One-Way Song'

Turing Tests and Chinese Rooms

In the first five chapters of this book I explored how engaging with qualia creates problems for critical interpretations of modernist fiction orientated towards a cognitive realist paradigm. To claim that qualia exist while maintaining that certain forms of literary discourse are able to convey those qualia to other minds without loss is to commit a category error, while to deny that qualia exist is to endorse a reductive view of consciousness that makes it difficult to make any special representational claims for the novel (or, indeed, for any other form of literature). Simply put: if qualia exist, then they cannot be contained in writing. But if they don't exist then there doesn't seem to be much difference – in terms of their ability to produce certain kinds of affect in their readers – between a highly 'literary' description of sensation and a clinical, objective, or otherwise 'scientific' one.

The narratives of reduction that so dominated modernist aesthetics in the early twentieth century had, as we have seen, their origins in the material conditions of modernity itself, especially in the medical and technical contexts associated with the new neurology, the material unconscious, and the aesthetics of the reflex arc. These conditions led directly to a conception of sensation which stressed its status as ephemeral and information-bearing, rather than as grossly material, and became in turn a fertile source of inspiration for Samuel Beckett. I want now to consider a more radical solution to the impasse produced by qualia than those explored previously, one that is associated with a school of psychology which emerged alongside the 'introspectionist' disciplines of phenomenology, Jamesian pragmatism and psychoanalysis. The doctrine of behaviourism – which rose to prominence more or less in parallel with modernism in the arts – denies qualia. It provides an altogether more mechanistic view of the human subject than was espoused by the introspectionists. As we shall see, behaviourism's radical proposal – that the problem of consciousness might be solved by denying interiority – creates a compelling justification for cognitive realism. Yet, in its stronger forms, in doing so it also denies the existence of those very qualities of consciousness which literature, uniquely, is often held to contain.

Though composed of a multifaceted set of theories, in its most extreme form behaviourism denies the existence of qualia altogether. Proponents of logical behaviourism (of the kind associated with Carnap and the logical positivists), argue that any mental state can be re-written as an indeterminate – but not infinite – series of logical 'if-then' statements. Methodological behaviourism, as described in the work of J. B. Watson (later developed by B. F. Skinner) proposes that the proper study of the psychologist should be not interiority but the behaviour of human beings, understood as bodies moving through space and time.[1] Introspection is considered by the methodological behaviourist to be an illegitimate psychological technique. Rather, from the behaviourist's perspective the mind should be treated as a 'black box': unknowable, impenetrable and forever out of reach. By denying that there are such things as mental states at all behaviourism provides a compelling paradigm for cognitive realism. If any mental state can be re-written, without loss, as a series of if-then statements, then the mind itself can be defined as constituting a literary – or at least a textual – object. For the behaviourist the mind doesn't consist of a set of nebulous, unshareable qualities or phenomena, but is instead an encodable series of potential behaviours. It becomes possible to copy and reproduce the mind as one would a spool of machine-code. Under the auspices of logical behaviourism the novel can be read not as psychologically accurate description of an imaginary inner life, but as a kind of cognitive instruction manual. If, as behaviourism would have it, all that can ever be known about a person is their outward behaviour, then the novel represents as good a record of that behaviour as any record can be. On this reading notions of literary style become irrelevant: according to the workings of the narratives of reduction, the information contained within a novel can be re-written in any number of ways without any real loss.

The implications of behaviourism – that we are affectless beings stuck in a mechanical world of pre-determined causality, and that our minds can be contained in their entirety within language – are therefore stark. Yet they also pull in productive ways against the psychologised claims of affective veracity made on behalf of modernism by many proponents of the inward turn and cognitive realism. If behaviourism is true, then it might be that the most efficient and straightforward way of conveying mental states to readers would not be to write novels about minds at all: it would be to transcribe them into the machine-code of logical behaviourism. Indeed, as we have seen, this is precisely what much modernist literature often conceived of itself as doing: reducing literary characters to a series of painstakingly recorded behavioural tics.

In this chapter I will show how these ideas manifest themselves in the work of Wyndham Lewis, an author violently opposed to what Jessica Burstein terms the psychologised 'hot modernisms' of interiority associated with the work of Virginia Woolf, Dorothy Richardson, James Joyce and Gertrude Stein, and yet an author committed, despite his frequent protestations to the contrary, to a recognisably behaviourist aesthetic, one which ultimately denies the very existence of qualia.[2] In this reading the modernist novel, like the subjects it hoped to describe, becomes reconfigured as a Turing machine, and the job of the reader becomes that of a participant in Turing's imitation game. Lewis's interest in the dynamic kinaesthetic of silent film in the 1920s provided one model for the exteriorising, expressionist narrative that so dominates his early novels. Yet his interest in behaviour was not merely aesthetic: it was technical and philosophical also.

As a novelist who engaged provocatively and in a sustained fashion with contemporary philosophical debates over the nature of consciousness, Lewis was well placed to recognise the profoundly anti-humanist paradox that lies at the heart of the idea of behaviourist narrative. 'That *Behaviourism* has its effects upon popular thought', he wrote in the second issue of his magazine the *Enemy*, 'or at least upon the fictionist, who is the middleman conveying philosophic notions to the minds of people not accessible to ideas in anything but a sensuous and immediate form, of that there is plenty of evidence.'[3] If Woolf had 'consumed' the philosophical arguments of Cambridge philosophy within her novels, and Joyce and Stein had applied what Lewis viewed as a misplaced Bergsonionism to the writing of fiction, for him the dominant mode of most post-war narrative prose was, loosely defined, behaviourist.

Yet, as many critics have noted, Lewis's portrayal of his characters as little more than puppets, automata, or moving lumps of matter stood at odds with his often virulent attacks on the burgeoning psychological theories of behaviourism in his non-fictional writing from the 1920s. Hugh Kenner notes that in *Time and Western Man* Lewis 'argued that the behaviourist, in reducing the person to a set of predictable gestures, was insulting the human race. In the same year [he] was producing a body of fiction on the premise that people were nothing else.'[4] Paul Scott Stanfield has extended Kenner's argument, writing, of Lewis's novel *Snooty Baronet,* that 'behaviorism is for Lewis no ordinary antagonist. [. . .] it is one from which he cannot extricate himself.'[5]

For Stanfield, the contradictions in Lewis's relationship with behaviourism can be explained by accepting that Lewis believed that while the tenets of behaviourism did accurately describe the minds of most people, certain individuals – in particular artists, geniuses and totalitarian dictators – *were* possessed of an interiority that undermined the blanket application of behaviourist doctrine. In his political reading of Lewis's aesthetic Stanfield argues that for Lewis it was only a few visionaries – those who avoided the 'aping' mimicry of the herd – who were possessed of actual interior lives: of qualia. *Hoi poloi* could be comfortably dismissed as automata, as mechanistic reactants without any consciousness to speak of, and it is these people (if, indeed, we can call them that) who are generally described in Lewis's novels in a behaviourist mode. For this reason, Stanfield concludes, the fact that Lewis attacked behaviorism while writing novels stuffed full of puppets and automata is 'not really a contradiction, for he believed that almost all people were exactly as behaviorism described them. Behaviorism, however, allowed for no exceptions, and for Lewis it was precisely on the exceptions that all depended.'[6]

Certainly it is true that the principal characters of Lewis's novels (the 'idiot-mute' Dan Boleyn of *The Apes of God*; the one-dimensional agents of *Tarr*) are largely devoid of interiority, indeed of any explicitly written consciousness, at least of a kind associated with modernism's turn inward. Similarly, those 'aping' the views of Pierpoint (a sort of Lewis manqué) in *The Apes of God*, who 'broadcast' his ideas second-hand, as actors might, are allowed to do so only because their source is always kept off-stage. But such characterisations may say more about Lewis's views of literature than they do about his views of politics. There is undoubtedly a political element to Lewis's views on consciousness. Denying interiority to people in general makes it easy to justify their inhuman treatment. But in taking this contradiction at face value Stanfield might have downplayed the philosophical complexity of Lewis's position, reducing his sophisticated epistemological theses to play second fiddle to an ideologically informed model of human consciousness. One reason that Lewis's work is now so neglected is that it challenges the neo-humanist assumptions that underpin so much contemporary literary analysis. Aesthetically, as well as politically, his work is still, as Fredric Jameson has noted, shocking in its modernity: his novels sometimes feel like fossilised pieces of avant-garde experimentalism that have largely resisted incorporation into the modernist canon.[7]

In this chapter I will suggest that these apparent contradictions in Lewis's thinking can be best understood with reference to the qualia debate and the limits of literary fiction as a record of consciousness. Throughout his career Lewis drew attention to the fact that fictional 'character' is always and inevitably composed of nothing more than behavioural report inscribed on the page. If qualia exist then novels can only *ever* present us with a composite of gestural and behavioural – and therefore ontologically objective rather than subjective – characteristics of capacities. Yet at the same time Lewis recognised more thoroughly than perhaps any of his contemporaries that the problem of other minds manifests itself only in relation to real people. The narrated mind – even if that narration makes overtures to some kind of interiority – consists of nothing more than a compendium of described behaviours. Paradoxically, a reductively materialist doctrine like behaviourism provides a strong philosophical foundation for some of the claims made on behalf of the novel by many of the literary critics who endorse neuroaesthetic or cognitive realist theories of literature. Logical behaviourism is anathema to such theories as it seems distressingly reductive, providing a singularly impoverished view of the 'human machine'. And yet at the same time behaviorism offers a theoretical justification precisely *for* the kinds of extravagant claims of phenomenological verisimilitude made by many of these critics on behalf of the literary monuments of high modernism.

The founding father of behaviourism, and one of Wyndham Lewis's great enemies, was the American psychologist J. B. Watson. Watson defined behaviourism as the thesis that:

> the most fruitful starting point for psychology is the study not of our own self but of our neighbour's behavior – in other words it assumes that the student should take the view that the most interesting and helpful method is the study of what other human beings do and why they do it.[8]

The proper study of mankind, according to Watson, was not Man but Man's actions: 'consciousness' was chimerical and misleading, a shadowy proxy for the soul that should have been chased out of analyses of personhood by the advances of science. 'Behaviorism claims that consciousness is neither a definite nor a useable concept', wrote Watson elsewhere, the 'behaviorist, who has been trained always as an experimentalist, holds . . . that belief in the existence of consciousness goes back to the ancient days of superstition and magic.'[9] According to Watson, the only legitimate area of study for the psychologist was that of the individual as a corporate behavioural organism. The student of behaviourism, he went on, 'is not confronted with definitions of "consciousness," "sensation," or of "image," "perception" and the like', therefore, but only 'with definite concrete problems which he can solve by observing the behavior of others.'[10]

Following Watson, Lewis defined consciousness as a necessary but ultimately unsatisfactory (and philosophically dubious) property, one that we seem compelled to attribute to any entities displaying complex behaviours, but which in reality didn't describe very much at all. As he noted in *Time and Western Man*:

> 'Consciousness' is perhaps the best hated 'substance' of all: but there is a technical specialist reason for that. Consciousness is the most troublesome common-sense *fact* of any scientific analysis. The hardiest investigators

approach it with trepidation, and apologize beforehand for the poor show they are likely to put up in grappling with it.[11]

Get rid of consciousness, however, and you are forced to radically revise what you consider the human person to consist of. 'In order to fit in with the only explanation of it that science is able to provide', Lewis continued, 'the mechanist, behaviourist explanation – the actual standard of human consciousness and human ambition will have to be indefinitely lowered and debased.'[12]

Watson's behaviourism, which treated human beings as discrete behavioural units, understood consciousness to consist (if it existed at all) merely of a set of interlocking stimulus-responses or dispositions to behave that could be expressed in straightforward 'if–then' statements. As John Searle describes this radical position:

> According to typical behaviorist analysis, to say that Jones believes it is going to rain just means the same as saying an indefinite number of statements such as the following: if the windows of Jones's house are open, he will close them; if the garden tools are left outside, he will put them indoors; if he goes for a walk he will carry an umbrella or wear a raincoat or both and so forth. The idea was that having a mental state was just being disposed to certain sorts of behavior and the notion of a disposition was to be analyzed in terms of hypothetical statements, statements of the form 'If p then q.'[13]

According to Searle, behaviourism thus denies what has been termed 'intentionality': the idea that mental states consist of more than mere syntax; that the mind does more than shuffle symbols around. Intentionality, as defined by Franz Brentano, is the idea that a mental state must always be *about* something. This creates a problem for theories of consciousness analogous to that which are posed by the problem of qualia. A machine can potentially be semantically and behaviourally perfect and yet be totally ignorant of the 'aboutness' of the symbols it shuffles. Yet under behaviourism's watchful eye, beliefs, desires, feelings and emotions could all be reduced without loss to symbolic equations, and could therefore be studied and conveyed to other minds in their entirety. With no underlying ineffable mental states to account for – no qualia – the behaviourist was freed from the apparent conundrums of dualist metaphysics to engage directly with the mind stripped of the trappings of superstition, or of psychoanalytical and phenomenological analysis (which, for Lewis, often amounted to the same thing).

Lewis's fiction is full of representations of the philosophical peculiarities of the behaviourist thesis. During an early scene in *Snooty Baronet*, the protagonist Sir Michael Kell-Imrie, a committed behaviourist (and himself a man-machine: a war wound means that he wears a silver plate in his head, and he has a wooden leg and a generally treacherous body) looks into the window of a hatter's shop and sees an automated advertising dummy. A crowd has gathered outside the window, leading Kell-Imrie to speculate about the difference between people and automata: 'it is absurd to say these things (if you insist upon calling them *things*) have no character. Those that are made to-day are, like characters in books, often much more real than live people.'[14]

Kell-Imrie then works himself into a salvo of philosophical speculation. 'The puppet looked like a man', he recalls, 'and that word *looked*, that was for me everything.'[15] Like Turing after him, Kell-Imrie here suggests that if an entity behaves enough to look as though it is conscious, its interiority cannot be denied, or, perhaps, that the denial of interiority becomes irrelevant. 'It was impossible as one watched him not to feel that he was in some real sense *alive*', he reports, at 'certain moments of course the imperfections of the apparatus would betray him. But is this not the case, for the matter of that, with the best of us?'[16]

The ability to tell the difference between a being actually possessed of consciousness and a machine that only behaves as though it is conscious is something that has come to dominate philosophical discussions over the possibilities of creating 'strong AI': artificial intelligence that encompasses all the properties of the human mind. As such Kell-Imrie's speculations have a bearing on the problem of qualia as manifested in behaviourist analyses and contemporary solutions to David Chalmers' 'hard problem' of consciousness. As we saw in Chapter 5, during the early to mid-twentieth century the mind was placed under intense scrutiny and came to have an almost symbiotic metaphorical relationship with technologies which threatened to better, and thus replace, its mnemonic capabilities. During the late nineteenth and early twentieth centuries people began to be conceived of as machines, and sensations as information. By 1950 the philosopher A. J. Ayer was able confidently to claim:

> The only ground I can have for asserting that an object which appears to be conscious is not really a conscious being, but only a dummy or a machine, is that it fails to satisfy one of the empirical tests by which the presence or absence of consciousness is determined.[17]

The camera (both as visual technology and as room) provided one compelling model for the kind of automatism that emerged directly from the internalisation of technological modes of seeing during the modernist moment. The black-box nature of the camera, doomed to wield its powers in the dark – indeed, failing to function at all if one tried to see precisely what is going on inside it – became a popular metaphor for consciousness-free cognition of the kind envisaged by Kell-Imrie. Jacob in his room, Mary in hers, Watt, Molloy and Murphy in their skullscapes: modernist fiction is full of representations of these technologically mediated Cartesian theatres. Before the mid-twentieth century, however, the technologies invoked to describe these theatres were mechanical. Thus in *The Monadology* Leibniz proposed his famous 'perceptual mill' thought experiment, asking us to imagine walking around inside a perceptual machine constructed according to mechanical principles. What we would experience were we to do so, he suggested, would not allow us in any way to discern how the phenomenon of perception worked.[18] Knowledge of the interiority of such a perceptual system would, argued Leibniz, get you no closer to understanding how perception itself worked, or what it consisted of: all you would be able to discern were you to enter such a mill would be mindless mechanical movements.

As John Searle has argued in updating Leibniz's argument, to identify the outward behaviour of a system as identical with the underlying principles which govern that system is to ignore the very thing that qualiaphile philosophers – and many proponents of the novel as a cognitive realist form – assert. In Searle's famous 'Chinese Room' thought experiment, outlined in his 1980 paper 'Minds, Brains and Programs', we are asked to imagine a human agent who speaks only English ensconced in a room and forced to perform a symbol-shuffling routine.[19] Chinese characters are passed into the room, and the agent must read through a list of instructions (written in English) before responding with appropriate replies. The whole system functions as a mechanical computer, but one with a conscious homunculus rather than an abstract symbol shuffling routine at its centre. Can we legitimately say, asks Searle, that in this instance either the person in the room or the system of which he is a part can 'understand' Chinese, no matter how coherent the responses seem to be? If 'the man in the room does not understand Chinese on the basis of implementing the appropriate program for understanding Chinese', argues Searle, 'then neither does any other digital computer solely on that basis because no computer, qua computer, has anything the man does not have.'[20]

Searle's thought experiment was a response to Alan Turing's famous question, asked in his 1950 paper 'Computing Machinery and Intelligence', 'can machines think?' Since 'thinking' proved so difficult to define, Turing had reframed the question, replacing it with another definition of consciousness 'which is closely related to it and is expressed in relatively unambiguous words ... Are there imaginable digital computers which would do well in the *imitation game*?'[21] The 'imitation game' was designed to test a computer's ability to fool a human interlocutor into thinking they were conversing with another human of the opposite gender. If the human judge couldn't tell apart her human and machine interlocutors then, argued Turing, the machine should be considered conscious. With the imitation game Turing asserted that all that can ever be tested of consciousness is its behavioural properties, and in doing so he consolidated a model of human cognition as behaviour that had been proposed by Watson and the behaviourists.

Yet according to Searle, those who claim that machines can have minds, and who hold that such thought could be tested in the way Turing suggested, commit a serious error. Despite a proficiency in Chinese, it would make no sense to speak of such a room as 'knowing' Chinese, just as it would make no sense to ascribe mental states to an interlocutor during the Turing test. Even if a machine *could* fool you into thinking you were having a conversation with another person, such a system offers no guarantee that what was being displayed amounted to consciousness. Such a system can be conceived as functioning in a way identical to a human agent but lacking in qualia, leading to the logical possibility of the 'philosophical zombie': an imagined creature behaviourally identical in every way to its human equivalent (including in its neurological processes), yet devoid of any interiority whatsoever.[22]

Many of these anxieties were prefigured in Lewis's fiction, and in his critical engagements with the work of Joyce and Woolf. His non-fictional writing was aligned with an epistemological project which sought to draw out the ethical implications of the qualitative emptiness of modernism's hollow men: affectless beings isolated from one another, and from the mob. His fiction dramatised these debates, exploring what a world structured around rooms, closed systems, and philosophical zombies would mean for those few who were in possession of consciousness. In *The Childermass*, for instance, Lewis explicitly asks Turing's question. When the two protagonists Satters and Pullman encounter one of the 'peons' who populate the desolate limbo of the novel they exist within directly, they can't decide whether they've encountered a living mind – that of their old friend Marcus – or the mere simulacra of a person:

> 'No really you must be wrong. It was Marcus right enough.'
> 'To all appearance!'
> 'But I know Marcus as well as I know you! If that wasn't Marcus –
> Pullman is sneering under his hat.
> 'That may be. Better, perhaps. But what is Marcus?'[23]

Knowing someone's behaviour doesn't seem to provide a guarantee that they are consciously present when you observe that behaviour, or, indeed, that they are that 'person' at all. Action, speech and gesture are not, suggests Satters here, necessarily identical with personhood. But it is all that we have access too. Such views align many of Lewis's protagonists with a behaviourist conception of consciousness. As Kell-Imrie declares in *Snooty Baronet*:

> I behave as a *Behaviorist* and as such I claim I should be accepted, and if there is nothing else that I can do to prove it, I will at least continue to behave as you have seen me behaving throughout these pages, and as all true behaviorists *must* behave.[24]

Behaviourism, clearly, is a broad church, with an often confused critical inheritance. The central question any theory of consciousness must answer – is there any difference between a person and something that behaves *exactly* like a person? – is, as Lewis realised, rather more complicated than it has often been interpreted in relation to fiction. 'Are we very different?' Satters goes on to ask of Marcus in *The Childermass*, 'I believe we only think we're so different.'[25]

Behaviourism's stark reductive analysis of the human organism had severe limitations, as Watson himself acknowledged. As well as intentionality, another of the properties of the mind it was difficult to reconcile with this model of consciousness was language. For Watson, according to Lewis, man was an 'animal, in every respect on the same footing as a rat or an antelope . . . except for what the Behaviourist terms his word-habit . . . man is *that* and no more.'[26] As Watson argued, behaviourist doctrine held that:

> being 'conscious' is merely a popular or literary phrase descriptive of the act of naming our universe of objects both inside and outside, and that 'introspecting' is a much narrower popular phrase descriptive of the more awkward act of naming tissue changes that are taking place i.e., movements of muscles, tendons, glandular secretions, respiration, circulation and the like. They must be looked on solely as literary forms of expression.[27]

Here the act of Jamesian introspection is redefined as solely a linguistic act, an act of discovering and giving voice to bodily actions, and by doing so allowing those actions to take their place in the pantheon of consciousness as conveyed through public language.

Yet, as Lewis realised, the 'word-habit' that Watson slips into his definition of the human as essentially identical to any other animal caused significant problems for behaviourist analyses of consciousness. For Watson, language, and thought, was itself a kind of 'implicit' behaviour: though it was unobservable, it nevertheless functioned to modify the bodily tissues and dispositions to behave which were, according to the logical behaviourists, all that consciousness consisted of. 'Word-habits make up the bulk of the *implicit* forms of behavior', argued Watson, in a passage seized upon by Lewis as evidence of the absurdities of behaviourism:

> Now it is admitted by all of us that words spoken or faintly articulated belong really in the realm of behavior, as do movements of the arms and legs. If implicit behavior can be shown to consist of nothing but word movements (or expressive movements of the word-type) the behavior of the human being as a whole is as open to objective control as the behavior of the lowest organism.[28]

Watson anticipated some obvious criticisms of his definition of consciousness as simply another manifestation of behaviour. 'How can you explain "thought" in behaviorist terms?' he asked rhetorically in a debate over the status of behaviorism with William McDougal. '[T]o do so requires considerable time.'[29] And not just time. To conceive of thought in behaviourist terms forced Watson into all sorts of conceptual contortions as he tried to square the state of contemporary neuroscientific knowledge with his rather holistic thesis of cognitive physiology. For instead of defining the firing of nerve fibres as instances of 'behaviour' (the solution proposed by many contemporary type-identity theorists), and thus allowing a 'thought' to be interpreted in relation to localised brain function, Watson preferred to define thinking as a form of unvocalised speech: 'thinking is merely talking but talking with concealed musculature ... We thus think and plan with the whole body.'[30] On this account 'thinking' is essentially linguistic or literary, and so thoughts are potentially as publicly accessible as hand gestures, facial expressions, and written language. Watson's doctrine of thought as unvocalised speech was widely mocked. 'Any doctrine identifying Thought with *muscular* movement', responded I. A. Richards in *The Philosophy of Rhetoric,* 'is a self-refutation of the observationalism that prompts it – heroic and fatal.'[31] But it was nonetheless influential, and it promised an intriguing solution to many of the problems posed by qualia.

Whatever the particular difficulties faced by behaviourist accounts of language, or of definitions of consciousness as merely the movements of the larynx and associated musculature, behaviourism quickly gained a foothold as a dominant theory and methodology within the psychological sciences. And yet the deeply misanthropic implications of Watson's doctrine continued to trouble psychology and culture more generally. For to play the Turing game on so large a scale as this, as Hugh Kenner observed in *The Counterfeiters,* was not only to make of society at large a mass of unconscious automata: it was to mechanise the perceiving subject herself. 'Turing's question had been asked, at least in principle, long before 1950', writes Kenner:

> But consider what actually happens when you elect to examine the nature of man while situating yourself outside of that nature: you yourself elect not to be human. You decide that what you know about yourself is best neglected. You are going to be an observer of man, and a recorder of facts about man, but you are not going to be a man, for fear of corrupting your observations with what you know already.[32]

Inside the Chinese room, under the auspices of behaviourism, both observer and observed are transformed into empty-headed machines engaged in a never-ending imitation game. It was this understanding of consciousness which became both a threat and an inspiration for modernist literature.

Cinema and the Aesthetics of Automatism

One needn't look far to see the effects of these doctrines on literature of the period. Near the beginning of John Rodker's *Adolphe 1920*, the narrator, Dick, walks through the crowd at a fair. A vague composite of Leopold Bloom and Septimus Warren Smith, Dick possesses a disturbed consciousness intent solely on registering the world of sensation in which he finds himself. He drifts through the crowd, passively cataloguing the smells and sights that modernity scores upon his consciousness. It's a wonderfully dense, and in some ways archetypal, evocation of the modern city as sensory *Gesamtkunstwerk*:

> The street was filling on all sides in a shuffling of feet, and from the booths like a twittering of birds rose the first timid cries of morning. And a sickly sweet smell of vanilla rose, cloying all the wet air, till some more violent blast from a passing woman washed it again. The road now lay between two rows of booths, where at intervals, stoves were frying potatoes in a sweet acrid smell of oil. All that like a crystal had grown about him since he awoke, and now part of it, drifting, he moved to and fro, half seeing but aware; his mind tall standards holding milky globes, a reverberation of deliberate feet on boards, faces drifting and featureless, pale in light, a sighing of sea, black close but unseen.[33]

Dick is both of the world and set apart from it: a component part of a social whole who is able to reflect on the smells and sights he experiences only through the prism of a mineral barrier that grows 'like a crystal' around him. The world remains resolutely outside, 'close but unseen'.

After some more solipsistic wondering Dick approaches one of the objects standing mutely around him at the fair, a 'man-eating one-leg' standing 'sombre, with dark square eyes staring from its breast'.[34] He walks up to what turns out to be a mutoscope machine and inserts a penny. It comes alive:

> A warm light moistened its eyes, lit up its chest. He put his eyes on its eyes, his heart on its heart, listening deeply, anxiously; forgetting his fair, his fellows reading other hearts around him . . . Where its heart was, a woman rose from a chair, smiled, patted her elaborate hair, unhooked a shoulder-of-mutton blouse, a petticoat or two, stood self-consciously for a minute in lace-edged draws, laced boots and black stockings, smiling a timid 1890 smile. She too in that darkness, from which for a moment he had called her. A coin brought her back: as though gratefully she shyly reappeared, went through all her senseless gestures, smiled and smiled. And darkness again, heavy, inevitable. That room, that sofa, filled his brain with warm shapes and comforting light, and the woman moved amicably through it.[35]

Dick's desperate need to connect leads him to further neglect the world of 'fellows reading other hearts' around him, all of who are engaged in their own onanistic attempts to commune with the world of machines. His brain, itself presented as an enclosed space – a Chinese room or Cartesian theatre – is filled with the image of another room, through which the ghost of a woman moves.

In this scene, written in the late 1920s, Rodker describes a visual technology which was by then already outdated. The mutoscope was a popular device at the late nineteenth-century fairground, generally used to show titillating stripshows. As Leopold Bloom muses in 'Nausicaa': 'mutoscope pictures in Capel Street: for men only. Peeping Tom. Willy's hat and what the girls did with it. Do they snapshot those girls or is it all fake? *Lingerie* does it.'[36] Dick's encounter in *Adolphe 1920* is therefore self-consciously historically mediated: the performer smiles 'a timid 1890 smile', and takes off her numberless layers of clothing against a backdrop of stuffy Victorian domesticity. Compared to Dick's consciousness, which registers every sensory bombardment the city can throw at it, her movements are literally 'senseless', both within the fictional world – as a staged scene within a novel – and in their rehearsal of a set of empty, ghost-like and strictly performative gestures.

As David Trotter has argued, mutoscopes were an important transitional technology in the development of literature's relationship with visual culture in the early twentieth century. Defiantly mechanical, they operated on the principles of the flip-book, and yet gave the first glimpses of the potential for the moving image to transcend the linear flicker of Zoetropism. 'Prufrock's visual technology of choice had been the magic lantern, a staple of Victorian home entertainment', writes Trotter in *Cinema and Modernism*; 'Tiresias's [in *The Waste Land*] is the mutoscope.'[37] It is therefore not difficult to see why Rodker invoked the mutoscope – colloquially known as the 'What the Butler Saw' machine – as a symbol of Dick's profound social and epistemological alienation. Mutoscopes explicitly position a solitary viewer in relation to an imagined scene. Unlike the cinema, they are viewed in private and therefore lend themselves to presentation of the illicit. And, as this extract suggests, they place great stress on focalisation: on implied and internalised (narrated) perspectives. For your penny you are allowed to *become* a voyeur: able to inhabit an imaginary point of view and see precisely what it was that the butler himself saw. The question of who is watching that is raised as soon as the cinema begins to develop its own more sophisticated narrative strategies is fudged in the case of the mutoscope, as the viewer is offered a narratological get-out-clause by being able to imagine herself watching the scene through a window or keyhole. It's a striking metaphor for fiction, especially for fiction which, like Rodker's, engages provocatively with questions of narrative perspective. Just as with reading, viewing a mutoscope forces you to construct an imagined relationship to that which is seen, producing (admittedly often flimsy) narratives about this positioning that justify the equally flimsy narrative set-up.

In his Trieste notebook James Joyce noted that the cinema was particularly suited to pornographic representation as it was able to stimulate the body directly through the sense organs.[38] The non-verbal languages which are constantly suggested and interrogated in *Ulysses* – the rituals of the Catholic Church, the symbolic richness of odours, the frequent references to Masonic lore – also suggest what Lynch identifies as Stephen Dedalus's 'Pornosophical philotheology', according to which 'gesture, not music not odours, would be a universal language'.[39] In *Adolphe 1920* Dick's experience of the mutoscope offers him a private glimpse into another world, one that is mirrored in the act of reading itself, but one that is also phenomenologically opposed to that very act, becoming instead a nightmarish, ghostly invocation of the *behaviour* of sex, with none of the accompanying qualia. The mutoscope retains the meaning of sex but fails to contain its phenomenal experience:

> Immutably the anthropophagi stood among them, a woman for a heart, tight round their secret lure for which no pain disease damnation were too much to pay. A woman walks into a room, she is alone and smiles, she seems a little mad; wears drawers and black boots, in 1890, and to the watcher all is miraculous. But his starting eyes touch glass. And behind, near, inferior, the talkers, singers; pensive, whispering if questioned. And on all sides large man-high voices blaring a full orchestra. Through the wild gaiety of the severe machines, men moved distracted, their fun dark chambers, chutes, distorted visions, the agonies of nightmare.[40]

Thus, despite the archaism of the mutoscope, in *Adolphe 1920* Rodker described a relationship with technology that was strikingly modern. Alienation is the dominant note: men are 'distracted' by the 'fun dark chambers' of the mutoscope, unable or unwilling to engage with each other as persons, instead preferring to spend their time with the 'severe machines'. The notion that people were themselves machines, and that they should be treated as such for experimental purposes, was, as I have argued, a dominant one in the period, but it must be noted that this was a conceit not unique to modernism. Man-like machines, mechanical automata, have for a long time exercised the philosophical imagination.[41] Nevertheless, technological progress provided modernism with a model of cognition that seemed to transcend the merely mechanical, or imitative. As Jessica Riskin has argued, early automata generally made no attempt to simulate perception, or the higher physiological faculties, instead operating by a process of analogy with the human.[42] The famous mechanised automata of the eighteenth and nineteenth centuries – Jacques de Vaucanson's 'Canard Digérateur [Digesting Duck]' and Wolfgang von Kempelen's 'Mechanical Turk' – were strictly conceived of as *performers*:

expressionist rather than impressionist in mode (and were ultimately proved to be hoaxes). Conversely, the mnemonic technologies associated with modernity made no attempt to replicate the outward *look* of the human organs they were models of (apart, arguably, from the telephone, imitative as it was of the principles of the tympanum, and that only internally), instead providing functional analogies of various sensory aspects of cognition: the camera saw; the telephone heard.

As such, and by virtue of their mysterious complexity, modernist machines re-vivified the debate over the possibilities of creating a mechanical form of consciousness. As machines reached a certain level of complexity they seemed to have the potential to contain within their dark and mysterious folds other properties, properties more generally associated with human consciousness. Thomas Edison called the brain 'a queer and wonderful machine', comparable in its operations to a phonographic cylinder.[43] 'The air is filled with strangely human birds', wrote Guillame Apollinaire in 1910 'machines, the daughters of man and having no mother, live a life from which passion and feeling are absent.'[44] The seeming feelinglessness of mechanised modernity provided an alternative and profoundly anti-sentimental model for cognition, a model seized upon by (among others) Futurists, Vorticists and, in psychology, behaviourists.

What technologies like the mutoscope, the telephone and gramophone therefore provided, as David Trotter argues in *Cinema and Modernism*, was a model of passive mechanical sensation that was quickly subsumed within literature. The literally senseless way in which the camera records a scene, or the mutoscope performer behaves, began to be reflected in fiction that endorsed notions of what Trotter terms modernism's 'will-to-automatism'.[45] Emerging visual technologies, and the 'reproducible neutrality' of film as a medium, led some writers to represent what Trotter calls the 'disembodiment of perception by technique'.[46] Much modernist literary fiction constituted a 'wilful inquiry into the age's wilful absorption in the kinds of automatic behaviour exemplified by machinery in general, and by the new technologies of perception in particular', he concludes.[47] The cinematic gaze thus brought about, as early neurology had before it, a tendency to conceive of visual processes as separate from and independent of a central processing consciousness.

Like Trotter, Sara Danius sees in the cinematograph the genesis of this self-sufficient vision. 'Early cinema', she says,

> was a medium of cultural production whose capacity for analogically reproducing the real as it moved through time stood in sharp contrast to its other tendency: the compartmentalization of the ways in which the five senses experience and process the real.[48]

Yet as we have seen the notion of 'the real' is particularly treacherous in relation to descriptions of mental processes. As Raymond Tallis notes in *In Defence of Realism*, the argument that cinema posed a threat to the realist paradigm in the way Danius describes here is not at all straightforward. As Tallis argues, to identify the 'reality' of a thing with an indexed visual image of the exterior of that thing is to vastly underestimate the project that 'realist' authors often felt themselves to be engaged in:

> if the role of words in a novel were the same as that of the camera in film – namely to replicate the visible surfaces of parts of the world – then there could be no doubt that cine-photography, which copies visible surfaces with effortless precision and the instantaneous inclusiveness of the eye, would be indisputably superior to the pen as an instrument for achieving the aims of realist fiction. The cameraman is better at reduplicating surfaces than the writer.[49]

The point is, Tallis concludes, that 'even realistic fiction does not attempt to *represent* reality. Words are not representational signs: they are expressive, not mimetic.'[50]

Many early commentators were similarly struck by film's limitations in replicating the 'real', noting that cinema was a spectre haunting the contemporary sensorium rather than an immersive and effortless stimulant *of* it. Maxim Gorky identified what, to borrow Jacques Derrida's term, we might call the 'hauntological' capacities of cinema. It 'is not life but its shadow', he wrote, 'it is not motion but its soundless spectre'.[51] Despite Virginia Woolf's suggestion that 'the pictures' presented things that felt 'more real, or real with a different reality from that which we perceive in daily life', for her that reality was fundamentally misleading for the cinematographic 'horse will not knock us down. The King will not grasp our hands. The wave will not wet our feet.'[52]

Wyndham Lewis and Cinema

Lewis, more than many of his contemporaries, incorporated the aesthetic and epistemological lessons learned from cinema into his work in order to test categories of the real. In his novels, metaphors provided by the new mnemonic technologies are used to present a radical vision of what fiction might be capable of were behaviourism true and qualia didn't exist. His fiction was among the earliest to be informed and conditioned by the burgeoning cinematic aesthetic that influenced the work of so many modernist authors subsequently. As Alan Munton notes, 'Lewis was alert to the cultural significance of cinema and the new media as soon as they became established commercially during the first decade of the twentieth century.'[53] And he used this awareness of the cultural significance of cinema to often radical ends.

Lewis frequently described his characters using the tropes of the cinema, which were, especially in the era of silent film, themselves clichés: exaggerations of gesture, movement and behaviour. Thus in his first novel, *Mrs. Dukes' Million*, Lewis described a chase by comparing it with a cinematic scene in an instance which Munton claims is the earliest explicit literary reference to cinematic action:

> This mad pursuit was like one of the cinematograph pictures that are seen in sixpenny 'Electric Palaces.' And it occurred to him at the same time that if he were stopped or caught he might pretend that this was what was really happening, that he was taking part in a cinematograph 'picture.'[54]

Here a chase scene (which has itself become a cliché of cinema) becomes its own justification or cover: the art of the cinema is both consumed and commented on from within the confines of the novel.

Like the cinema, Lewis quickly grasped that the train and the car were primarily, as Sara Danius characterises them, 'technologies of perception', and had much in common with the cinematograph in terms of their visual function. In his short story 'The Crowd Master', for instance, Lewis described a train journey from Dover to London in which the window of the train is reinterpreted as a cinema screen, with the world a magic lantern throwing scenes and vistas onto it: 'Blenner, still smiling, looked out of the window. There the landscapes were sliding, like a White City by-show worked by a strong dynamo. Sometimes things licked out of view with stoical violence near the windows.'[55]

In *The Revenge for Love*, a similar thing happens as a pair of young revolutionaries attempt to escape the Spanish police by car:

> trees, rocks, and telegraph-poles stood up dizzily before her and crashed down behind. They were held up singly in front of her astonished eyes, then snatched savagely out of the picture. Like a card-world clocked cinematographically through its static permutations by the ill-bred fingers of a powerful conjurer, everything stood upon end and then fell flat.[56]

Here the world becomes mutoscopically presented to the senses in a flicker: a static landscape taking life. 'The motorists experience a visual event whose delightful nature is a function of speed', writes Sara Danius of Proust's essay 'Impressions de route en Automobile', the 'windshields delimit the view of the landscape, transforming it into an object of visual pleasure – a mobile panorama.'[57] As Danius notes, the visual effect of driving depends on the animation of inanimate matter, on the fact that things that should not move (the outside world; trees and telegraph poles) seem to be moving in relation to the car, rather than vice versa. With such descriptions 'the narrator insists on what his eyes perceive and not on what he knows, all in an effort to render the lived experience of speed and the delicious perception of the landscape through which the car races.'⁵⁸ Proust's essay therefore 'addresses a representational problem', argues Danius: 'how to render the lived experience of speed and movement.'⁵⁹ As in Proust, so in Lewis: these are profoundly and artificially cinematic scenes themselves, and they indebted both to the tropes and to the visual architecture of film.

The cinematic gaze, modifying the landscape on which it was cast, was only one way in which film manifested its influence in Lewis's work. Just as the cinema screen made landscape and movement legible in a way previously occluded, so too did the silent film of the twenties enshrine behaviour at the heart of its representative system. 'Kinesis was the rhetoric of [the 1920s]', argues Hugh Kenner in *The Counterfeiters*:

> when Americans did with pure motion what the English did about 1600 with language, and the French about 1880 with color. For those few years, before American eyes, the Newtonian universe flowered like a languid rose, disclosing, before its petals dropped away, all its intricate repertory of action, reaction, equilibrium. Man and machine, in that enchanted truce, meet nearly as equals ... The collaboration between audience and kinetic mime was nearly ideal. No one had trouble understating how the snagged log with Buster clinging to its end could pivot up like a mast and then out over the waterfall's lip like a bowsprit; nor why, swinging down from its end on a rope to rescue the girl, he launched himself not toward her but away from her; nor by what conversion of potential energy he is carried up, having snatched her from her ledge, exactly to that handy shelf of rock.⁶⁰

In Lewis's novels the kinaesthetic and the behaviourist impulses fuse to create a vision of the person as no more (but also no less) than a compendium of behaviours. Alongside behaviourism, Lewis's other great interests, topics he returned to frequently in his non-fiction essays throughout the 1920s, were Charlie Chaplin and German Expressionist cinema. 'Chaplin is probably the greatest figure on the stage today', he wrote in 1924. ⁶¹ The tramp was for Lewis a figure of both admiration and disdain. He frequently used 'Chaplinesque' as a term of abuse. Of Proust he wrote 'the "I" of his books is that small, naïf, Charlie Chaplin-like, luxuriously indulged, sharp-witted, passionately snobbish, figure'.⁶² But as David Trotter has argued, Lewis was mainly interested in Chaplin's mimicry: his skilful behavioural impersonation which, taken to its extreme, seemed to celebrate the notion of imitation for imitation's sake in an act that Trotter calls 'hyper-mimesis'.⁶³ This fertile counterfeiting, which Lewis diagnosed everywhere he looked, was seen by him as pernicious, threatening to eradicate difference and leading to a behavioural tyranny of the majority.

One implication of behaviourism therefore, and of the behaviourist imperative enshrined in silent film, was that it allowed for the potential existence of a literally mindless class of person. Under the auspices of behaviourism the mass could be conceived of as sub- or unconscious, and then dismissed as belonging to a realm outside of ethical consideration. It is not so much of a step from Eliot's famous declaration in 'Tradition and the Individual Talent' that 'only those who have personality and emotions know what it means to want to escape from these things' to argue that there exists a class of people who lack not just 'emotions and personality', but any conscious mental states whatever.[64] Modernism's will-to-automatism has therefore been seen by many commentators as politically dubious. The distillation of all consciousness to a single property and the notion that the human person was nothing more than the sum of her behaviours, allowed for a stark binary debate over the status of personhood to emerge. These anxieties manifested themselves across all fields of literary production, from Karel Čapek's critique of mechanised man in *R.U.R*, to the aesthetics of exclusion that Andreas Huyssen has argued were so symptomatic of high modernism, to Charlie Chaplin's mockery of the mechanisation of production in *Modern Times*.

Thus Lewis's behaviourist aesthetic was intimately bound up with the political. In 'A Room Without a Telephone', for instance, a short story that appeared in the collection *Rotting Hill*, Lewis outlined a vision of nationalised healthcare which treated bodies as opposed to people, the doctor becoming a mere mechanic of the flesh. In this view the NHS is an example of a general 'Bolshevik tendency' which treats man 'as if he were a machine. When a machine wears out you push it on to the scrap-heap. When a man's body wears out there is still a man inside it.'[65] Lewis was fearful too of the loss of privacy that such a realignment of the relationship between doctor and patient might cause: under the auspices of behaviourism the inside of our heads, last bastion of the un-broadcasted action, was itself under attack. This was a typical move, according to Trotter, one that reaches back as far as John Stuart Mill's fear of the vanishing of difference in contemporary society.[66] But it manifested itself in particularly intriguing ways within modernist discourse. 'The politics and the sociology of Anglo-American modernism's anti-mimesis', Trotter argues, 'amounted to an anxiety about the wholesale suppression of differences.'[67]

Lewis's dismissal of the mob as mere automata was certainly reactionary, establishing a hierarchy of the mental which placed the majority of people on the bottom rung, blindly and mechanically acting and using language in plodding, clichéd and repetitive ways. But his dismissal of the mind of the mob was also heavily informed by and contained within the philosophical tradition, most notably by the Cartesian tradition of equating man with machine. As Lewis himself noted,

> Descartes called animals *machines*: they had not the rational spark. But men use their rational spark so unequally, and are so much machines too,

that, on the face of it, that generalisation is a very superficial one ... Many animals, indeed most, are more dignified, much freer, and more reasonable than men, in the conduct of their lives: and the 'language habit,' as the behaviourist calls it, is a servitude for those who are unable to use it, but have to be content to be used by it. It is not a thing to boast about that you *talk*, and the elephant does not. It depends on what you say.[68]

Similarly, Lewis's faith in the redemptive power of individual genius certainly had a political edge, and he frequently reduced movements to individuals, describing himself as a 'personal appearance artist', and arguing that 'Hitlerism is Hitler' and that Nazism 'is rather a person than a doctrine.'[69] In the catalogue to the 1956 retrospective of the Vorticist movement in the Tate he claimed that: 'Vorticism, in fact, was what I, personally, did, and said, at a certain period', much to his collaborators' consternation.[70] And he frequently stressed that to be an artist, or a dictator, was to be a *doer*, someone opposed to the unthinking rump, to the 'spectators' who made up the bulk of contemporary society:

> Art is not here defended for its own sake: *art-for-art's-sake,* of Walter Pater, is nothing to do with art – it is a spectator's doctrine, not an artist's: it teaches how to enjoy, not how to perform. I am a performer. It is as a performer that I shall speak.[71]

Thus for Lewis actions often spoke far louder than words, and the provocative sympathy he occasionally displayed to dictators was based on the fact that the 'society of today' was 'essentially an actor's world'.[72]

More than most arts, cinema embodied these ideals of individualism, performance and the celebration of action over thought. As a form, silent film is utterly dependent on gesture and movement: on the outward appearance of the body (often modified with heavy make-up and exotic costume) and on what Kenner calls the 'rhetoric of kinesis'. And, although there are certainly other precedents for modernism's interest in bodily action as an end in itself (one thinks, in particular, of W. B. Yeats's interest in dance, and of Ezra Pound's fascination with Japanese Noh plays), in its means of reproduction and dissemination the cinema was undoubtedly unique and distinctive to modernism.

Lewis's theory of laughter (derived in large part from the work of Henri Bergson), as outlined in *The Wild Body*, was likewise based on the distinction between animate and inanimate matter as dramatised by the cinema and conditioned by the commodification of action. Satire is an art of the outside and the Turing test, Hugh Kenner argues, is essentially satirical, in a Swiftian mode. It is not difficult to see how the physical comedy of Charlie Chaplin is based primarily on what Trotter calls 'hypermimesis' on the body as impersonator and mirror of other bodies; on behaviour as a shared cultural experience. Silent film for a brief period reduced the art of acting to that of gesture, and reduced the actor to an insensible lump of matter engaged in amusing actions and devoid of any suggestion of interiority. As Lewis summarised in his essay on 'The Meaning of the Wild Body':

> The root of the Comic is to be sought in the sensations resulting from the observations of a *thing* behaving like a person. But from that point of view all men are necessarily comic: for they are all *things*, or physical bodies, behaving like *persons*. It is only when you come to deny that they are 'persons,' or that there is any 'mind' or 'person' there at all, that the world of appearance is accepted as quite natural, and not at all ridiculous.[73]

In many of his novels, then, Lewis dramatises this tension between personhood and matter, describing his characters as dummies, machines, puppets, or automata. In *Revenge for Love*, a novel which obsesses over counterfeiting and falsity (the original title was to be *False Bottoms*, but Lewis was forced to change it after a reader from Boots circulating library objected) nearly all of the central characters are, at one point or another, presented as nothing more than vacuous shells. And frequently Lewis invoked images from the cinema as metaphors for this cognitive emptiness. At a gathering of artists and hangers-on in *Revenge for Love* a young confused groupie observes the crowd around her:

> They were not so much 'Human persons,' as she described it to herself, as big portentous wax-dolls, mysteriously doped with some impenetrable nonsense, out of a Caligari's drug-cabinet, and wound up with wicked fingers to jerk about in a threatening way – their mouths backfiring every other second, to spit out a manufactured hatred, as their eyeballs moved.[74]

The reference to Robert Wiene's 1922 film *The Cabinet of Dr Caligari* is particularly striking, contained as it is within a novel imbued with the expressionist aesthetic of that film. In Wiene's movie a travelling showman sets up his somnambulist sideshow at a country fair, after which a series of gruesome murders occur in the village. Suspicion falls on the showman-doctor, and so a villager takes it upon himself to keep watch over Caligari and his cabinet one night. When, sure enough, another murder is committed, the villager swears that the somnambulist has remained in his cabinet. Eventually it transpires that Dr Caligari keeps a dummy in his cabinet, sending his somnambulist slave to commit nocturnal murders for him. A doubled dummying has occurred: a doll acts as stand-in for an already unconscious human agent. At the end of the film it is revealed that Caligari is the head of a local lunatic asylum, and, in a final narrative twist, that the narrator is himself an inmate of that asylum.

Wiene's film is rightly celebrated for its narrative innovations and wonderful design. But it encompasses a broader preoccupation within German Expressionism, one that intersects with the essential philosophical underpinnings of Lewis's fiction. In *Time and Western Man* Lewis referred to Sigmund Freud as 'like a sort of Mephistophelian Dr. Caligari', and visually, Hermann Warm's angular set (with shadows and perspective painted directly onto the scenery) looks very much like some of Lewis's own paintings.[75] Wiene's film evokes Lewis's description of the limbo-landscape of his novel *The Childermass* also, a landscape described by Satters, the Joyce manqué trapped with his fag Pullman in the strange Beckettian skullscape of that novel as 'a flat daguerreotype or . . . a pre-war film.'[76]

Marshall McLuhan declared that with *The Childermass* 'Lewis used the medium of the talking picture before it had been invented', calling it 'a talkie in full colour.'[77] The world described in *The Childermass* is that of a mechanical hell inhabited by crowds of empty mechanical and sub-human 'peons'. Near the beginning of the novel Satters encounters one of these 'man sparrows' who 'multiplies precise movements, an organism which in place of speech has evolved a peripatetic system of response to a dead environment. It has wandered beside this Styx, a lost automaton rather than a lost soul.'[78] Throughout the novel Lewis reduces movement to its component parts in this way, in an anguished attempt to atomise gestures that again owes much to the exaggerated movement of silent film. *The Childermass* describes a world populated by creatures of senseless responses, reacting rather than acting, dwelling in a world of Potemkin villages and one-dimensional, sprite-like cut-outs. It was a type of world that, Lewis feared, was quickly eroding our conception of the real.

The cinematograph thus provided Lewis with an endlessly attractive model for a kind of qualia-free cognition of the kind that was formally instantiated with Turing's test, and was challenged by Searle's Chinese Room. Lewis's novels were engaged in a productive yet protean argument with the central tenets of behaviourism, a psychological system and philosophical position which placed the machine-mind – the automaton – at the centre of its analysis, and in doing so denied qualia. Lewis's 'puppets', like T. S. Eliot's hollow men, are examples of a more pronounced and general interest in the potential emptiness of bodies in the period, therefore. Mnemonic technologies such as the cinema provided the behaviourists with a compelling model for the qualia-free mind, raising the spectre of automata as near-total simulacra of human bodies, lacking only one essential quality: conscious mental states.

THE GREAT WITHOUT

As we have seen Lewis's overriding concern, as both artist and philosopher, was with exteriors. In both his fiction and in his painting he was preoccupied with surfaces: with the body as agent – an active component of the physical world – but also as barrier, with the skin as the interface between internal mental states and their public interpretation. James Joyce declared that 'modern man has an *epidermis* rather than a soul', invoking the skin as both a locus of sensation and as a publicly 'readable' organ, but unlike Joyce, whom he criticised for being overly concerned with the inner lives of his characters, Lewis's aesthetic was fundamentally of the epidermis.[79] 'Skin and Intestines', the title of one of the chapters of *The Art of Being Ruled*, described the counterintuitive dichotomy he saw as the essential difference between art and science: 'I have defined art as the science of the *outside* of things', he wrote, 'and natural science as the science of the *inside* of things.'[80] His paintings are celebrations of what he elsewhere called an 'orgy of the externals of this life of ours': stylised portraits of bodies in motion, or abstract scenes implying mechanistic movement.[81] Similarly, the typographic virtuosity of *Blast* celebrated the concrete dynamism of the written, drawing attention to the way words looked on the page as much as to the sense they contained.

But the surface of the body is more than the formal frontier of human consciousness: it is also the source of a generalised but specific sense-modality, that of touch. In his ongoing battles with Bloomsbury, Lewis frequently attempted to re-evaluate the primacy of the visual sense in contemporary philosophy and art. For Woolf *et al.* sight might have been the most privileged of the senses, synonymous with sensation in general, but for Lewis, concerned as he was with challenging the claims made on behalf of philosophers of what he called the 'time-school', touch was an ally. It was the 'enemy of the time-school' because 'the eye is . . . the *private* organ; the hand the *public* one.'[82] This was a claim that, though it remained implicit in much of Lewis's fiction, can be seen as informing his approach to the paradoxes of the relationship between mind, language and sensation throughout his work.

In his 1921 manifesto of tactilism, F. T. Marinetti had called for the development of a new art based on the sense of touch. Identifying the moment of his aesthetic awakening with an experience in the trenches during the First World War, he claimed that in the modern world:

> A Visual sense is born in the fingertips. X-ray vision develops, and some people can already see inside their bodies. Others dimly explore the inside of their neighbours' bodies. They all realize that sight, smell, hearing touch and taste are modifications of a single keen sense: touch, divided in different ways and localized in different points.[83]

For Marinetti, touch was not only the basis of all sensation, but potentially the source of novel and exciting new modes for art. He felt that the 'return' to tactility he had identified with modernity was intimately bound up with our consumption of visual and moving images. Following Marinetti, Marshall McLuhan, a friend and admirer of Lewis near the end of his life, described the autonomy of the eye as a direct effect of technological developments such as photography which threatened the unity of the sensorium in the late nineteenth century. 'Photography', he observed in 'Inside the Five Sense Sensorium', 'gave separate and, as it were, abstract intensity to the visual, a development which called for and received swift compensating strategy in the arts'.[84] For McLuhan (using words and concepts conspicuously similar to those employed by Lewis – here we find the 'child cult' of primitive cultures interpreted in an anthropological context), tactility was the basic linking sense and the foundation of all synaesthetic experience. Touch had been divorced from visual experience by the advent of photography, but could be reunited with vision through the rise of television.[85]

That tactility could be considered the fundamental basis of all sense-modalities is something that is reflected at the level of language, of course. Things that we 'feel' are generally opposed to those more abstract mental states such as imagining or hallucinating, whether or not the 'felt' is haptic in origin. As Mark Patterson and others have argued, the basic state of embodied consciousness is one which is intimately and continually bound up with tactility. Touch refers not only to the exteroceptive sensations (to the ways in which our skin processes the main characteristics of external bodies by cataloguing heat, roughness, pressure and so on) but to the interoceptive characteristics of our bodies (the somatic states that are described by the inner ear as balance, for instance, or our awareness of moving our limbs through space, and so on).[86]

Lewis worked many of these ideas into his novels, and into his theories of fiction. In *Men Without Art* he had argued that what he called the 'external' approach to narrative fiction was a method which 'more and more, will be adopted in the art of writing.'[87] The external approach, Lewis suggested, is 'classical'; the internal, as wielded by Joyce and Woolf, 'romantic'. The external approach is of the eye, the internal is suffused with 'hellenic naturalism'. Finally the external method possesses a 'masculine formalism', whereas the internal monologue is 'a phenomenon of decadence'.[88] The stream-of-consciousness method – telling things from the inside in a doomed effort to describe the workings of the mind – was for Lewis nothing more than a 'tumultuous stream of evocative, spell-bearing, vocables, launched at your head – or poured into your Unconscious', and was 'finally, a dope only.'[89] 'Dogmatically, then', he concludes, 'I am for the Great Without, for the method of *external* approach – for the wisdom of the eye, rather than that of the ear.'[90]

In his fiction this interest in 'the great without' was registered in the care with which he obsessed over physiognomy, appearances, performance, clothing, and, above all, behaviour. Of *The Apes of God* he wrote 'no book has ever been written that has paid more attention to the *outside* of people. In it their shells, or pelts, or the language of their bodily movements, come first, not last.'[91] The following description of Hobson from *Tarr* is typical of the kind of atomised, deconstructed description that Lewis perfected in his novels in the late 1920s:

> He was very athletic, and his dark and cavernous features had been constructed by Nature as a lurking place for villainies and passions. But he slouched and ambled along, neglecting his muscles: and his dastardly face attempted to portray delicacies of commonsense, and gossamerlike backslidings into the Inane, that would have puzzled a bile-specialist.[92]

Hobson is described forensically and almost phrenologically, his outer form clearly and unambiguously announcing the dispositions of his character. He 'ambles' along, his face an independent agent 'attempting' (and, we must assume, failing) to 'portray the delicacies of commonsense'. Consciousness is split here, fragmented into various pieces which are then placed in competition with one another. Yet they are still contained within a single moving body. Hobson, wherever or whoever *he* might be, neglects his muscles, becoming a Cartesian outrider trapped within the machine of his own body. Later in the novel this same body 'stop[s] in front of Tarr of its own accord' and slinks 'up, ashamed of its plight, its gait, its clothes'.[93] Transformed into a Vorticist composite 'of sinister piston rods, organ-like shapes, heavy drills', Hobson's body acts on its own inscrutable impulses, largely devoid of agency: an automaton to which a feeble mind has become momentarily attached.[94]

The protagonist of Lewis's early novel *Snooty Baronet*, Kell-Imrie, is introduced to us in similarly alienating fashion, 'the' (not 'his') 'eye somewhat closed up – this was a sullen eye', and 'the nose upon the face indicated strength of character if anything . . . the mouth, which did not slit it or crumple it, but burst out of it (like an escaped plush lining of rich pink), that spelled sensitiveness'.[95] Yet as the paragraph continues, it becomes clear that this is a self-portrait, and the objective distancing achieved by the use of the third person by the apparently omniscient narrator is undermined by the presence of an arranging self-consciousness. As Kell-Imrie continues, 'the face was mine. I must apologize for arriving as it were incognito upon the scene.'[96] In much of Lewis's work, particularly in what Hugh Kenner calls the 'puppet fictions' written in the 1920s and 1930s, people are again and again described in this way, presented explicitly as little more than the mechanical, unconscious agents which, as literary characters, they ultimately are.[97]

In framing his narratives in this way Lewis drew attention to the artificiality of the third-person/first-person narrative divide, a divide seen subsequently, as I have shown, by many critics as central to modernism's proposed solutions to the problem of qualia. In these novels Lewis's characters amount to little more than atomised lumps of insensible matter. As he defined such beings in *The Wild Body*, they are:

> not creations but puppets. You can be as exterior to them, and live their life as little, as the showman grasping from beneath and working about

a Polichinelle. They are only shadows of energy, and not living beings. Their mechanism is a logical structure and they say nothing about that.[98]

These are creatures we are as readers doomed forever to be external to; doomed to look upon rather than to inhabit or know in the first person. Their reported behaviours, conveyed to us through the Turing imitation game of the novel, come to replace any notion of 'character' or conscious inner life. And yet this is just as it should be, argues Lewis, for this is all the novel can *ever* consist of. Externalities and behaviours are all literature can contain, and all we can ever know of each other.

As Michael Levenson has noted, Lewis's idiosyncratic aesthetic was therefore profoundly anti-impressionist, and as such confronted a suite of philosophical arguments from the period concerned with the relationship between sensation, qualia and literature. Throughout his fiction Lewis made no attempt to present readers with reified 'minds' or with fictional versions of synthesised consciousnesses, instead choosing to concentrate on

> absurdly purposive lumps of matter that behave autonomously and *intelligently*, without any signs of direction from the mind, indeed often in leering opposition to its biddings. The body acts as an independent agent with, as it were, a mind of its own.[99]

Yet here Levenson's definition of Lewis's art is a curiously dualist one, and draws attention to the fact that we are used to being presented (or to believing that we are being presented) with *minds* in fiction. When they are *not* 'presented', when the motivating desires and thoughts associated with a character's behaviour are ignored by the novelist, then we tend to read the processes governing that behaviour as 'automatic'. However, our bodies do, of course, have minds of their own, and in highlighting the distinction between the various terms we use to describe these minds – character, or consciousness, or thought – Lewis was aligning himself with a quite specific vision of literary consciousness. In the debate between the Bailiff and Hyperides in *The Childermass*, Hyperides declares it 'is not people that interest me so much as the principles that determine their actions', and it is by replacing an interest in the notion of 'consciousness' with an interest in the principles governing his character's actions that Lewis most thoroughly challenged the prevailing aesthetic assumptions of modernism, in the process proposing a radical solution to the problem of qualia.[100]

In doing so Lewis endorsed a model of cognition which was deeply influenced by the material conditions of modernity. In many of his novels 'thought' is presented less as a question of experience than as one of processing ability. Many of Lewis's characters register the world rather than see it. In *Revenge for Love* Don Alvaro is described as a kind of proto-computer or Turing machine:

> his eye fastened upon this lazily moving object, Don Alvaro studied the profiled countenance, as you watch an advertisement flashed upon a safety-curtain before the beginning of a play. Since it is presented to you, you lend it your attention – all is grist to the mill of the senses, there is nothing that is refused in a vacant mind.[101]

Later in the novel Don Alvaro recognises a face as 'an important puzzle, that taxed his recording machinery, like a question of mislaid fingerprints'; and a woman walking down the stairs is described as a 'slowly tramping contraption'.[102] In *Snooty Baronet* Kell-Imrie is described as though we are being given a schematic of a computing machine: 'the left eye kept a sullen watch: it was counting. Numbers clicked-up in its counting box, back of the retina, in a vigesimal check-off.'[103]

When Lewis's characters are aged or mentally infirm this tendency towards cognitive mechanisation is even more pronounced. Lady Fredigonde, the ageing 'ape' whose narrative opens *The Apes of God*, is described in terms resolutely committed to treating her merely as dead (or at any rate dying) matter:

> Her fixed eye was bloodless and without any animation, a stuffed eagle's sham optic in fact, or a glass eye in the head of a corpse – though the bellows plainly worked still, the shoulders slowly grinding on, blown up and let down with the labour of the breath. Gradually however her personality made its appearance. Fragment by fragment she got it back, in rough hand-over-hand, a bitter salvage.[104]

Lady Fredigonde's body is here described as one inhabited only occasionally by a complete and healthy consciousness, and the waxing and waning of her mind is conveyed in this 'prelude' to the novel with some sensitivity, as an italicised interior monologue. But pretty soon the method is contextualised, and self-consciously explained away within the terms of established literary convention. Fredigonde, whose ailing mind drifts in and out of contact with her body, is cut off 'from the optic or tactile connections' and passes

> most of her time in her mental closet, a hermit in her own head. Sometimes she would Stein away night and morning to herself, making patterns of conversations, with odds and ends from dead disputes, and cat's-cradles of this thing and that – a veritable peasant industry, of personal chatterboxing and shortsighted nonsense.[105]

It is not consciousness which is being evoked here, then, but style: the 'Stein-stutter' of the repetitious interior monologue which Lewis was so scathing of elsewhere. This is a satirical intervention, with Lewis skilfully employing a familiar literary technique (with some mastery) only to undermine its claims to faithfully reify consciousness in a cognitive realist mode. As he suggested elsewhere, satire can *only* tell its stories behaviourally, from the outside, and attempting to do otherwise is precisely what is being satirised here:

> To let the reader 'into the minds of the characters', to 'see the play of their thoughts' – that is precisely the method least suited to satire. That it must deal with the *outside*, that is one of the capital advantages of this form of literary art – for those who like a resistant and finely-sculptured surface, or sheer words.[106]

A reader's report from his publisher endorsed by Lewis compared his method, favourably, to that of Henry James, noting that in his work 'everything is told from the outside. To this extent it is the opposite of, say, James, who sought to narrate from the *inside* the character's mind. James, in short, was a Bergsonian, where you are a Berkeleyan'.[107] Lewis defended his occasional use of the interior monologue in similar terms, claiming that 'its use (for the purposes of projecting this brain-in-isolation, served only by the senses paralysed with age) is an exposure of the literary dogma of the "internal monologue," regarded as a *universal* method.'[108]

According to Lewis, the narration of interiority could only legitimately be applied to certain minds, to describing the thoughts of '(1) the extremely aged; (2) young children; (3) half-wits; and (4) animals' – individuals cut off from their sensory inputs, or unable to process them rationally.[109] It was these exceptions that proved the rule.

Thus in his novels Lewis established a compromised epistemology, rejecting the 'infantilisation' of raw sensation as a legitimate field for literature in favour of something altogether more complicated, and conflicted. In Lewis's conception, qualia could never be conveyed, so there was little point in attempting to write them (if that meant indulging in the reductive, impressionistic impulses of Woolf and Joyce) at all. As Hugh Kenner summarises, Lewis's most stable position was that instead one must 'retain one's aloofness from the hot time-world of the senses.'[110] Lewis's aversion to the 'hot time-world of the senses' was, as Fredric Jameson notes, a truly revolutionary aesthetic, but it never became as popular as he hoped, perhaps because its ultimate implications were so challenging. 'Anglo-American modernism', writes Jameson, 'has indeed traditionally been dominated by an impressionistic aesthetic, rather than that – externalizing and mechanical – of Lewis's expressionism. The most influential formal impulses of canonical modernism have been strategies of inwardness.'[111] Perhaps one reason Lewis's lessons were largely ignored is that they had such troubling implications for the status of most twentieth-century fiction. If such inwardness is shown to be inherently unworkable – if the mind is indeed impossible to convey – then the last few hundred years of western literary development might appear to have been wasted.

In place of naïve impressionism, with its faith in the veridical possibilities of language, Lewis exploited the performative artificiality of prose fiction, insisting on the interpretive temporality of the reading process. The syntactical difficulty of his writing, like its partial and atomistic descriptive strategies, forces the reader to slow down and *assemble* meaning in a painstaking, active and (inevitably) incomplete way. In a brief article on 'Lewis's Prose Style' Marshall McLuhan endorsed his methods in terms very similar to those associated by many critics with the impressionist literary aesthetic, arguing that:

> For readers who are accustomed to action in prose narrative Lewis is baffling. Especially his early novels provide passage after passage which are like nothing so much as a package of materials with directions for making a painting . . . A good deal is left for the reader. But the result enables the reader to *see*.[112]

For McLuhan, in Lewis's work logical behaviourism's definition of consciousness as a series of if–then statements is turned into a style which was able to capture human character in its totality. But McLuhan's conclusion – that the result enables the reader to see – leads as back to where we began, with Conrad's assertion, in the preface to *The Nigger of the 'Narcissus'*, that making his readers 'see' was one of his central aims as a novelist. This position, as we have seen, is difficult to sustain. 'Lewis the painter', McLuhan claims,

> turned to literature in an age of passive mechanical photography. As a writer he set out to educate the eye by means of deft organisation of gestures. He translates what he sees into terms of painting, and translates this in turn into words which embody, in embryo, as it were, the same gestures.[113]

Yet this satirical atomisation of perception, this commitment to a radical form of delayed decoding, can only ever be sustained if behaviourism is true, and if qualia do not exist.

Lewis's novels challenge and interrogate the premises of cognitive realism in many ways, therefore, all of which tend to mark the limits of fiction and its relation to consciousness. His insistence on materiality at the level of the sentence is perhaps the most striking example of this resistance. Fredric Jameson describes Lewis's technique as 'the painstaking anatomy of the external world and of gesture' and 'a kind of tireless visual inventory'.[114] Offering a political reading of this style, of the excessive anatomical deconstruction of the human body into its constituent parts, and constituent actions, Jameson goes on to argue that

> the step-by-step dismantling of the body's gestural machine implies that reality itself is infinitely divisible, that its smallest atomic units can themselves be further and further subdivided by an infinitely expandable accretion of sentences, towards some unimaginable infinitesimality.[115]

Lewis's streams of description stand as a monument, according to Jameson, to the sheer open-ended industriousness of the human mind in the age of the machine: 'The Apes of God is indeed a kind of ambiguous monument to this illimitable sentence-producing capacity, which is itself a figure for human productive power in the industrial age.'[116] But, as I have suggested, it is also possible to read Lewis's style as a response to the ontological confusion engendered by modernism's inward turn.

'Realism pressed to an extreme capsizes into its opposite', writes Terry Eagleton, the 'more scrupulously you detail human action in this relentlessly externalising way, the more you estrange it.'[117] Lewis's wary relationship with language was borne largely of his fear of cliché: his fear of uttering something that had been uttered before, and by doing so contributing to language's status as a set of tokenistic stand-ins for action on the behaviourist model. Sometimes, for instance, his inverted commas function to distance his narrators from the clichés of speech, as in *The Childermass*, where Satters's face is described as '"grave as a judge"'.[118] Elsewhere, they add a hidden layer to our glossing of Lewis's performative sentences. *Revenge for Love* is full of this authorial distancing; 'O'Hara looked "rueful," as it is called in the vocabulary of the book-stall', we are told, 'as his British respectability was his long suit now, a certain obscure touchiness as to "appearances".'[119] When the revolutionary Serafin is shot in *Revenge for Love* his own uncertainty over what has occurred is shared by the reader. All he can say for sure is that 'something had "occurred".'[120] Lewis used inverted commas as a way of masking, of slipping in cliché (itself a form of mask, to hide the lack of thought behind an expression) and therefore reclaiming the mask, the expression, the tired phrase and worn gesture and, in the process, making it new. Placed in inverted commas, utterances are flagged as nothing more than tokens.

Elsewhere Lewis's insistent materialism is encoded in a syntax which treats dialogue merely as the inevitable outcome of the mechanical deployment of preconceived utterances: phrases and solecisms which occur ready-made in the mind to be unleashed on other minds. The Germanic inflections which pepper *Tarr* call attention to this, and force us, sentence-by-sentence, to construct meanings for ourselves. It is laborious work, certainly, but ultimately, Lewis acknowledges, it is no more 'faithful' to lived experience than the easy solecisms of other writers, or the often anguished laments for the little languages of interiority and sensory reification of the impressionists. French and German sayings, confined by the controlling presence of inverted commas, as well as the idiomatic undercurrents encoded in the 'rôles' people play, all make up a Lewisian style, which, as Jameson continues, enacts at the level of the sentence the very irreducibility of felt sensation to language:

> since it cannot tell us what to see, it will rather tell us what we would have seen had it been able to do so. Since there exists no adequate language for 'rendering' the object, all that is left to the writer is to tell us how he would have rendered it had he had such a language in the first place.[121]

Just as behaviourism reduced the human subject to an ever more atomised description of behavioural processes, then, so Lewis's fiction sought to show how the introspectionist, impressionist paradigms endorsed by Woolf, Joyce and Stein were, at least in terms of cognitive realism, doomed to failure. Hugh Kenner identifies in this style Lewis's

> war with Time – especially with the time past that his heroes emphatically disown – a war which underlies every manifestation of his genius, from the galvanic absolutism of his prose syntax (which, at its most characteristic, works by systematic denial of the existence of sequence) to his obsession with the empty machine-minds of modernity.[122]

But what Lewis ultimately records with his tortuous syntax, his obfuscatory metaphor-making, and his inverted allegories is the very impossibility of language to ever convey that which so many of his contemporaries wanted it to: the human mind.

It is wrong to speak of narratives – such as Lewis's – that are primarily concerned to 'stage' the behaviour of their protagonists rather than using an 'inner method' to tell us what they are thinking as 'behaviourist', therefore. The distinction between the 'exterior' and 'interior' methods, as Lewis characterised them, is one of style or epistemology (the satirical as opposed to the sentimental, perhaps) rather than of ontology. All language is methodologically behaviourist, in that it necessarily presents us with descriptions of things rather than those things themselves. But if behaviourism as a philosophical doctrine were true then the feeling of externality that characterises certain types of narrative fiction would cease to feel like anything of the sort. Similarly, though externalities were for Lewis all that could legitimately be portrayed in fiction, this does not necessarily mean that he conceived of real individuals as devoid of qualia and interior mental lives. Indeed he could be read as arguing quite the opposite. By skimming over surfaces and penetrating into the mental lives of his characters only when such a practice served to demonstrate their limited mental faculties, Lewis can be read as an author who worked expressly within – indeed who took as his subject – the limits of language rather than the limits of personhood. Perhaps Lewis resisted what he termed the 'inner method' in his fiction because he realised that 'writing the mind', in any mimetic sense, was a hopeless and impossible task.

One of the reasons that Lewis's work is so often ignored by critics, therefore, is that it flirts with a rather frightening possibility. If logical behaviourism is true then qualia cannot exist, and the kinds of problems presented by cognitive realist readings of fictional representations of mind can be solved in quite straightforward terms. But at the same time such explanations threaten to remove from the critical task the very quality which the humanist critical project is said to be seeking in narrative fiction: call it feeling, or affect, or qualia.

Notes

1. See, in particular, John B. Watson, 'Psychology as the Behaviorist Views It', *Psychological Review*, 20.2 (1913), 158–177.
2. Jessica Burstein, *Cold Modernism: Literature, Fashion, Art* (Pennsylvania, PA: Pennsylvania University Press, 2012), p. 22.
3. Wyndham Lewis, 'Behaviourist "Summer Conversation"', in *The Enemy: A Review of Arts and Literature*, ed. by Wyndham Lewis, 3 vols (Santa Rosa, CA: Black Sparrow Press, 1994), vol. II, p. 42.
4. Hugh Kenner, *Wyndham Lewis* (London: Methuen & Co., Ltd, 1954), p. 107.
5. Paul Scott Stanfield, '"This Implacable Doctrine": Behaviorism in Wyndham Lewis's "Snooty Baronet"', *Twentieth Century Literature*, 47.2 (2001), 241–267 (p. 242).
6. Stanfield, 'This Implacable Doctrine', p. 250.
7. See Fredric Jameson, *Fables of Aggression: Wyndham Lewis, the Modernist as Fascist* (Berkeley, CA, Los Angeles, CA and London: University of California Press, 1979), p. 2.
8. John B. Watson, *Psychology from the Standpoint of a Behaviorist* (Philadelphia, PA: J. B. Lippincott Company, 1919), p. xii.
9. John B. Watson, *Behaviorism* (Chicago, IL: University of Chicago Press, 1930), p. 2.
10. Watson, *Behaviorism*, p. 2.
11. Wyndham Lewis, *Time and Western Man*, ed. by Paul Edwards (Santa Rosa, CA: Black Sparrow Press, 1993), p. 301 (emphasis in original).
12. Lewis, *Time and Western Man*, p. 302.
13. John R. Searle, *Mind: A Brief Introduction* (Oxford: Oxford University Press, 2004), p. 52.
14. Wyndham Lewis, *Snooty Baronet* (London: Cassell and Company, Ltd, 1932), p. 155.
15. Lewis, *Snooty Baronet*, p. 161.
16. Lewis, *Snooty Baronet*, p. 156.
17. A. J. Ayer, *Language, Truth and Logic* (Harmondsworth: Penguin, 1971), p. 130.
18. Gottfried Wilhelm Leibniz, *The Monadology and Other Philosophical Writings*, trans. by Robert Latta (Oxford: The Clarendon Press, 1898), pp. 227–228.

19. John R. Searle, 'Minds, Brains and Programs', *Behavioral and Brain Sciences*, 3.3 (1980), 417–424.
20. Searle, 'Minds, Brains, and Programs', p. 421.
21. Alan Turing, 'Computing Machinery and Intelligence', *Mind*, 59.236 (1950), 433–460 (pp. 433, 442).
22. That such beings are conceivable is taken by some philosophers itself as sufficient evidence of the existence of qualia. See especially David Chalmers, *The Character of Consciousness* (Oxford: Oxford University Press, 2010).
23. Lewis, *The Childermass: Section 1* (London: Chatto & Windus, 1928), p. 29.
24. Lewis, *Snooty Baronet*, p. 309.
25. Lewis, *The Childermass*, p. 31.
26. Walter Michel and C. J. Fox, eds, *Wyndham Lewis on Art* (London: Thames and Hudson, 1969), p. 155.
27. Watson, *Behaviorism*, p. 212.
28. Qtd in Wyndham Lewis, *The Art of Being Ruled*, ed. by Reed Way Dasenbrock (Santa Rosa: Black Sparrow Press, 1989), p. 340; orig. in John B. Watson, 'Image and Affection in Behavior', *Journal of Philosophy, Psychology and Scientific Methods*, 10 (1913), 421–428 (p. 424).
29. John B. Watson, *The Battle of Behaviorism: an Exposition and an Exposure* (London: Kegan Paul, Trench, Trubner & Co. Ltd, 1928), p. 34.
30. Watson, *The Battle of Behaviorism*, pp. 34–35, 40.
31. I. A. Richards, *The Philosophy of Rhetoric* (New York and London: Oxford University Press, 1936), p. 13.
32. Hugh Kenner, *The Counterfeiters* (Bloomington, IN: Indiana University Press, 1968), p. 124.
33. John Rodker, *Adolphe 1920* (London: The Aquila Press, 1929), pp. 11–12.
34. Rodker, *Adolphe 1920*, p. 18.
35. Rodker, *Adolphe 1920*, pp. 18–19.
36. James Joyce, *Ulysses*, ed. by Hans Walter Gabler (London: The Bodley Head, 1986), 13.794. All references to James Joyce's *Ulysses* are to the Gabler synoptic edition, and are given in the form [episode number.line number].
37. David Trotter, *Cinema and Modernism* (Oxford: Blackwell Publishing, 2007), p. 12.
38. See James Joyce, 'Trieste Notebook', in *The Workshop of Daedalus: James Joyce and the Raw Materials for 'A Portrait of the Artist as a Young Man'*, ed. by Robert Scholes and Richard M. Kain (Evanston, IL: Northwestern University Press, 1965), pp. 92–105.
39. Joyce, *Ulysses*, 15.105–107.
40. Rodker, *Adolphe 1920*, p. 138.
41. For a good account of the history of literature's relationship with automata, see Deirdre Coleman and Hilary Fraser, eds, *Minds, Bodies, Machines 1770–1930* (Basingstoke: Palgrave Macmillan, 2011).
42. Jessica Riskin, 'Eighteenth-Century Wetware', *Representations*, 83.1 (2003), 97–125 (p. 118).
43. Qtd in Laura Salisbury, 'Linguistic Trepanation: Brain Damage, Penetrative Seeing and a Revolution of the World', in *Minds, Bodies, Machines 1770–1930*, ed. by Deirdre Coleman and Hilary Fraser (Basingstoke: Palgrave Macmillan, 2011), p. 183.

44. Guillaume Apollinaire, *Selected Writings*, trans. by Roger Shattuck (New York: New Directions, 1971), p. 232.
45. Trotter, *Cinema*, p. 10.
46. Trotter, *Cinema*, p. 10.
47. Trotter, *Cinema*, p. 10.
48. Sara Danius, *The Senses of Modernism: Technology, Perception, and Aesthetics* (Ithaca, NY and London: Cornell University Press, 2002), p. 147–148.
49. Raymond Tallis, *In Defence of Realism* (London: Edward Arnold, 1988), p. 33.
50. Tallis, *In Defence of Realism*, p. 33.
51. Qtd in Colin Harding and Simon Popple, *In the Kingdom of Shadows: A Companion to Early Cinema* (London: Cygnus Arts, 1996), pp. 5–6.
52. Virginia Woolf, 'The Cinema', in *The Essays of Virginia Woolf Volume IV: 1925–1928*, ed. by Andrew McNeillie (London: The Hogarth Press, 1994; repr. 2009), p. 349.
53. Alan Munton, 'From Charlie Chaplin to Bill Haley: Popular Culture and Ideology in Wyndham Lewis', in *Wyndham Lewis the Radical: Essays on Literature and Modernity*, ed. by Carmelo Cunchillos Jaime (New York and Oxford: Peter Lang, 2007), p. 160.
54. Wyndham Lewis, *Mrs. Dukes' Million* (London: George Prior Publishers, 1980), p. 349.
55. Wyndham Lewis, *Blast*, 2 vols (Santa Rosa, CA: Black Sparrow Press, 1915; repr. 1981), vol. II, p. 101.
56. Wyndham Lewis, *The Revenge for Love*, ed. by Reed Way Dasenbrock (Santa Rosa, CA: Black Sparrow Press, 1991), p. 314.
57. Danius, *The Senses of Modernism*, p. 131.
58. Danius, *The Senses of Modernism*, p. 132.
59. Danius, *The Senses of Modernism*, p. 130.
60. Kenner, *The Counterfeiters*, p. 47.
61. Wyndham Lewis, 'The Strange Actor', *The New Statesman*, 22.563 (1924), 474–476.
62. Wyndham Lewis, 'The Revolutionary Simpleton', in *The Enemy: A Review of Art and Literature*, ed. by Wyndham Lewis, 3 vols (Santa Rosa: Black Sparrow Press, 1994), vol. I, p. 76.
63. Trotter, *Cinema*, p. 11.
64. T. S. Eliot, 'Tradition and the Individual Talent', in *Selected Prose*, ed. by Frank Kermode (London: Faber and Faber, 1975), p. 43.
65. Wyndham Lewis, *Rotting Hill* (London: Methuen & Co. Ltd, 1951), p. 126.
66. See Trotter, *Cinema*, p. 183.
67. Trotter, *Cinema*, p. 183.
68. Lewis, *Time and Western Man*, p. 303.
69. Wyndham Lewis, *Hitler* (New York: Gordon, 1972), p. 31.
70. Wyndham Lewis, 'Introduction', in *Wyndham Lewis and Vorticism* (London: Tate Gallery, 1956), p. 3.
71. Wyndham Lewis, *Men Without Art* (Santa Rosa, CA: Black Sparrow Press, 1987), p. 13 (emphasis in original).
72. Lewis, *Time and Western Man*, p. 342.

73. Wyndham Lewis, 'The Meaning of the Wild Body', in Lewis, *The Complete Wild Body*, ed. by Bernard Lafourcade (Santa Barbara, CA: Black Sparrow Press, 1982), p. 158.
74. Lewis, *Revenge for Love*, p. 153.
75. Lewis, *Time and Western Man*, p. 301.
76. Lewis, *The Childermass*, p. 7.
77. Marshall McLuhan, 'Lewis's Prose Style', in *Wyndham Lewis: A Revaluation*, ed. by Jeffrey Meyers (London: The Athlone Press, 1980), p. 66.
78. Lewis, *The Childermass*, p. 7.
79. James Joyce, *James Joyce in Padua*, ed. and trans. by Louis Berrone (New York: Random House, 1977), p. 21.
80. Lewis, *The Art of Being Ruled*, p. 349.
81. Wyndham Lewis, *Wyndham Lewis: Anthology of Prose*, ed. by E. W. F. Tomlin (London: Methuen, 1969), p. 282.
82. Lewis, *Time and Western Man*, p. 393 (emphases in original).
83. F. T. Marinetti, 'The Manifesto of Tactilism', *Comœdia*, 11 January 1921.
84. Marshall McLuhan, 'Inside the Five Sense Sensorium', *Canadian Architect*, 6.6 (1961), pp. 49–54.
85. McLuhan, 'Sensorium', p. 46.
86. For a good account of the various ways in which types of touch have been classified, see Mark Patterson, *The Senses of Touch* (Oxford and New York: Berg, 2007), pp. 1–14.
87. Wyndham Lewis, *Men Without Art*, ed. by Seamus Cooney (Santa Rosa, CA: Black Sparrow Press, 1987), p. 103.
88. Lewis, *Satire and Fiction* (London: The Arthur Press, 1930), p. 52.
89. Lewis, *Satire and Fiction*, pp. 52–53.
90. Lewis, *Men Without Art*, p. 105.
91. Lewis, *Satire and Fiction*, p. 46.
92. Wyndham Lewis, *Tarr*, ed. by Paul O'Keeffe (Santa Rosa, CA: Black Sparrow Press, 1990), p. 22.
93. Lewis, *Tarr*, p. 22.
94. Lewis, *Tarr*, p. 23.
95. Lewis, *Snooty Baronet*, p. 15.
96. Lewis, *Snooty Baronet*, p 130.
97. Kenner, *Wyndham Lewis*, p. 97.
98. Wyndham Lewis, *The Complete Wild Body*, ed. by Bernard Lafourcade (Santa Barbara, CA: Black Sparrow Press, 1982), p. 150.
99. Michael Levenson, 'Form's Body Wyndham Lewis's Tarr', *Modern Language Quarterly*, 45.3 (1984), 241–262 (p. 246) (emphasis in original).
100. Lewis, *The Childermass*, p. 289.
101. Lewis, *Revenge for Love*, p. 19.
102. Lewis, *Revenge for Love*, pp. 20, 21.
103. Lewis, *Snooty Baronet*, p. 42.
104. Wyndham Lewis, *The Apes of God* (London: Penguin 1965), p. 29.
105. Lewis, *The Apes of God*, p. 18.

106. Lewis, *Men Without Art*, p. 95 (emphasis in original).
107. Qtd in Lewis, *Men Without Art*, p. 97 (emphasis in original).
108. Lewis, *Men Without Art*, p. 98 (emphasis in original).
109. Lewis, *Men Without Art*, p. 98.
110. Kenner, *Wyndham Lewis,* p. 87.
111. Jameson, *Fables of Aggression*, p. 2.
112. McLuhan, 'Lewis's Prose Style', p. 64.
113. McLuhan, 'Lewis's Prose Style', p. 64.
114. Jameson, *Fables of Aggression*, p. 31.
115. Jameson, *Fables of Aggression*, p. 31.
116. Jameson, *Fables of Aggression*, p. 32.
117. Terry Eagleton, 'An Octopus at the Window', *London Review of Books*, 19 May 2011, pp. 23–24.
118. Lewis, *Childermass*, p. 6.
119. Lewis, *Revenge for Love*, p. 31.
120. Lewis, *Revenge for Love*, p. 49.
121. Jameson, *Fables of Aggression*, pp. 85–86.
122. Kenner, *Wyndham Lewis*, p. 6.

CONCLUSION: MODERNISM, QUALIA AND THE NARRATIVES OF BEHAVIOURISM

> One could also put it this way: How would a human body have to act so that one would not be inclined to speak of inner and outer human states? Again and again I think: 'like a machine.'
> Ludwig Wittgenstein, *Last Writings on the Philosophy of Psychology*, vol. II

As we have seen, the anxiety articulated in debates over qualia is one conditioned by the vast technological and material changes that threatened the unity of the sensorium in the late nineteenth and early twentieth centuries. Broadly I share Sara Danius's view that 'classical modernism' inculcated a 'shift from idealist theories of aesthetic experience to materialist ones, or, which ultimately amounts to the same thing, that the emergence of modernist aesthetics signifies the increasing internalization of technological matrices of perception.'[1] But the particular form this argument takes within contemporary philosophy of mind (and within critical theories which seek to apply it to literature) is, as I also hope to have shown, paradigmatic of modernist anxieties about the limits of positivism, and about the relationship between knowledge and sensation more generally. This is an anxiety that we have inherited from the modernist moment, and is one that still dominates discussions over the nature of consciousness, and the relationship between textual representations of the mind and what it might be that those representations are supposed to be representing. What we think we know about the essential characteristics of consciousness are, I would suggest, largely derived from those descriptions of consciousness and subjectivity that modernist fiction is often celebrated for providing us with. Far from developing more successful strategies for the representation of qualia, therefore, I would contend that modernist fiction 'wrote the mind' in a more straightforward sense: by giving us the models or metaphors of cognition which still, in a diverse range of forms and contexts, dominate the way in which the mind–body distinction is framed.

In making this argument I would certainly not deny that the development of the novel is intimately associated with the origins of modern consciousness. But it would seem equally valid to argue that modernist novels strike us as particularly representative of how our minds work not because they, for the first time in human history, captured something essential and unchanging about minds, but because they have in some sense *caused* us to think that our minds work in the way that they do. On this reading the novel – and the modernist novel in particular – doesn't describe consciousness at all: it causes it to exist by defining its qualities and properties, reifying the mind and thus bringing it into being as a conceptual entity that is then read back in to the history of the novel, and also the history of consciousness.

The contested two-way locus of interaction between fiction and the mind is, as I have shown, clearly evident in the 'sensory crisis' which so marks the philosophical and aesthetic projects of the early twentieth century. A wide variety of critical approaches to modernism – from its own manifestos, through the psychologised modernism associated with the critical narrative of an 'inward turn' which held sway from the mid- to late twentieth century, to contemporary neuroaesthetic and cognitive approaches to modernist fiction – have sought to read the senses (interpreted both as a source of knowledge of the external world, and as stand-alone phenomenological experiences) – back into literature. As I have shown, this is an impulse which emerged directly from the material, scientific and cultural conditions of modernity, and which tended to divide the sensorium along classical Aristotelian lines (distinguishing between the five classical senses) by invoking models provided by mnemonic technologies. Informed by what Sara Danius calls the 'technological matrices of perception', many accounts of modernism's minds have appropriated the perceptual metaphors associated with scientific reductionism (and with the mnemonic technologies that were increasingly able to accurately recreate sense-data) and applied them to the literary realm.[2] This tendency was fertilised by the close links between philosophy and fiction in the period (manifested particularly in the work of Virginia Woolf and Wyndham Lewis), and by the way in which the novel-form has subsequently often been interpreted as uniquely able to reunite a fragmented sensorium by 'evoking', 'describing', 'rendering' or 'writing' consciousness. In doing so the novel has come to be defined as a literary form primarily concerned to provide an answer to the question of 'what it is like to be' another mind.

At the same time these very contexts made the limitations of reductive approaches to consciousness, within both philosophy of mind and literary criticism, ever more apparent. The 'neuromodernist turn' examined in previous chapters led to a conception of sensation as consisting solely of 'information' or 'data', and thus reinforced characterisations of the sensorium as something that was reducible to poetically compressed statements or, ultimately, to mathematical formulas. It is these reductions that seem so vexed within contemporary neuroaesthetic and cognitive approaches to the reading of fiction.

Recently, I have argued, the material contexts of 'neuromodernism' have reinvigorated these established cognitive realist interpretive models, and this reinvigoration has been accompanied by a wide-ranging interrogation and reappraisal of modernism's afterlives and legacies. Gabriel Josipovici's enquiry, in his 2010 book of the same name, into 'whatever happened to modernism?' has been accompanied by a renewed interested in experimental writing that is often explicitly framed in terms of a neo- or historical-modernist aesthetic, an impulse detectable in the work of contemporary British and Irish novelists such as Will Self, Eimear McBride, Tom McCarthy and many others.

At the same time, during the last twenty years or so there has been a noticeable attempt to turn against – or at least to tame – some of the formal and stylistic innovations associated with modernist literature: to render them inert by incorporating them into novels which in other ways read as quite straightforwardly realist. In his essay 'The Rise of the Neuronovel' Marco Roth points out that in a host of contemporary novels which take as their basis the neurological substrate of broken or damaged minds and brains, the languages of modernist experimentalism have become associated not with everyday consciousness, but with cognitive atypicality. Of Jonathan Lethem's *Motherless Brooklyn* – a detective novel which takes as its central character Lionel Essrog, a character with Tourette's syndrome who speaks in a fragmented modernist word stream – Roth points out that 'the very act of medicalization marginalizes the experimental impulse, marking any remnant modernism as a case for abnormal psychology.'[3] Where once fragmented internal narration seemed to democratise consciousness – making no formal distinctions between sensory and analytical knowledge, or between healthy and broken minds – in many contemporary novels that engage with modernism's stylistic legacies, the stream of consciousness is used to signal neuro-atypicality or flawed character traits.[4]

My larger point in this book has been to ask what influence a conception of consciousness informed by an acceptance (or at least an awareness) of qualia has on our readings of modernist narratives of consciousness. But the implications of my enquiry have something to tell us about the various theoretical approaches to reading literature which have sprung up in the last two decades or so also, both within modernist studies and more generally. Rather than having a straightforwardly mimetic relationship with the mind, I have argued that modernist narratives of sensation are important constituent parts of a nexus of cultural forces that allowed the idea of a reified mind – stable and essentially unchanging – to take hold within literary criticism in the latter half of the twentieth century, despite the anti-essentialising impulses of those fields of enquiry which were united under the broad term of postmodernism. Modernism, therefore, can be seen to have set (or at least to have contributed to setting) the terms of many of the debates still current both within neuroaesthetic approaches to literature and within contemporary philosophy of mind. This influence – whether philosophers acknowledge it or not – is a pervasive one: Daniel Dennett describes his anti-qualia model of consciousness (rather oxymoronically) as the 'Joycean machine'; in *The Blank Slate* Stephen Pinker misquotes Virginia Woolf to argue that her statement 'on or about December 1910' human 'nature' changed is absurd.[5]

The unsatisfactory nature of many of these positions has, I hope, been made evident. Modernism's various attempts to 'write consciousness' should not necessarily be interpreted as instances of visionary Whiggish discovery, in which writers anticipated scientific truths about the functions of the brain by describing the 'true' nature of what it is to have a mind, but as creative acts, the influences of which are still being felt. Perhaps modernist narrative fiction didn't describe a stable and unchanging object – the mind – at all, but rather equipped us with the metaphors by which this object became thinkable, and with the discourses with which we, in many different disciplines and discourses, continue to describe it. Yet the 'cognitive turn' in criticism, like the critical narrative of an 'inward turn' which held sway before it, often obfuscates precisely what an ontologically 'realistic' account of consciousness, either scientific, philosophical or literary, would or could consist of. Perhaps we only think that we are being presented with particularly veridical portraits of consciousness within modernist fiction because modernist fiction has taught us what such portraits *should* look like. I don't believe it is facetious to suggest that modernism invented not just modernity, but modern minds too.

As we have seen, many contemporary manifestations of cognitive realism are interested in applying psychological theories derived from neuroscience to the novel. Often these approaches invoke 'theory of mind': our supposedly uniquely human ability to interpret internal mental states from a person's (either real or fictional) outward behaviour. Some critics view this as the main evolutionary justification for fiction, believing that, as Lisa Zunshine summarises 'fiction engages, teases, and pushes to its tentative limits our mind-reading capacity', and that this engagement and teasing is socially beneficial.[6] For Zunshine fiction should be valued for its ability to give out theory of mind a 'rigorous workout'. On this account the way we read novels is akin to the ways in which we interpret other peoples' consciousnesses from their behaviour more generally.

To conclude my discussion of modernism's narratives of sensation I want to challenge this understanding of literary 'mind-reading', drawing attention to a distinction that can be made between methodological behaviourism and 'behaviourist narrative' as the term is employed in some contemporary narrative theory, and which seems to have further complicated the ontological assumptions of many cognitive realists in relation to the question of qualia. Whether or not they exist, writing qualia is impossible: to suggest otherwise is to commit a simple category mistake. Yet if we endorse qualia, does it make any sense to argue, as does Alan Palmer, that in 'behaviorist narratives very little direct access to minds is given, the behaviour of the characters only makes sense when it is read as the manifestation of an underlying mental reality'?[7] If minds are something distinct from behaviours then it remains unclear precisely how 'direct access to minds' could *ever* be given, in *any* narrative, either scientific, psychological, or literary.[8] Under the auspices of the qualia thesis their very unknowableness, as we saw in Chapter 2, is what makes them minds.

With the cognitive turn in literary criticism, in line with what Patricia Waugh has described as a general 'biologisation' of culture, the relationship between consciousness and its representation in fiction seems therefore to have come full circle.[9] At the same time cognitive narratologists have begun to invoke something like Wyndham Lewis's notion of behaviourist narrative to describe a form of narrative that purports to be less interested in writing the 'insides' of a character's mind than in reporting their actions. According to Gerald Prince such 'behaviourist narrative' can be defined as: 'objective narrative; a narrative characterized by external focalization and thus limited to the conveyance of the character's behaviour (words and actions but not thoughts and feelings), their appearance, and the setting against which they come to the fore.'[10]

In Chapter 5 we saw how, as a psychological doctrine, behaviourism was (like Lewis's own novels), borne of a dissatisfaction with the perceived subjective bias of introspectionist psychology and what Hugh Kenner calls the 'hot time-world of the senses'.[11] As a narrative strategy it supposed that the only proper way of evoking character in fiction was to report behavioural interactions and reactions. In this the doctrine directly addresses critical anxieties which are central to modernism's own conception of narrative and sensation. It is undoubtedly the case that, as Alan Palmer goes on to suggest, a 'good deal of twentieth-century narration is characterized by a reluctance to make the decoding of action too explicit and a disinclination to use too much indicative description or contextual thought report.'[12] But the question of whether this resistance really leads to the creation of 'behaviourist narrative', in anything other than a loose metaphorical sense, is complicated by the curious ontology of written minds, and by the possible existence of qualia. More persuasively,

Joshua Gang has recently used the intellectual history of behaviourism to challenge critical accounts of modernism's 'inward turn', finding that our notion of the 'modernist mind' as 'knowable and introspective' is derived only from one fairly narrow strain of modernist literature – that associated with Proust, James and Woolf. In contrast, argues Gang, we should attend to the parallel strain in modernist literature exemplified by the work of Samuel Beckett (and also, as I have argued above, by that of Wyndham Lewis), to ask what the novel would look like 'if it were mindless and had no access to mental states'.[13]

With the rise of cognitive and neuroaesthetic approaches to reading modernist fiction the inward turn has therefore been refigured as only one side of a representational divide, part of a division that allegedly became more pronounced with modernism, but which has in the years since been flattened to suggest that psychological 'inwardness' was the major legacy of modernist fiction. Thus when 'Woolf shows Clarissa observing Peter's body language', writes Lisa Zunshine of Virginia Woolf's *Mrs Dalloway*, 'she has an option of providing us with a representation of either Clarissa's mind that would make sense of Peter's physical action . . . or of Peter's own mind.'[14] In choosing to describe behavioural actions rather than inner mental states, argues Zunshine, Woolf is drawing attention to the fact that, as readers and as human beings, we are able to posit those thoughts, desires and beliefs that motivate Peter's actions, 'reading' the minds of characters through the behaviour they display, and giving our 'Theory of Mind' a 'rigorous workout'.[15] 'Woolf is able to imply', writes Zunshine,

> that her representations of Hugh's, Lady Bruton's, and Richard's minds are exhaustive and correct because, creatures with a Theory of Mind that we are, we just know that there must be mental states behind the emotionally opaque body language of the protagonists.[16]

But here, as in much neuroscientifically informed literary criticism, the tension between 'reading' a mind and 'inhabiting' or 'having' one is never finally resolved. Zunshine suggests not only that we are condemned always to be mere 'readers' of the conscious states of other people, but that sometimes, somehow, we can transcend the ontological limits of subjectivity by reading *better*.

Much neuroaesthetic criticism itself therefore endorses a doctrine that might be defined as neo-behaviourist. Affect is sought in the fMRI scanner rather than in the reader's response; rather than interpreting works of fiction as the products of complex historical and cultural forces (and as contributing to our formulation of these categories themselves) such approaches seek to uncover the 'essential' properties of literature by interpreting them solely in terms of brain function. Generally these accounts are defiantly ahistorical: uninterested in the philosophical and cultural origins of their own methodologies. In relation to the ontology of consciousness and the question of qualia, distinguishing between literary representations of the 'behaviour' of characters and their 'thoughts' is largely meaningless, however. For if qualia do exist, then representations of behaviour and representations of consciousness occupy precisely the same area of representation – the literary. And if qualia do not exist, then it seems unclear why the novel (rather than, say, a scientific paper, or a poem, or a mathematical equation) would constitute the best way of accessing the minds of others through language. The distinction between presenting character from the 'outside' and from the 'inside', between portraying 'action' rather than 'thought' must in the end be stylistic rather than ontological in nature. To suggest otherwise while maintaining the existence of qualia is to commit a category mistake. This kind of slippage – mistakenly interpreting stylistic virtuosity or differences in narrative technique as ontologically significant in relation to the question of the mind – recurs across much twentieth-century literary criticism.

What is striking about neuroaesthetic definitions of narrative, then, is how historically indebted they are to the philosophy of the early twentieth century. Many of these approaches share their methodology with the reductive impulses of behaviourism as a psychological doctrine, and face many of the problems associated with logical behaviourism as a theory of consciousness. Such readings seem to invoke the notions of stimulus and response as a principle of reading: the novel-form, in many of these accounts, is functionally identical with the set of formal statements about dispositions to behave contained within it, and the job of the reader is to decode these descriptions and re-experience or re-imagine another mind in light of them. Thus, like many of the critical accounts of the inward turn in narrative fiction which preceded them, neuroaesthetic approaches to the novel often tend to argue that the mind is a stable and unchanging entity isolated from the influences of culture more generally, and that its essential nature can be conveyed through language.

Such approaches therefore have much in common with the behaviourist method itself, as applied to the novel rather than to the study of other people. By suggesting that all mental states can be reduced to descriptions of behaviour or dispositions to behave, behaviourism, and its application to literary criticism, does not imply that we are doomed forever to have an external, an ontologically objective, relationship with the lives of others. Far from it. Instead a full-blooded behaviourism would maintain that qualia do not exist, and thus that accounts of consciousness provided by reports of external behaviour (whether in a psychological paper or in a novel) are all that mental states can ever consist of.

It is of course understandable that literary critics often feel compelled to make special representational claims for the novel by endorsing, however obliquely, a behaviourist model of consciousness. But often these claims directly contradict other assumptions they hold about the status of representation elsewhere. It is inconsistent to deny reductive forms of materialism – deny that the mind can be reduced to a symbolic representation of a set of physical processes or behaviours without loss – while at the same time maintaining that literature is able to overcome those limitations and present us with actual qualia, and thus simulate living minds.

My central claim here is that if they exist then qualia, by definition (and whether understood as equivalent with sensations, impressions, or with the mind and consciousness itself) are not objects that can be 'captured' in language at all. I certainly do not seek to deny that modernism's narratives positioned or advertised themselves as engaging with subjectivity, experientiality, time and all the other properties of the phenomenon of mind that have traditionally been associated with them. But I *do* deny that if qualia exist the mind is a stable, if elusive, object, unchanging through time, that was finally pinned down by the dagger-definitions which were unsheathed by modernist novelists. Instead it might make more sense to think of minds as rhetorical, linguistic and literary constructions. To pursue a cognitive realist interpretation of modernist fiction might be to domesticate, tame and misrepresent the work of novelists who often explicitly rejected the idea that their work aimed to 'represent' or 'render' or 'recreate' anything at all.

Notes

1. Sara Danius, *The Senses of Modernism: Technology, Perception, and Aesthetics* (Ithaca, NY and London: Cornell University Press, 2002), p. 2.
2. Sara Danius, *The Senses of Modernism*, p. 2.
3. Marco Roth, 'The Rise of the Neuronovel', in *Say What You Mean: The n+1 Anthology*, ed. by Christian Lorentzen (London: Notting Hill Editions, 2012), p. 102.
4. For an excellent discussion of how these issues play out in the work of Ian McEwan, see Laura Salisbury, 'Narration and Neurology: Ian McEwan's Mother Tongue', *Textual Practice*, 24.5 (2010), 883–912.
5. See Stephen Pinker, *The Blank Slate* (London: Allen Lane, 2002), pp. 409–410.
6. Lisa Zunshine, *Why We Read Fiction: Theory of Mind and the Novel* (Columbus, OH: Ohio State University Press, 2006), p. 4.
7. Alan Palmer, *Fictional Minds* (Lincoln, NE and London: University of Nebraska Press, 2004), p. 140.
8. Palmer, *Fictional Minds*, p. 140.
9. See Patricia Waugh, 'Writing the Body: Modernism and Postmodernism', in *The Body and the Arts*, ed. Corinne Saunders, Ulrika Maude and Jane Macnaughton (Basingstoke: Palgrave Macmillan 2009), pp. 131–147.
10. Gerald Prince, *Dictionary of Narratology* (Aldershot: Scolar, 1988), p. 10.
11. Hugh Kenner, *Wyndham Lewis* (London: Methuen & Co., Ltd, 1954), p. 87.
12. Palmer, *Fictional Minds*, p. 216.
13. Joshua Gang, 'Mindless Modernism', *Novel*, 46.1 (2013), 116–132 (p. 128).
14. Lisa Zunshine, *Why We Read Fiction: Theory of Mind and the Novel* (Columbus, OH: Ohio State University Press, 2006), p. 22.
15. Zunshine, *Why We Read Fiction*, p. 23.
16. Zunshine, *Why We Read Fiction*, p. 208.

BIBLIOGRAPHY

Agamben, Giorgio, *The Open Man and Animal*, trans. by Kevin Attell (Stanford, CA: Stanford University Press, 2004).

Albright, Daniel, *Quantum Poetics: Yeats, Pound, Eliot and the Science of Modernism* (Cambridge: Cambridge University Press, 1997).

Alexander, Jennifer Karns, *The Mantra of Efficiency: from Waterwheel to Social Control* (Baltimore, MD: The Johns Hopkins University Press, 2008).

Antliff, Mark, *Inventing Bergson: Cultural Politics and the Parisian Avant-Garde* (Princeton, NJ: Princeton University Press, 1993).

Apollinaire, Guillaume, *Selected Writings*, trans. by Roger Shattuck (New York: New Directions, 1971).

Aquinas, St Thomas, *Summa Theologica*, 22 vols (London: Burns, Oates & Washburne, 1918–1928), vol. II.

Ardoin, Paul, Gontarski S. E, and Mattison Laci, eds, *Understanding Bergson, Understanding Modernism* (New York, Bloomsbury, 2013).

Armstrong, D. M., *A Materialist Theory of Mind* (London: Routledge & Kegan Paul, 1968).

Armstrong, Tim, *Modernism, Technology, and the Body: A Cultural Study* (Cambridge: Cambridge University Press, 1998).

Auerbach, Erich, *Mimesis: The Representation of Reality in Western Literature*, trans. by Willard R. Trask (Princeton, NJ: Princeton University Press, 1953).

Ayer, A. J., *Language, Truth and Logic* (Harmondsworth: Penguin, 1971).

Banfield, Ann, *The Phantom Table: Woolf, Fry, Russell and the Epistemology of Modernism* (Cambridge: Cambridge University Press, 2000).
Barthes, Roland, *Sade, Fourier, Loyola* (Paris: Editions du Seuil, 1980).
Beckett, Samuel, 'Dante . . . Bruno. Vico . . . Joyce', *Our Exagmination Round His Factification for Incamination of Work in Progress* (Paris: Shakespeare and Company, 1929).
Beckett, Samuel, *Murphy* (London: George Routledge & Sons Ltd, 1938).
Beckett, Samuel, *Watt* (London: John Calder, 1976).
Beckett, Samuel, *Collected Shorter Plays* (London: Faber & Faber, 1984).
Beckett, Samuel, *The Expelled; The Calmative; The End; with First Love*, ed. by Christopher Ricks (London: Faber & Faber, 2009).
Beckett, Samuel, *Three Novels: Molloy, Malone Dies, The Unnameable* (New York: Grove Press, 2009).
Beer, Gillian, ed., *Open Fields: Science in Cultural Encounter* (Oxford: Clarendon Press, 1996).
Beja, Morris, Gontarski, S. E. and Astier, Pierre, eds, *Samuel Beckett: Humanistic Perspectives* (Columbus, OH: Ohio State University Press, 1983).
Bennet, M. R. and Hacker, P. M. S., *The Philosophical Foundations of Neuroscience* (Oxford: Blackwell Publishing, 2003).
Bergson, Henri, *Time and Free Will: An Essay on the Immediate Data of Consciousness*, trans. by F. L. Pogson (London: George Allen & Company, Ltd, 1910).
Bergson, Henri, *Creative Evolution*, trans. by Arthur Mitchell (London: Macmillan and Co., Ltd, 1911).
Bergson, Henri, *An Introduction to Metaphysics*, trans. by T. E. Hulme (London: Macmillan and Co., Ltd, 1913).
Blackburn, Simon, *The Oxford Dictionary of Philosophy*, 2nd edn (Oxford: Oxford University Press, 2008).
Block, Ned, 'Mental Paint', *Reflections and Replies: Essays on the Philosophy of Tyler Burge*, ed. by Martin Hahn and Bjørn Ramberg (Cambridge, MA: The MIT Press, 2003).
Borck, Cornelius, 'Communicating the Modern Body: Fritz Kahn's Popular Images of Human Physiology as an Industrialized World', *Canadian Journal of Communication*, 32.3–4 (2007), 495–520.
Boring, E. G., *The Physical Dimensions of Consciousness* (New York and London: The Century Co., 1933).
Boswell, James, *The Life of Samuel Johnson: Including a Journal of a Tour to the Hebrides*, ed. by John Wilson Croker, 2 vols (London: Carter, Hendee and Company, 1832), vol. I.
Bowling, Lawrence Edward, 'What is the Stream of Consciousness Technique?', *PMLA*, 65.4 (1950), 333–345.

Broad, C. D., *The Mind and Its Place in Nature* (London: Kegan Paul, Trench, Trubner & Co. Ltd, 1923; repr. 1937).
Budgen, Frank, *James Joyce and the Making of Ulysses* (Bloomington, IN: Indiana University Press, 1960).
Burstein, Jessica, *Cold Modernism: Literature, Fashion, Art* (Pennsylvania, PA: Pennsylvania University Press, 2012).
Burwick, Frederick and Douglas, Paul, eds, *The Crisis in Modernism: Bergson and the Vitalist Controversy* (Cambridge: Cambridge University Press, 1992).
Cajal, Santiago Ramon y, *Histology of the Nervous System of Man and Vertebrates*, trans. by L. Azoulay, Neely Swanson and Larry W. Swanson, 2 vols (New York and Oxford: Oxford University Press, 1995).
Capitan, W. H., and Merrill, D. D., eds, *Art, Mind, and Religion* (Pittsburgh, PA: University of Pittsburgh Press, 1967).
Carnap, Rudolf, *The Logical Structure of the World: Pseudoproblems in Philosophy*, trans. by Rolf A. George (London: Routledge & Kegan Paul, 1967).
Cave, Terence, *Thinking with Literature: Towards a Cognitive Criticism* (Oxford: Oxford University Press, 2016).
Chalmers, David, 'Facing Up to the Problem of Consciousness', *Journal of Consciousness Studies*, 2.3 (1995), 200–219.
Chalmers, David, *The Conscious Mind: In Search of a Fundamental Theory* (New York and Oxford: Oxford University Press, 1996).
Chalmers, David, *The Character of Consciousness* (Oxford: Oxford University Press, 2010).
Churchland, Patricia Smith, Neurophilosophy: Toward a Unified Science of the Mind–Brain (Cambridge, MA and London: The MIT Press, 1986).
Cobley, Evelyn, *Modernism and the Culture of Efficiency: Ideology and Fiction* (Toronto and London: University of Toronto Press, 2009).
Coleman, Deirdre and Fraser, Hilary, eds, *Minds, Bodies, Machines 1770–1930* (Basingstoke: Palgrave Macmillan, 2011).
Conrad, Joseph, *The Nigger of the 'Narcissus'* (London: Penguin Classics, 1988).
Crane, Tim and Patterson, Sarah, eds, *The History of the Mind–Body Problem* (London: Routledge, 2000).
Crick, Francis, *The Astonishing Hypothesis: The Scientific Search for the Soul* (New York: Charles Scribner's Sons, 1994).
Danius, Sara, *The Senses of Modernism: Technology, Perception, and Aesthetics* (Ithaca, NY and London: Cornell University Press, 2002).
Das, Santanu, *Touch and Intimacy in First World War Literature* (Cambridge: Cambridge University Press, 2005).
Davies, Paul, *The Ideal Real: Beckett's Fiction and Imagination* (London: Associated University Presses, 1994).

Deleuze, Giles, *Bergsonism*, trans. by Hugh Tomlinson and Barbara Habberjam (New York: Zone Books, 1988).

Dennett, Daniel C., *Consciousness Explained* (London: Allen Lane, The Penguin Press, 1992).

Dennett, Daniel C., 'Quining Qualia', in *Consciousness in Contemporary Science*, ed. by A. J. Marcel and E. Bisiach (New York: Oxford University Press, 1988), p. 44.

Dingle, Herbert, *Relativity for All* (London: Methuen & Co. Ltd, 1922).

Eagleton, Terry, 'An Octopus at the Window', *London Review of Books*, 19 May 2011, pp. 23–24.

Eagleton, Terry, *The Ideology of the Aesthetic* (Oxford: Blackwell, 1990).

Eccles, John, *How the Self Controls Its Brain* (Berlin and London: Springer-Verlag, 1994).

Eddington, Arthur, *The Nature of The Physical World* (Cambridge: Cambridge University Press, 1928).

Edel, Leon, *The Psychological Novel: 1900–1950* (London: Rupert Hart-Davis, 1955).

Eliot, T. S., 'Tradition and the Individual Talent', in *Selected Prose*, ed. by Frank Kermode (London: Faber & Faber, 1975).

Eliot, T. S., 'The Love Song of J. Alfred Prufrock', in *The Poems of T. S. Eliot Volume I: Collected and Uncollected Poems*, ed. by Christopher Ricks and Jim McCue (London: Faber & Faber, 2015).

Ellmann, Richard, *Ulysses on the Liffey* (London: Faber & Faber, 1972).

Eno, Henry Lane, *Activism* (Princeton, NJ: Princeton University Press, 1920).

Fernihough, Anne, 'Consciousness as a Stream', in *The Cambridge Companion to the Modernist Novel*, ed. by Morag Shiach (Cambridge: Cambridge University Press, 2007).

Fleming, Bruce E., 'The Smell of Success: A Reassessment of Patrick Süskind's "Das Parfum"', *South Atlantic Review*, 56.4 (1991), 71–86.

Fletcher, John, 'Samuel Beckett and the Philosophers', *Comparative Literature*, 17 (1965), 43–56.

Fludernik, Monika, *Towards a 'Natural' Narratology* (London and New York: Routledge, 1996).

Forster, E. M., *Virginia Woolf* (Cambridge: Cambridge University Press, 1942).

Foucault, Michel, *Madness and Civilization: A History of Insanity in the Age of Reason*, trans. by Richard Howard (London and New York: Routledge, 1989).

Frattarola, Angela, 'Developing an Ear for the Modernist Novel: Virginia Woolf, Dorothy Richardson, and James Joyce', *Journal of Modern Literature*, 33.1 (2009), 132–153.

Freud, Sigmund, *The Psychopathology of Everyday Life*, trans. by A. A. Brill (London: T. Fisher Unwin, 1914).

Friedman, Melvin, *Stream of Consciousness: A Study in Literary Method* (New Haven, CT: Yale University Press, 1955).
Fuller, David and Waugh, Patricia, eds, *The Arts and Sciences of Criticism* (Oxford: Oxford University Press, 1999).
Gaedtke, Andrew, 'Cognitive Investigations: The Problems of Qualia and Style in the Contemporary Neuronovel', *Novel: A Forum on Fiction*, 45.2 (2012), 184–201.
Gang, Joshua, 'Mindless Modernism', *Novel*, 46.1 (2013), 116–132.
Genette, Gérard, *Narrative Discourse: An Essay in Method*, trans. by Jane E. Lewin (Ithaca, NY: Cornell University Press, 1980).
Gillespie, Diane F., *The Sisters' Arts: The Writing and Painting of Virginia Woolf and Vanessa Bell* (Syracuse, NY: Syracuse University Press, 1988).
Gillies, Mary Ann, *Henri Bergson and British Modernism* (Montreal and London: McGill-Queen's University Press, 1996).
Goncourt, Edmond de, *Pages from the Goncourt Journal*, ed. and trans. by Robert Baldick (London: Oxford University Press, 1962).
Greenberg, Clement, 'Complaints of an Art Critic', *Artforum*, October 1967, 38–39.
Greenberg, Clement, *The Collected Essays and Criticism*, ed. by John O'Brian, 4 vols (Chicago, IL and London: The University of Chicago Press, 1993), vol. 4, *Modernism with a Vengeance 1957–1969*.
Grote, John, *Exploratio Philosophica: Rough Notes on Modern Intellectual Science* (London: Bell and Daldy, 1865).
Hahn, Martin and Ramberg, Bjørn, eds, *Reflections and Replies: Essays on the Philosophy of Tyler Burge* (Cambridge, MA: The MIT Press, 2003).
Hardin, Clyde L., 'Qualia and Materialism: Closing the Explanatory Gap', *Philosophy and Phenomenological Research*, 48.2 (1987), 281–298.
Harding, Colin and Popple, Simon, *In the Kingdom of Shadows: A Companion to Early Cinema* (London: Cygnus Arts, 1996).
Harrington, Anne, *Reenchanted Science Holism in German Culture from Wilhelm II to Hitler* (Princeton, NJ, Princeton University Press, 1996).
Helmholtz, H. L. F. von, 'The Recent Progress of the Theory of Vision', *Popular Scientific Lectures*, trans. by. P. H. Pye-Smith (New York: Dover Publications, 1962).
Herman, David, *Basic Elements of Narrative* (Chichester: Wiley-Blackwell, 2009).
Herman, David, ed., *The Emergence of Mind: Representations of Consciousness in Narrative Discourse in English* (Lincoln, NE and London: University of Nebraska Press, 2011).
Herman, David, 'Modernist Life Writing and Nonhuman Lives: Ecologies of Experience in Virginia Woolf's Flush', *Modern Fiction Studies*, 59.3 (2013), 547–568.

Honderich, Ted, *The Oxford Companion to Philosophy* (Oxford: Oxford University Press, 1995).

Hulme, T. E., *The Collected Writings of T. E. Hulme*, ed. by Karen Csengeri (Oxford: Clarendon Press, 1994).

Humphrey, Robert, *Stream of Consciousness and the Modern Novel* (Berkeley and Los Angeles, CA: University of California Press, 1962).

Husserl, Edmund, *Logical Investigations*, ed. by Dermot Moran, trans. by J. N. Findlay, 2 vols (London and New York: Routledge, 2001), vol. I.

Idhe, Don, ed., *The Conflict in Interpretations: Essays in Hermeneutics* (Evanston, IL: Northwestern University Press, 1974).

Jackson, Frank, 'Epiphenomenal Qualia', *The Philosophical Quarterly*, 32.127 (1982), 127–136.

Jackson, Frank, 'What Mary Didn't Know', *The Journal of Philosophy*, 83.5 (1986), 291–295.

Jaime, Carmelo Cunchillos, ed., *Wyndham Lewis the Radical: Essays on Literature and Modernity* (New York and Oxford: Peter Lang, 2007).

James, Henry, *What Maisie Knew*, ed. by Douglas Jefferson (Oxford: Oxford University Press, 1966).

James, William, *Principles of Psychology*, 2 vols (London: Macmillan and Co. Ltd, 1907), vol. I.

James, William, 'The Stream of Consciousness', in *Writings 1878–1899* (New York: Library of America, 1992).

Jameson, Fredric, *Fables of Aggression: Wyndham Lewis, the Modernist as Fascist* (Berkeley, CA, Los Angeles, CA and London: University of California Press, 1979).

Jayne, Edward, 'I. A. Richards: Theory of Metaphor, Theory as Metaphoric Variation Affective Criticism: Theories of Emotion and Synaesthesis in the Experience of Literature' (Dissertation, SUNY at Buffalo, 1970).

Jeans, James, *The Mysterious Universe* (Cambridge: Cambridge University Press, 1930).

Joyce, James, *Finnegans Wake* (London: Faber & Faber, 1939).

Joyce, James, *Letters of James Joyce*, ed. by Stuart Gilbert, 3 vols (London: Faber & Faber; Viking, 1957), vol. I.

Joyce, James, *Stephen Hero: Part of the First Draft of 'A Portrait of the Artist as a Young Man'*, ed. by Theodore Spencer (London: Jonathan Cape, 1960).

Joyce, James, The Workshop of Daedalus: James Joyce and the Raw Materials for 'A Portrait of the Artist as a Young Man', ed. by Robert Scholes and Richard M. Kain (Evanston, IL: Northwestern University Press, 1965).

Joyce, James, *James Joyce in Padua*, ed. and trans. by Louis Berrone (New York: Random House, 1977).

Joyce, James, *Ulysses*, ed. by Hans Walter Gabler (London: The Bodley Head, 1986).

Joyce, James, *Ulysses*, ed. by Jeri Johnson (Oxford: Oxford University Press, 1993).
Kahler, Eric, *The Inward Turn of Narrative*, trans. by Richard and Clara Winston (Princeton, NJ: Princeton University Press, 1973).
Kenner, Hugh, *Wyndham Lewis* (London: Methuen & Co., Ltd, 1954).
Kenner, Hugh, *Samuel Beckett: A Critical Study* (New York: Grove Press, 1961).
Kenner, Hugh, *The Counterfeiters* (Bloomington, IN: Indiana University Press, 1968).
Kenner, Hugh, *The Mechanic Muse* (New York and Oxford: Oxford University Press 1987).
Kittler, Friedrich A., *Discourse Networks 1800–1900*, trans. by Michael Metteer and Chris Cullens (Stanford, CA: Stanford University Press, 1990).
Kittler, Friedrich A., *Gramophone, Film, Typewriter*, trans. by Geoffrey Winthrop-Young and Michael Wutz (Stanford, CA: Stanford University Press, 1999).
Knight, Christopher J., *The Patient Particulars: American Modernism and the Technique of Originality* (Lewisburg, PA: Bucknell University Press; London: Associated University Press, 1995).
Knowlson, James, *Damned to Fame: The Life of Samuel Beckett* (London: Bloomsbury, 1996).
Kumar, Shiv, *Bergson and the Stream of Consciousness Novel* (London and Glasgow: Blackie & Son, 1962).
Lawrence, D. H., *Fantasia of the Unconscious* (London: M. Secker, 1930).
Lawrence, D. H., *Study of Thomas Hardy and Other Essays*, ed. by Bruce Steele (Cambridge: Cambridge University Press, 1985).
Leibniz, Gottfried Wilhelm, *The Monadology and Other Philosophical Writings*, trans. by Robert Latta (Oxford: The Clarendon Press, 1898).
Levenson, Michael H., *A Genealogy of Modernism A Study of English Literary Doctrine 1908–1922* (Cambridge: Cambridge University Press, 1984).
Levenson, Michael H., 'Form's Body Wyndham Lewis's Tarr', *Modern Language Quarterly*, 45.3 (1984), 241–262.
Levine, George, ed., *One Culture: Essays in Science and Literature* (Madison, WI: The University of Wisconsin Press, 1987).
Levine, Joseph, 'Materialism and Qualia: The Explanatory Gap', *Pacific Philosophical Quarterly*, 64.4 (1983), 354–361.
Lewis, C. I., *Mind and the World Order* (New York: Dover Publications, Inc., 1929).
Lewis, Wyndham, *Blast*, 2 vols (Santa Rosa, CA: Black Sparrow Press, 1915; repr. 1981).
Lewis, Wyndham, 'The Strange Actor', *The New Statesman*, 22.563 (1924), 474–476. .

Lewis, Wyndham, *The Childermass: Section 1* (London: Chatto & Windus, 1928).
Lewis, Wyndham, *Snooty Baronet* (London: Cassell and Company, Ltd, 1932).
Lewis, Wyndham, *One-Way Song* (London: Faber & Faber, 1933).
Lewis, Wyndham, *Rotting Hill* (London: Methuen & Co. Ltd, 1951).
Lewis, Wyndham, *Wyndham Lewis and Vorticism*, exhibition catalogue (London: Tate Gallery, 1956).
Lewis, Wyndham, *The Apes of God* (London: Penguin 1965).
Lewis, Wyndham, *Wyndham Lewis: Anthology of Prose*, ed. by E. W. F. Tomlin (London: Methuen, 1969).
Lewis, Wyndham, *Hitler* (New York: Gordon, 1972).
Lewis, Wyndham, *Mrs. Dukes' Million* (London: George Prior Publishers, 1980).
Lewis, Wyndham, *The Complete Wild Body*, ed. by Bernard Lafourcade (Santa Barbara, CA: Black Sparrow Press, 1982).
Lewis, Wyndham, *Men Without Art*, ed. by Seamus Cooney (Santa Rosa, CA: Black Sparrow Press, 1987).
Lewis, Wyndham, *The Art of Being Ruled*, ed. by Reed Way Dasenbrock (Santa Rosa, CA: Black Sparrow Press, 1989).
Lewis, Wyndham, *Tarr*, ed. by Paul O'Keeffe (Santa Rosa, CA: Black Sparrow Press, 1990).
Lewis, Wyndham, *The Revenge for Love*, ed. by Reed Way Dasenbrock (Santa Rosa, CA: Black Sparrow Press, 1991).
Lewis, Wyndham, *Time and Western Man*, ed. by Paul Edwards (Santa Rosa, CA: Black Sparrow Press, 1993).
Lewis, Wyndham, *The Enemy: A Review of Arts and Literature*, ed. by Wyndham Lewis, 3 vols (Santa Rosa, CA: Black Sparrow Press, 1994).
Lewis, Wyndham, 'The Revolutionary Simpleton' in *The Enemy: A Review of Art and Literature*, ed. by Wyndham Lewis, 3 vols (Santa Rosa, CA: Black Sparrow Press, 1994), vol. I.
Locke, John, *An Essay Concerning Human Understanding*, ed. by Peter H. Nidditch (Oxford: Clarendon Press, 1975).
Lodge, David, *Thinks . . .* (London: Secker & Warburg, 2001).
Lodge, David, *Consciousness and the Novel* (London: Secker & Warburg 2002).
Lorentzen, Christian, ed., *Say What You Mean: The n+1 Anthology* (London: Notting Hill Editions, 2012).
Lukács, Georg, *Realism in Our Time: Literature and the Class Struggle* (New York: Harper Torchbooks, 1971).
Mach, Ernst, *Popular Scientific Lectures,* trans. by Thomas J. McCormack (Chicago, IL: The Open Court Publishing Company, 1898).
Mach, Ernst, *The Analysis of Sensations and the Relation of the Physical to the Psychical*, trans. by C. M. Williams (Chicago, IL and London: The Open Court Publishing Company, 1914).

Malabou, Catherine, *What Should We Do With Our Brain?* (Ashland, OH: Fordham University Press, 2008).

Marcel, A. J. and Bisiach E., eds, *Consciousness in Contemporary Science* (New York: Oxford University Press, 1992).

Marinetti, F. T., 'The Manifesto of Tactilism', *Comœdia,* 11 January 1921.

Marinetti, F. T., *Let's Murder the Moonshine: Selected Writings,* ed. by R. W. Flint, trans. by R.W. Flint and Arthur A. Coppotelli (Los Angeles, CA: Sun and Moon Press, 1991).

Marinetti, F. T., *Selected Poems and Related Prose,* trans. by Elizabeth R. Napier and Barbara R. Studholme (New Haven, CT and London: Yale University Press, 2002).

Marinetti, F. T., 'Destruction of Syntax – Wireless Imagination – Words-in-Freedom', trans. by Lawrence Rainey, in *Modernism: An Anthology,* ed. by Lawrence Rainey (Oxford: Blackwell, 2005).

Marshall, Edward, '"No Immortality of the Soul" Says Thomas A. Edison', *The New York Times,* 2 October 1910.

Martson, William, King, C. D. and Marston, E. H., *Integrative Psychology; A Study of Unit Response* (London: Harcourt, Brace & World, 1931).

Matz, Jesse, *Literary Impressionism and Modernist Aesthetics* (Cambridge: Cambridge University Press, 2001).

Matz, Jesse, 'T. E. Hulme, Henri Bergson, and the Cultural Politics of Psychologism', in *The Mind of Modernism: Medicine, Psychology and the Cultural Arts in Europe and America 1880–1940* (Stanford, CA: Stanford University Press, 2004).

Maude, Ulrika, *Beckett, Technology and the Body* (Cambridge: Cambridge University Press, 2009).

Maude, Ulrika, 'Pavlov's Dogs and Other Animals in Beckett' in *Beckett and Animals,* ed. by Mary Bryden (Cambridge: Cambridge University Press, 2013).

McEwan, Ian, interview with Michael Silverblatt, Bookworm, KCRW, 11 July 2002.

McLuhan, Marshall, *The Gutenberg Galaxy: The Making of Typographic Man* (Toronto: University of Toronto Press, 1962).

McLuhan, Marshall, 'Inside the Five Sense Sensorium', *Canadian Architect,* 6.6 (1961), pp. 49–54.

Merleau-Ponty, Maurice, *Sense and Non-Sense,* trans. by. Hubert L. Dreyfus and Patricia Allen Dreyfus (Evanston, IL: Northwestern University Press, 1964).

Meyers, Jeffrey, ed., *Wyndham Lewis: A Revaluation: New Essays* (London: Athlone Press, 1980).

Micale, Mark S., ed., *The Mind of Modernism: Medicine, Psychology and the Cultural Arts in Europe and America 1880–1940* (Stanford, CA: Stanford University Press, 2004).

Michel, Walter and Fox, C. J., eds, *Wyndham Lewis on Art* (London: Thames and Hudson, 1969).

Moore, G. E., Philosophical Studies (London: Kegan Paul, Trench, Trubner & Co. Ltd, 1922).

Moore, G. E., *Some Main Problems of Philosophy* (London: George Allen & Unwin Ltd, 1953).

Muller, Hebert, 'Impressionism in Fiction: Prism vs. Mirror', *The American Scholar*, 7.3 (1938), 355–367.

Müller, Johannes, *Elements of Physiology*, trans. by William Baly, 4 vols (Bristol: Thoemmes, 2000), vol. I.

Murry, John Middleton, *Still Life* (London, Constable and Company Ltd, 1918).

Musil, Robert, *On Mach's Theories*, trans. by Kevin Mulligan (Washington, DC: Catholic University of America Press, 1882).

Musil, Robert, *Precision and Soul: Essays and Addresses,* ed. and trans. by Burton Pike and David S. Luft (Chicago, IL and London: University of Chicago Press, 1990).

Musil, Robert, *The Man Without Qualities*, trans by. Sophie Wilkins, 2 vols (London: Picador, 1995), vol. I.

Nagel, Thomas, 'What is it Like to be a Bat?', *The Philosophical Review*, 83.4 (1974), 435–450.

Nochlin, Linda, ed., *Impressionism and Post-Impressionism 1874–1904: Sources and Documents* (Englewood Cliffs, NJ: Prentice-Hall, 1966).

Nordau, Max, *Degeneration* (London: William Heinemann 1913).

Ong, Walter J., *Orality and Literacy: The Technologizing of the Word* (London: Methuen, 1982).

Oppenheim, Lois, ed., *Samuel Beckett and the Visual Arts: Music, Visual Arts, and Non-Print Media* (New York: Garland, 1998).

Palmer, Alan, *Fictional Minds* (Lincoln, NE and London: University of Nebraska Press, 2004).

Paris, John Ayrton, *The Life of Sir Humphrey Davy*, 2 vols (London: Colburn & Bentley, 1831), vol. I.

Pater, Walter, *The Renaissance: Studies in Art and Poetry*, ed. by Adam Phillips (Oxford: Oxford University Press, 1986).

Patterson, Mark, *The Senses of Touch* (Oxford and New York: Berg, 2007).

Pearson, Karl, *The Grammar of Science* (London: Walter Scott, 1892).

Pinker, Stephen, *The Blank Slate* (London: Allen Lane, 2002).

Place, U. T., 'E. G. Boring and the Mind–Brain Identity Theory', *British Psychological Society, History and Philosophy of Science Newsletter*, 11 (1990), 20–31.

Plock, Vike Martina, *Joyce, Medicine, and Modernity* (Gainesville, FL: University Press of Florida, 2010).

Pound, Ezra, *Literary Essays* (New York: New Directions, 1935; repr. 1968).
Power, Arthur, *Conversations with James Joyce*, ed. by Clive Hart (London: Millington, 1974).
Price, H. H., *Perception* (London: Methuen & Co. Ltd, 1932).
Prieto, Eric, *Listening In: Music, Mind and the Modernist Narrative* (Lincoln, NE and London: University of Nebraska Press, 2002).
Prince, Gerald, *Dictionary of Narratology* (Aldershot: Scolar, 1988).
Quine, Willard Van Orman, *From a Logical Point of View: 9 Logico-Philosophical Essays* (Cambridge, MA: Harvard University Press, 1953).
Ramachandran, V. S., and Blakeslee, S., 'Three Laws of Qualia: What Neurology Tells Us about the Biological Functions of Consciousness, Qualia and the Self', *Journal of Consciousness Studies*, 4.5–6 (1997), 429–457.
Ramachandran, V. S., and Blakeslee, S., *Phantoms in the Brain: Probing the Mysteries of the Human Mind* (New York: William Morrow & Co, 1998).
Reynolds, Joshua, *Discourses*, ed. by Roger Fry (London: Seeley & Co. Limited, 1905).
Richards, I. A., *Principles of Literary Criticism* (London: Kegan Paul, Trench, Trubner & Co., Ltd, 1925).
Richards, I. A., *The Philosophy of Rhetoric* (New York and London: Oxford University Press, 1936).
Ricks, Christopher, *Beckett's Dying Words* (Oxford: Clarendon Press, 1993).
Riskin, Jessica, 'Eighteenth-Century Wetware', *Representations*, 83.1 (2003), 97–125.
Robbins, Stephen E., 'Time, Form and the Limits of Qualia', *The Journal of Mind and Behavior*, 28.1 (2007), 19–43.
Rodker, John, *Adolphe 1920* (London: The Aquila Press, 1929).
Rosenbaum, S. P., ed., *English Literature and British Philosophy* (Chicago, IL and London: The University of Chicago Press, 1971).
Rosenthal, David M., *Materialism and the Mind–Body Problem* (Englewood Cliffs, NJ; London: Prentice-Hall, 1971).
Rousseau, George S., *Nervous Acts: Essays on Literature, Culture and Sensibility* (Basingstoke: Palgrave Macmillan, 2004).
Russell, Bertrand, *Our Knowledge of the External World* (London: George Allen & Unwin Ltd, 1922).
Russell, Bertrand, *The Problems of Philosophy* (London: Thornton Butterworth Ltd, 1912).
Russell, Bertrand, *The Analysis of Mind* (London: George Allen & Unwin, 1921).
Russell, Bertrand, *The ABC of Relativity* (London and New York: Routledge, 1997).
Rutherfurd-Dyer, R., 'Homer's Wine-dark Sea', *Greece & Rome Second Series*, 30.2 (1983), 125–128.

Salisbury, Laura, *Samuel Beckett: Laughing Matters, Comic Timing* (Edinburgh: Edinburgh University Press, 2012).

Salisbury, Laura, 'Narration and Neurology: Ian McEwan's Mother Tongue', *Textual Practice*, 24.5 (2010), 883–912.

Salisbury, Laura and Shail, Andrew, eds, *Neurology and Modernity* (Basingstoke: Palgrave Macmillan, 2010).

Saunders, Corinne, Maude, Ulrika and Macnaughton, Jane, eds, *The Body and the Arts* (Basingstoke: Palgrave Macmillan, 2009).

Searle, John R., 'Minds, Brains and Programs', *Behavioral and Brain Sciences*, 3.3 (1980), 417–424.

Searle, John R., *The Mystery of Consciousness* (London: Granta, 1997).

Searle, John R., *Mind: A Brief Introduction* (Oxford: Oxford University Press, 2004).

Searle, John R., 'The Mystery of Consciousness Continues', *The New York Review of Books*, 9 June 2011.

Sebastian, Thomas, *The Intersection of Science and Literature in Musil's The Man Without Qualities* (Rochester, NY: Camden House, 2005).

Shepherd-Barr, Kirsten and Shepherd, Gordon M., 'Madeleines and Neuromodernism: Reassessing Mechanisms of Autobiographical Memory in Proust', *Auto/ Biography Studies*, 13.1 (1998), 39–60.

Sinclair, May, 'The Novels of Dorothy Richardson', *The Egoist*, 5.4 (1918), 57–59.

Smart, J. C. C., *Philosophy and Scientific Realism* (London: Routledge & Kegan Paul, 1963).

Snaith, Anna and Kenyon-Jones, Christine, 'Tilting at Universities: Virginia Woolf at King's College London', *Woolf Studies Annual*, 16 (2010), 1–44.

Solomons, Leon M. and Stein, Gertrude, 'Normal Motor Automatism', *Psychological Review*, 3.5 (1896), 492–512.

Stanfield, Paul Scott, '"This Implacable Doctrine": Behaviorism in Wyndham Lewis's "Snooty Baronet"', *Twentieth Century Literature*, 47.2 (2001), 241–267.

Stanzel, F. K., *A Theory of Narrative* (Cambridge: Cambridge University Press, 1984).

Steiner, George, *On Difficulty and Other Essays* (Oxford: Oxford University Press, 1978).

Stephen, Karin, *The Misuse of Mind: A Study of Bergson's Attack on Intellectualism* (London: Kegan Paul, Trench, Trubner & Co., Ltd, 1922).

Tajiri, Yokishi, *Samuel Beckett and the Prosthetic Body: The Organs and Senses in Modernism* (Basingstoke: Palgrave Macmillan, 2007).

Tallis, Raymond, *In Defence of Realism* (London: Edward Arnold, 1988).

Tallis, Raymond, *Aping Mankind: Neuromania, Darwinitis and the Misrepresentation of Humanity* (Durham: Acumen Publishing Ltd, 2011).

Thompson, Evan, *Mind in Life: Biology, Phenomenology, and the Sciences of Mind* (Cambridge, MA: Harvard University Press, 2007).
Trilling, Lionel, *The Liberal Imagination: Essays on Literature and Society* (London: Secker and Warburg, 1951).
Troscianko, Emily, *Kafka's Cognitive Realism* (London: Routledge, 2016).
Trotter, David, *Cinema and Modernism* (Oxford: Blackwell Publishing, 2007).
Turing, Alan, 'Computing Machinery and Intelligence', *Mind*, 59.236 (1950), 433–460.
Uexküll, Jakob von, *A Foray into the Worlds of Animals and Humans: with A Theory of Meaning*, trans. by Joseph D. O'Neill (Minneapolis, MN: University of Minnesota Press, 2010).
Watson, John B., 'Image and Affection in Behavior', *Journal of Philosophy, Psychology and Scientific Methods*, 10 (1913), 421–428.
Watson, John B., 'Psychology as the Behaviorist Views It', *Psychological Review*, 20.2 (1913), 158–177.
Watson, John B., *Psychology from the Standpoint of a Behaviorist* (Philadelphia, PA: J. B. Lippincott Company, 1919).
Watson, John B., *The Battle of Behaviorism: An Exposition and an Exposure* (London: Kegan Paul, Trench, Trubner & Co. Ltd, 1928).
Watson, John B., *Behaviorism* (Chicago, IL: University of Chicago Press, 1930).
Watt, Ian, *The Rise of the Novel Studies in Richardson, Defoe, Fielding* (London: Chatto & Windus, 1957).
Whitehead, Alfred North, *Science and the Modern World: Lowell Lectures, 1925* (New York: Mentor Books, 1925).
Whitworth, Michael H., *Einstein's Wake: Relativity, Metaphor, and Modernist Literature* (Oxford: Oxford University Press, 2001).
Whitworth, Michael H., *Virginia Woolf* (Oxford: Oxford University Press, 2005).
Wittgenstein, Ludwig, *Last Writings on the Philosophy of Psychology*, vol. II, ed. by G. H. von Wright and H. Nyman, trans. by C. G. Luckhardt and M. A. E. Aue (Oxford: Blackwell, 1992).
Woolf, Virginia, *Jacob's Room* (London: The Hogarth Press, 1922).
Woolf, Virginia, *To the Lighthouse* (London: The Hogarth Press, 1927).
Woolf, Virginia, *A Room of One's Own* (London: The Hogarth Press, 1929).
Woolf, Virginia, *The Waves* (London: The Hogarth Press, 1931).
Woolf, Virginia, *Flush* (London: The Hogarth Press, 1933).
Woolf, Virginia, *The Flight of the Mind: The Letters of Virginia Woolf Volume I: 1882–1912*, ed. by Nigel Nicolson (London: The Hogarth Press, 1975).
Woolf, Virginia, *A Reflection of the Other Person: The Letters of Virginia Woolf Volume IV: 1929–1931*, ed. by Nigel Nicolson (London: The Hogarth Press, 1978).

Woolf, Virginia, *The Diary of Virginia Woolf Volume I: 1915–19*, ed. by Anne Oliver Bell (Harmondsworth: Penguin, 1979).
Woolf, Virginia, *The Sickle Side of the Moon: The Letters of Virginia Woolf Volume V: 1932–1935*, ed. by Nigel Nicolson (London: The Hogarth Press, 1979).
Woolf, Virginia, *The Diary of Virginia Woolf Volume IV: 1931–35*, ed. by Anne Olivier Bell (Harmondsworth: Penguin, 1983).
Woolf, Virginia, *A Sketch of the Past*, ed. by Jeanne Schulkind (London: The Hogarth Press, 1985).
Woolf, Virginia, *The Essays of Virginia Woolf Volume III: 1919–1924*, ed. by Andrew McNeillie (London: The Hogarth Press, 1988).
Woolf, Virginia, *The Essays of Virginia Woolf Volume IV: 1925–1928*, ed. by Andrew McNeillie (London: The Hogarth Press, 1994; repr. 2009).
Woolf, Virginia, *A Haunted House: The Complete Shorter Fiction*, ed. by Susan Dick (London: Vintage, 2003).
Woolf, Virginia, *The Essays of Virginia Woolf Volume V: 1929–1932*, ed. by Stuart N. Clarke (London: The Hogarth Press, 2009).
Woolf, Virginia, *The Essays of Virginia Woolf Volume VI: 1933–1941*, ed. by Stuart N. Clarke (London: The Hogarth Press, 2011).
Woolf, Virginia, *The Pargiters*, New York Public Library, Berg Coll., MSS Woolf, M42, vol. V.
Wright, Edmond, ed., *The Case for Qualia* (Cambridge, MA: The MIT Press, 2008).
Young, Kay, *Imagining Minds: The Neuro-Aesthetics of Austen, Eliot and Hardy* (Columbus, OH: The Ohio State University Press, 2010).
Zunshine, Lisa, *Why We Read Fiction: Theory of Mind and the Novel* (Columbus, OH: Ohio State University Press, 2006).

INDEX

aesthetics
  the category of the 'impression', 2–3
  of Impressionism, 49–50, 52, 53
  principles of efficiency, 111, 114
  scientific discourse, philosophy and literary aesthetic interrelations, 18–22, 36, 37
  see also neuroaesthetics
Alexander, Jennifer Karns, 111
Apollinaire, Guillaume, 80
arts, visual
  Impressionist aesthetic, 49–50, 52, 53
  perceptions of colour, 39–40
  reading modern art, 20
aurality
  aural reductive thesis, 117–19
  information theory and, 114–15, 122, 123
  of internal monologues, 120
  in modernism, 117
  musical notation, 116, 117–18
  in Samuel Beckett's work, 120, 122–3
  in *Ulysses* (Joyce), 117, 118, 119

automatism
  alienation of mutoscopes, 142–4
  the camera and, 137–8
  Cartesian tradition of body as machine, 149–50
  early automata, 144–5
  in early cinema, 145–6
  mechanical consciousness, 137, 138–9, 141, 144–5
  the mob as automata, 134, 149
Ayer, A. J., 137

Banfield, Ann, 23, 34, 35, 47
Beckett, Samuel
  Cartesian conception of consciousness, 120–1
  on James Joyce, 72–3, 111
  linguistic failure in, 126–7
  Malone Dies, 124–5, 126–7
  material bodies in, 120–1
  Murphy, 120–1, 122, 124
  narratives of reduction, 119, 122–3, 132
  radio plays, 123–4

Beckett, Samuel (*cont.*)
  representation of hearing, 120, 123
  trope of the room, 121
  The Unnameable, 120
  Watt, 122, 124, 125–6
  words as sense-data, 121, 124–6
behaviourism
  Alan Turing's 'Imitation Game', 124, 133, 138–9, 156–7
  behaviourist narratives, 171–2, 173
  conceptions of thought, 140–1
  defined, 135
  denial of qualia/interiority, 132–3, 135–6, 141, 171
  language as word-habits, 140
  methodological behaviourism, 132
  the mob as automata, 148–9, 151, 152
  problem of consciousness in, 132–3, 135–6, 141
  silent film and, 148–9
  Wyndham Lewis's relationship with, 133–4, 135, 136–7, 139–40, 149, 160, 171
Bennett, M. R., 107
Bergson, Henri
  on the absolute as perfection, 72
  action/sensation dichotomy, 20–1, 22
  critiques of, 22
  durée and *temps*, 19–20
  influence of, 18–19, 150
  theories of in relation to qualia, 19–20
biosemiotics, 59–61
Block, Ned, 4, 25–6
the body
  autonomous behavioural systems, 95–6, 99
  cinematic kinaesthetics, 148, 150–1
  embodied consciousness, 154
  exteriority in Wyndham Lewis's work, 152–3, 154–5
  language's relation to, 5, 15–16
  legibility of, 86

  materiality of the nervous system, 84–5, 93–5
  mind–body problem, 4, 26–7, 34, 73, 83–4, 86, 95–6, 99, 104–5
  in Samuel Beckett's work, 120–1
  in *Ulysses* (Joyce), 73
  see also aurality
Boring, E. G., 89, 91–2, 95
Broad, C. D., 40–1, 97

Cambridge analytic tradition, 5, 15, 18, 33, 38
Carnap, Rudolf, 109–10, 132
Cave, Terence, 6, 14
Chalmers, David, 3–4, 88, 137
Chaplin, Charlie, 148, 150
Churchland, Patricia, 48, 107–9
Churchland, Paul, 48
cinema
  The Cabinet of Dr Caligari (Wiene), 151–2
  the cinema aesthetic in Wyndham Lewis's work, 133, 146–8, 151–2
  individualism in, 150
  silent film, 133, 146, 148–9, 150–1
  as a threat to the realist paradigm, 145–6
  transport tropes, 147–8
Cobley, Evelyn, 110–11
cognitive realism
  James Joyce's work as, 73, 75
  narrative realism of modernism, 13–14
  neuroaesthetics and, 7
  portrayal of consciousness, 6, 7, 12, 23–4
  qualia debate and, 23–7, 171
  reductionist/maximalist tensions, 111–13
  in relation to behaviourism, 132
  representative logic of, 12
  as stream of consciousness, 12–13, 111, 114
  theory of mind and, 170–1

Conrad, Joseph, 111, 159
consciousness
　Alan Turing's 'Imitation Game', 124, 133, 138–9, 156–7
　cinema's challenge to, 145–6
　cognitive realism, 23–4
　denial of interiority in behaviourism, 132–3, 135–6, 141
　double aspect theory of, 90–1
　embodied consciousness, 154
　identity thesis, 89, 91–2
　interpretation of the umwelt, 59–60
　the 'Joycean machine', 76, 170
　literary representations of, 11–14, 112
　matter as a construct of, 15, 45–7
　mechanical consciousness, 137, 138–9, 141, 144–5
　mind–body problem, 4, 26–7, 34, 73, 83–4, 86, 95–6, 99, 104–5
　mind–brain relationship, 80–1, 82–6, 89–92
　in modernist narrative fiction, 13–14, 170
　the momentary consciousness, 3
　the neurological unconsciousness, 95–7
　in the novel, 6, 23–4
　reductive theories of, 15–17, 23, 40–1, 89
　reflex arc, 95–6, 99
　in relation to qualia, 4, 5, 6–7
　in relation to the senses, 1–3
　Samuel Beckett's Cartesian tradition of, 120–1
　as sense-impressions, 96
　see also neuroscience; qualia
Crick, Francis, 107

Danius, Sara, 1, 2, 3, 67, 72, 94, 117, 145, 147–8, 167
defamiliarisation, 21–2
Dennett, Daniel, 4, 76, 170
Derrida, Jacques, 121–2, 146

dissociation, 96–7
double aspect theory, 90–1

Eagleton, Terry, 26–7, 160
Eliminative Materialism, 48
Eliot, T. S., 86, 149
Ellmann, Richard, 75
Eno, Henry Lane, 92
epistemology
　Cambridge philosophy and, 38
　external to internal transition, 15–16
　in James Joyce's works, 18, 67–9, 72, 111, 116
　and scientific enquiry into the senses, 82, 86, 88
　in Virginia Woolf's works, 18, 33, 34–5, 42, 43–4, 47, 121
　Wyndham Lewis's epistemological theses, 134, 139, 146, 158–9
　see also knowledge

Forster, E. M., 52, 111
Foucault, Michel, 84, 93
Freud, Sigmund, 152

Gall, Franz Joseph, 84, 85
gender
　female modernist neuroscientist figure, 41–2
　gendered dichotomy of knowledge, 42–4, 45, 47
　'Mary' (Jackson), 34–5, 40, 41
Golgi, Camillo, 85, 86, 93
Grote, John, 37

Hacker, Peter, 65, 107
Hall, Marshall, 95, 96
Hayles, N. Katherine, 114, 122, 123, 124
Helmholtz, Hermann von, 3, 37, 85, 86
Herman, David, 7, 12, 13–14, 44, 66, 74, 86

Hirstein, William, 90–1
Hulme, T. E., 19, 20–1, 22, 26
Humphrey, Robert, 12
Husserl, Edmund, 22, 49

identity thesis, 89, 91–2
Impressionism
　aesthetics of, 49–50, 52, 53
　the half-closed eye and, 40, 53

Jackson, Frank, 4, 34–5, 40, 41, 50
James, Henry, 18, 50–1, 158
James, William, 18, 37, 50–1, 81, 99, 110
Jameson, Fredric, 134, 158, 159–60, 161
Joyce, James
　on cinema and pornography, 144
　Finnegans Wake, 72–3, 119
　Samuel Beckett on, 111
　see also Ulysses (Joyce)
'Joycean machine', 76, 170

Kenner, Hugh, 119, 120, 133, 141, 148, 150, 155, 158, 161, 171
Kittler, Friedrich, 2, 31, 41, 82, 86, 94, 95, 115, 118
knowledge
　actual vs virtual knowledge, 20–1
　experiential/descriptive knowledge dualism, 18, 37–9, 40
　gendered dichotomy of knowledge, 42–4, 45, 47
　hierarchical organisation of, 115
　the knowledge argument for qualia, 32–3, 35, 36–7, 40
　the naïve eye, 49–51
　and the novel, 31–3
　objective/subjective distinction, 24–5, 32
　seeing as knowing, 35–6, 45
　sensations as objects of knowledge, 39–40
　technology's impact on understandings of, 31, 37
　Virginia Woolf's engagement with economies of knowledge, 18, 33, 34–5, 42, 43–4, 47, 121
　'What is it Like to be a Bat?', 63–7
　see also epistemology

language
　aurality of the internal monologue, 120
　descriptionism, 3, 15–17, 40, 85, 90, 113–14
　experiential/descriptive knowledge dualism, 18, 37–9, 40, 42–4
　fears of pseudo-scientific discourse, 105–6
　figurative language, 25–6
　of literary modernism in scientific discourse, 18
　literary narratives of reduction, 106, 110, 131–2
　musical notation, 116–19
　narratives of reduction in Samuel Beckett's work, 119, 122–3, 132
　onomatopoeia, 118
　phonic properties of, 117–18
　in relation to the body, 5, 15–16
　for representation of qualia, 24–6, 32, 47–8, 90–1
　scientific narratives of reduction, 106–10, 113
　sensation in literary language, 21–2
　as a system of notation, 116
　as word-habits in behaviourism, 140
Lawrence, D. H., 31, 32, 83–4, 104–5, 111
Leibniz, Gottfried Wilhelm, 138
Levenson, Michael, 20, 156
Levine, Joseph, 88, 89, 97
Lewis, C. I., 5, 17
Lewis, Wyndham
　The Apes of God, 134, 154, 157, 160

aurality of the internal monologue, 120
behaviourist aesthetic, 133–4, 135, 136–7, 139–40, 149, 160, 171
belief in individual genius, 134, 150
Cartesian tradition of man as machine, 149–50
The Childermass, 139, 140, 152, 156
the cinema aesthetic, 133, 146–8, 151–2
cognitive mechanisation, 156–7
definition of consciousness, 135–6
denial of interiority in, 134, 157–8, 161–2
external approach of, 152–3, 154–5, 157–8, 161–2
on Henri Bergson, 19, 22
interest in Charlie Chaplin, 148, 150
on James Joyce, 74–5
literary style of, 158–61
the mob as automata, 134, 149, 151, 152
model of consciousness, 139–40
Mrs. Dukes' Million, 147
opposition to interiority, 133
qualia debate and, 134–5, 156, 158
radical solution to the problem of qualia, 156, 158
Revenge for Love, 156–7, 160
Snooty Baronet, 136–7, 139–40, 155, 157
Tarr, 154–5, 160
theory of laughter, 150–1
third-person/first-person narrative divide, 155–6
Time and Western Man, 22, 133, 135–6, 152
The Wild Body, 150, 151, 155–6
literary fiction
break with musicality, 116–17
challenges of interpretation, 114
cinema's challenge to, 145–6
consciousness in narrative fiction, 13–14
and the explanatory gap, 87–92
interaction with psychological case studies, 82
mutoscope metaphor, 142–4, 145
naïve eye trope, 18
neuroaesthetics, 2
qualia in modernist narrative fiction, 32, 167–8, 173–4
reductionist/maximalist tensions, 111–14
third-person/first-person narrative divide, 24–5, 68–9, 74, 84, 155–6
see also language; the novel
Littlefield, Melissa, 92, 93
Locke, John, 15, 36, 37, 41
Lodge, David, 6, 23–4, 25, 66–7, 74
Lukács, George, 111
lyric poetry, 23, 25, 26

Mach, Ernst, 3, 15–17, 40, 85, 90, 113–14
McLuhan, Marshall, 5–6, 152, 153–4, 159
Marinetti, F. T., 83, 86, 104, 118, 153
Marston, William, 93
materialism, 13, 112, 113
Matz, Jesse, 2, 18–19, 20, 22, 49
Merleau-Ponty, Maurice, 49
Micale, Mark S., 11, 12, 82
modernism
culture of efficiency, 110–11, 114
defamiliarisation and, 21–2
inward turn of, 2, 5, 6, 7, 11–14, 22–3, 82, 85, 172
the nature of sensation, 1–3, 5–6
reductive impulses, 21, 22, 106–10
renewed interest in, 169–70
representations of consciousness, 11–14
use of figurative language, 26
see also neuromodernism

Monet, Claude, 52
Moore, G. E., 5, 16, 33, 34, 39–40, 49
Murry, John Middleton, 87–8, 89
music
  music, silence and technology, 121–2
  musical notation, 116–18
Musil, Robert, 115

Nagel, Thomas, 4, 6, 13–14, 25, 63–7
neuroaesthetics
  approaches to modernist fiction, 172–3
  cognitive realism and, 7
  defined, 82
  narratives of reduction and, 106–7
  overview of, 2, 5
neurology, 81–2
neuromodernism
  autonomous writing, 99
  emergence of, 81, 82
  female modernist neuroscientist figure, 41–2
  identification of brain states and sensory states, 88–9
  literature/psychology case study interactions, 82–3
  narratives of, 86
neurons
  and the explanatory gap, 88–90, 91
  impact on modernity, 81–2
  mapping of the neuronal system, 83, 84–5, 88, 93
  the psychon and, 93
  reductionism and, 83
  the reflex arc and, 95
neuroscience
  behaviourist conceptions of thought, 141
  and the explanation of consciousness, 81
  fears of reductionism of, 104–5
  impulse notion, 98
  materiality of the nervous system, 84–5, 93–5

mind–brain relationship, 80–1, 82–6, 89–92
narratives of reduction, 106–8
the neurological unconsciousness, 95–7
psychons, 92–3
reductive methodologies of, 82–6, 89–90
the novel
  as a cognitive instruction manual, 132
  consciousness in, 6, 23–4
  knowledge and, 31–3
  to live in another mind, 63, 65, 169
  the mind in, 167–70
  neurology, 75
  neuronovels, 2, 169
  as a Turing machine, 133
  see also literary fiction

Ong, Walter J., 5–6
onomatopoeia, 118

Palmer, Alan, 32, 171
Pater, Walter, 3, 118
Pearson, Karl, 94, 95–6
Perloff, Marjorie, 123
phenomenology
  of animal consciousness, 59–60, 64
  epoché, 54
  in 'The Mark on the Wall' (Woolf), 43
  modernism's reductionism and, 22
  the naïve eye and Impressionism, 49
  reductive brain/mind identity projects, 85, 91–2
  sensory experiences and, 12, 15, 23, 25, 43, 73, 110
philosophy
  descriptionism, 16–17, 90
  form of the thought experiment, 44–5, 65
  the nature of sensation, 1–2, 3
  nature of 'sense-data' debates, 15

scientific discourse, philosophy and literary aesthetic interrelations, 18–22, 36, 37
Plock, Vike, 75, 86
Price, H. H., 17, 84, 90
Prieto, Eric, 116
Proust, Marcel, 147, 148
psychoanalysis, 105–6
psychons, 92–3

qualia
  cognitive realism and, 23–7
  defamiliarisation and, 21–2
  defined, 3–4
  denial of in behaviourism, 132, 136
  as a disputed concept, 4–5, 14–15, 89
  and the explanatory gap, 88–9
  expressed through lyric poetry, 23, 25, 26
  the 'Joycean machine', 76, 170
  the knowledge argument, 32–3, 35, 36–7, 40
  literary criticism and, 23–7
  as metaphysical rupture/explanatory gap, 4
  and the mind–body problem, 4, 26–7, 34, 73
  in modernist narrative fiction, 32, 167–8, 173–4
  musical notation and, 117, 118–19
  of pain, 88
  in philosophy of mind, 4, 5, 6–7, 17
  as prelapsarian consciousness, 18, 51–2
  the 'problem' of, 6, 115, 131
  as properties of language, 24–6, 32, 47–8, 90–1
  qualia of sound, 123–7
  reductionist explanations for, 23, 107–9
  in relation to Henri Bergson's theories, 19–20, 21–2
  in *Ulysses* (Joyce), 67–8

'what-is-it-like-ness' of consciousness, 6, 13–14, 25, 63–7
  in Wyndham Lewis's work, 134–5, 156, 158
Quine, W. V. O., 109–10

Ramachandran, V. S., 90–1
Ramón y Cajal, Santiago, 85
reductionism
  aural reductive thesis, 117–19
  culture of efficiency, 114
  defined, 107
  descriptionism and, 114
  explanations of qualia, 23, 107–9
  information theory and, 114–16
  intertheoretic reduction, 107–9
  literary narratives of reduction, 110, 131–2
  of modern medicine, 104–5
  modernism's fears over, 104–6, 112
  modernism's narratives of, 21, 22, 106–10
  narratives of reduction in Samuel Beckett's work, 119, 122–3, 132
  neuroscientific methodologies, 82–6, 89–90
  radical reductionism, 110
  reductionist explanations for qualia, 23, 107–9
  scientific narratives of reduction, 106–10, 113
  stream of consciousness and, 111, 114
  tension with maximalism, 111–13
  theories of consciousness, 15–17, 23, 40–1, 89
Richards, I. A., 3, 98, 141
Rodker, John, 73, 142–3, 144
Roth, Marco, 2, 169
Rousseau, George, 84
Russell, Bertrand, 5, 16, 34, 38–9, 40, 45

Salisbury, Laura, 2, 81, 84, 86, 96
sciences
  descriptionism, 3, 15–17, 40, 85, 90, 113–14
  nature of 'sense-data' debates, 15
  scientific discourse, philosophy and literary aesthetic interrelations, 18–22, 36, 37
  the sensory crisis and, 36
  see also neuroscience
Searle, John, 3, 4, 24, 25, 136, 138, 139
sense-data
  within Cambridge philosophy, 33, 38–9, 47
  mimetic theory of sense-perception, 90
  nature of 'sense-data' debates, 14–17, 19, 20, 21–2, 47
  stored in mnemonic technologies, 2, 114, 118, 168
  vitality of, 84, 90
  words as in Samuel Beckett's work, 121, 124–6
the senses
  the category of the 'impression', 2–3
  descriptionism, 3, 15–17, 40, 85, 90, 113–14
  the eye in Bloomsbury, 35, 153
  neuroscientific analysis of, 82–4
  primacy of sight, 153, 154
  reinterpretation of in modernism, 1–2, 5–6, 168–70
  seeing as knowing, 35–6, 45
  tactility, 45–7, 153–4
  see also aurality
Shail, Andrew, 81, 84, 86
Shannon, Claude, 114, 122
Shepherd-Barr, Kirsten, 82
Sinclair, May, 12, 13
Stanfield, Paul Scott, 133–4
Stein, Gertrude, 41, 99, 133
Stephen, Karin, 20

stream of consciousness, 12–13, 81, 111, 114
subjectivity
  epistemic, 24
  intrapsychic subjectivity, 82–3
  ontological, 24–5
  of perception and the umwelt, 59–60

Tallis, Raymond, 107, 145–6
technology
  Alan Turing's 'Imitation Game', 124, 133, 138–9, 156–7
  the camera and, 137–8
  the gramophone in *Ulysses* (Joyce), 32, 122
  impact on understandings of knowledge, 31, 37
  information theory, 114–15, 123
  introspective technologies, 82
  mechanical consciousness, 137, 138–9, 141
  mnemonic technologies, 2, 31–2, 82, 114, 118
  music, silence and technology, 121–2
  mutoscopes, 142–4, 145
  photography, 154
  see also automatism
Thompson, Evan, 59
time, 19–20
trauma, 96–7
Trilling, Lionel, 105–6
Trotter, David, 143, 145, 147, 149
Turing, Alan, 123, 124, 133, 138, 150

Uexküll, Jakob von, 59–62, 71
Ulysses (Joyce)
  the body in, 73
  as cognitive realism, 73, 75
  convolutions of the grey matter, 99–100

epistemological thought experiments, 18, 67–9, 72, 111, 116
the gramophone in, 32, 122
'Hades' episode/recorded people, 31–2
Leopold Bloom's mindworld, 6, 59, 68–71, 76, 120
as a map, 71, 72
mathematical catechism of 'Ithaca,' 116
mutoscopes, 143
non-verbal language, 144
perception over knowledge, 72
'Sirens', 117, 118
sound, sight and meaning interplay, 119
third-person and first person discourse, 74–5
see also Joyce, James
Umwelt theory
animals in, 60–1
the blind man's Umwelt, 71
concept of, 59–60
perception marks, 61, 62
and the reading of environments, 61–2

vitality
Bergsonian notion of, 84, 93
and the double aspect theory, 90–1
of sense-data, 84, 90

Watson, J. B., 132, 135, 136, 140–1
Waugh, Patricia, 27, 32, 171
Whitehead, Alfred North, 15
Whitworth, Michael, 49, 114
Wiene, Robert, 151–2
Wittgenstein, Ludwig, 167
Woolf, Virginia
'On Being Ill', 47–8, 105
'Blue & Green', 39

consciousness as perspective, 33, 40
critique of materialists, 13, 112, 113
epistemological enquiry, 18, 33, 34–5, 42, 43–4, 47, 121
Flush, 65
gendered dichotomy of knowledge, 42–4, 45, 47
impressionist descriptions, 52–3
interiority and, 133
Jacob's Room, 34, 47, 112–13
'The Journal of Mistress Joan Martyn', 42
'Kew Gardens', 52, 53
knowledge of Bergson's philosophy, 20
To the Lighthouse, 45, 46, 51
linguistic expressions of qualia, 47–8
'The Mark on the Wall', 43–4
'Modern Fiction', 50, 60
'Monday and Tuesday', 44
'Mr Bennett and Mrs Brown', 13, 112
Mrs Dalloway, 172
'Phases of Fiction', 46
portrayals of childhood, 51–2
the relationship between mind and matter, 45–7
A Room of One's Own, 34–5, 41
sensory experiences in writing, 50, 52–5
'A Society', 42
story-like thought experiments, 44–5
trope of the room, 121
use of one word, 112–13
The Waves, 24, 46, 47, 53–4, 113
The Years, 65–6

Young, Kay, 25, 26

Zunshine, Lisa, 170, 172

EU representative:
Easy Access System Europe
Mustamäe tee 50, 10621 Tallinn, Estonia
Gpsr.requests@easproject.com

www.ingramcontent.com/pod-product-compliance
Lightning Source LLC
Chambersburg PA
CBHW070356240426
43671CB00013BA/2530